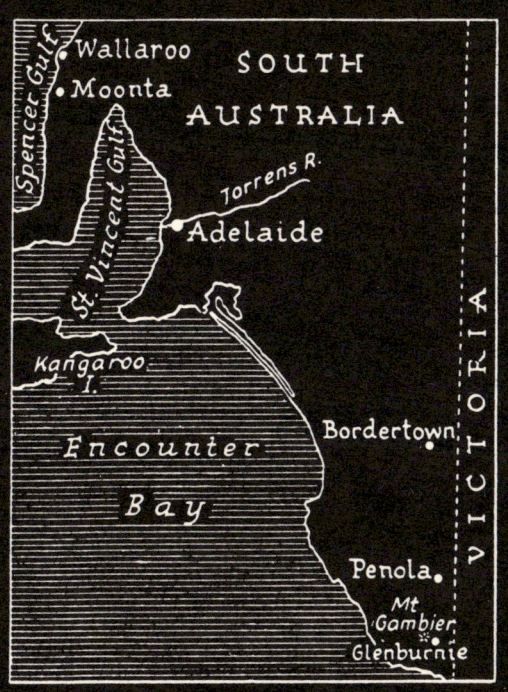
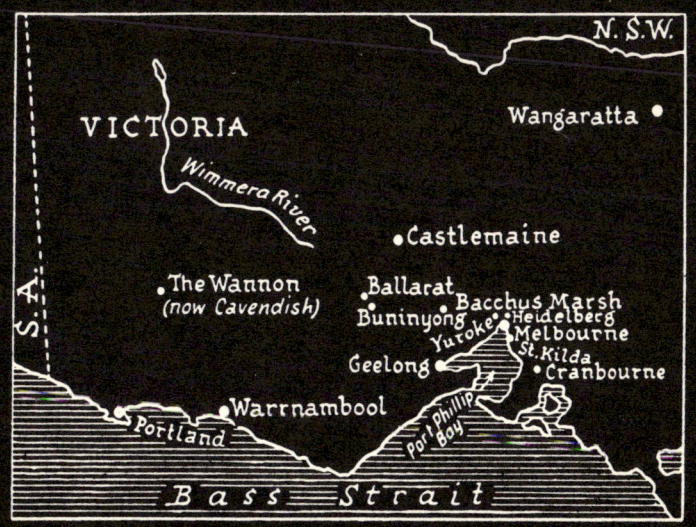

AUSTRALIAN EDUCATION
1788–1900

ROYAL COMMISSION ON TECHNICAL EDUCATION, VICTORIA, 1899–1901

(*See reverse of half-title for biographical notes*)

Australian Education
1788–1900

Church, State and Public Education in Colonial Australia

A. G. Austin
Third Edition

GREENWOOD PRESS, PUBLISHERS
WESTPORT, CONNECTICUT

Library of Congress Cataloging in Publication Data

Austin, Albert Gordon.
  Australian education, 1788-1900.

  Reprint of the 3d ed. published by Pitman,
Carlton, Vic., issued in series: Pitman Pacific
books.
  Bibliography: p.
  Includes index.
  1. Education--Australia--History. I. Title.
LA2101.A8 1976   370'.994   75-36359
ISBN 0-8371-8629-3

LA
2101
.A8
1976

© *A.G. Austin 1961, 1972*

This edition originally published in 1972 by Pitman
Pacific Books, Melbourne, Australia

Reprinted with the permission of Pitman Publishing Pty. Ltd.

Reprinted in 1976 by Greenwood Press,
a division of Williamhouse-Regency Inc.

Library of Congress Catalog Card Number 75-36359

ISBN 0-8371-8629-3

Printed in the United States of America

Preface to the Third Edition

IN THE Preface to the first edition of this book (1961) I pointed out that it was not a complete history of Australian education, as it ended in 1900 and made almost no reference to the private schools, the colonial universities, the Mechanics' Institutes, or the evolution of secondary (including technical) education. It was, however, I also pointed out, a complete statement of one important chapter in our social history—the evolution of a system of public, elementary education; to be that it also had to be an analysis of Church-State relations as they affected education.

The other claim that I originally made for this book was that it was the first attempt to trace the evolution of this system in the nation at large, and I pointed to the historiographical difficulties involved in locating and collating material which was scattered throughout the archives, libraries and private collections of this vast continent.

When I came to prepare a second edition in 1963 (though, by an unhappy accident, it was not published until 1965), I made no attempt to enlarge the book's scope, but concentrated instead on a reconsideration of its main theme. I was pleased to find that though I had much to be grateful for in the findings of recent historians, I had no cause to alter the essential argument of the book.

By late 1971, when I began to prepare this third edition, I had had some ten years' experience of using the book with university classes; that experience, and that of my colleagues in other universities and in teachers' colleges, convinced me that the essential argument was still sound. I have therefore concentrated on incorporating in footnotes (and in the bibliography) references to secondary sources which have been published since mid-1963; here and there I have cleared up minor blemishes and I have occasionally re-framed a section to give it more point.

The Mitchell Library of New South Wales has, of course,

been the most important single source of my material, but I must also acknowledge the help I have received from the trustees and librarians of the Oxley Memorial Library of Queensland, the South Australian and Tasmanian Archives, the J. S. Battye Library of Western Australia, the State Library of Victoria, the Parliamentary Libraries of South Australia and Victoria and the library of Trinity College, University of Melbourne.

It will be apparent to the reader how heavily indebted I am to Associate-Professor K. C. Cable, Rev. Bro. Ronald Fogarty and Dr J. S. Gregory whose unpublished theses I have used extensively, and to Mr Kelvin Grose, Professor A. W. Martin and Mr P. A. Howell for forming my views on Bishop Broughton, Henry Parkes and Thomas Arnold respectively. I have also had the benefit of discussions with Dr J. M. Tregenza (on C. H. Pearson) and with Mr H. Nixon (on the appointment of the Fink Commission). They are not, of course, responsible for the interpretation I have put upon these matters. Professor J. A. La Nauze (now of the Australian National University) kindly provided me with a summary of Alfred Deakin's appointments in the latter part of 1898. In Chapters 2 and 4 I have drawn upon material originally published in my *George William Rusden* (M.U.P., 1958), and in my article 'The Bush Boarding School in the Port Phillip District', *Journal of Education* (V.I.E.R.), Vol. 3, No. 3.

The successive volumes of Professor Manning Clark's *A History of Australia* (M.U.P., Vol. 1, 1962; Vol. 2, 1968; others to follow) and of the *Australian Dictionary of Biography* (M.U.P., Vol. 1, 1966; Vol. 2, 1967; Vol. 3, 1969; others to follow) provide an invaluable source of background information on events and characters in this book.

A. G. AUSTIN

UNIVERSITY OF MELBOURNE

Contents

		PAGE
Preface to the Third Edition		v
1. Teacher, Chaplain and Governor, 1788–1833		1
2. Church, State and Common School in New South Wales, 1833–1851		33
3. Church, State and Common School in Van Diemen's Land, Western Australia and South Australia, 1829–1851		72
4. Church, State and Public School System in the Eastern Mainland Colonies, 1851–1866		112
5. Church, State and Public School System in Tasmania, Western Australia and South Australia, 1851–1871		139
6. Defining the Constitutional Code of Public Education, 1872–1895		173
7. Interpreting the Constitutional Code of Public Education, 1872–1900		238
Select Bibliography		278
Index		293

Abbreviations

A.N.U.	Australian National University.
B.L.E.P.S.	British Library of Economics and Political Science, London School of Economics.
D.N.B.	*Dictionary of National Biography.*
H. of A.	House of Assembly.
H.R.A.	*Historical Records of Australia.* The letters H.R.A. are followed by the number of the series and the number of the volume, e.g. *H.R.A.*, I, xv.
H.R.N.S.W.	*Historical Records of New South Wales.*
J.S.B.	The J. S. Battye Library, Western Australia.
M. & V. & P.	*Minutes and Votes and Proceedings.*
M.L.	Mitchell Library of New South Wales.
P.P.	*Papers Presented to Parliament.*
Parl. Deb.	*Parliamentary Debates.*
Proc. Parlt.	*Proceedings of Parliament.*
P.R.O.	Public Record Office, London.
R.A.H.S.	Royal Australian Historical Society.
S.A.A.	South Australian Archives.
S.L.V.	State Library of Victoria.
T.C.C.	The Trinity College Collection of Rusden Papers.
T.S.A.	Tasmanian State Archives.
V. & P.	*Votes and Proceedings.*
V. & P. & P.	*Votes and Proceedings and Papers.*

Note. The term "public school" has been used throughout in one sense in which it is defined in the *Shorter Oxford English Dictionary*, i.e. "a school provided at the public expense and managed by public authority, as part of a system of public (and usu. free) education".

1

Teacher, Chaplain and Governor
1788–1833

DURING the last week of January and the first week of February 1788 Captain Arthur Phillip disembarked some 1,030 British migrants at Sydney Cove. Exactly how many survived the passage out on the First Fleet is in dispute, but nearly three-quarters of the survivors appear to have been convicts, and the remainder Marines and government officers; seventeen of them were convicts' children, nineteen were Marines' children.[1] Nowhere in Phillip's Commissions or Instructions was any mention made of these children, or of the child convicts whom the British Government saw fit to transport,[2] for it was alien to the official mind of the late eighteenth century to feel any interest in the welfare of these children. By 1809 the War Office had been persuaded to appoint regimental schoolmasters, and by 1833 the Colonial Office was prepared to sanction an experiment in the reformation of child convicts in Van Diemen's Land,[3] but in 1788 the education of these children formed no part of the business of any department of State.

British Government Attitude to Popular Education

The British Government, in fact, was not concerned at all with the education of the lower orders. In France La

Australian Education, 1788-1900

Chalotais might preach the doctrine of secular education as a State monopoly, and in England Adam Smith might urge that the State should encourage "the instruction of the inferior ranks of people" to make them less prone to rebellion,[4] but neither argument had much influence on the official British attitude. Conservative opinion, while seized with the need to suppress incipient rebellion, was convinced that education was exactly the wrong remedy to apply, and agreed wholeheartedly with the Bishop of London's conviction that it was "safest for both the Government and the religion of the country to let the lower classes remain in that state of ignorance in which nature has originally placed them".[5] In the Commons, Davies Giddy warned the nation:

> However specious in theory the project might be, of giving education to the labouring classes of the poor, it would, in effect, be found to be prejudicial to their morals and happiness; it would teach them to despise their lot in life . . . it would render them factious and refractory . . . it would enable them to read seditious pamphlets . . . it would render them insolent to their superiors; and, in a few years, the result would be, that the legislature would find it necessary to direct the strong arm of power towards them. . . .[6]

In this atmosphere, anyone who undertook the education of the poor became an object of suspicion. It only needed Wesley to praise Robert Raikes's Sunday schools to confirm Anglican suspicions that they were nurseries of Dissent, and even the devout Hannah More had to defend her schools against charges of Methodism, Calvinism and subversion. "My plan of instruction is extremely simple and limited", she protested to the Bishop of Bath and Wells.

> They learn . . . such coarse work as may fit them for servants. I allow of no writing for the poor. My object is not to make fanatics, but to train up the lower classes in habits of industry and piety. . . . My attachment to the established church is, and has been, entire, cordial, inviolable, and, until now, unquestioned.[7]

Teacher, Chaplain and Governor, 1788-1833

Opposition to a system of national education was not confined to High Church Tories, for the Dissenter and the liberal (so often the one person) had their own reasons for resisting government intervention in education. Distrustful of the State and fearful of its alliance with the Established Church, the liberal-Dissenter rejected any suggestion that Government should provide or control public education. "Education is a branch of civil liberty which ought by no means to be surrendered into the hands of a civil magistrate", Priestley advised in 1768. ". . . the best interests of society require that the right of conducting it be inviolably preserved to individuals".[8] Nearly a century later John Stuart Mill still thought it necessary to warn his readers that "A general State education . . . establishes a despotism over the mind . . . ."[9]

Pitt's Tory government thus had every reason to resist the few theorists who advocated State intervention in education. Not only did the project bristle with difficulties, but even to contemplate it was foreign to a party which had been tutored so well by Edmund Burke in the virtues of "prescription". Burke, it is true, had been more concerned to protect the Whig oligarchy than to establish the theoretical foundations of political conservatism, but the arguments he developed to support the proposition that "Prescription . . . is a presumption in favour of any settled scheme of government against any untried project . . ." could scarcely have been more opportune for a conservative party on the threshold of fifty years of office.[10] The members of Pitt's first Ministry saw no reason to meddle in the upbringing of other people's children, and no reason to suppose that the governor they were dispatching to New South Wales would be presumptuous enough to dispute their opinion.

Education under the Early Governors

The early governors of New South Wales, however, soon found it necessary to contradict their masters at Westminster, for Botany Bay was not a fragment of English society transplanted to the Antipodes, but a military and penal garrison

Australian Education, 1788-1900

in which they were responsible for every detail of daily life. In a settlement where the maintenance of discipline, the regulation of food production, the rationing of supplies, the employment of labour and the administration of justice were necessarily committed into one man's hands, there was no room for that *laissez-faire* indifference which characterized the conduct of public affairs in the Mother Country. Even if the early governors had wished to ignore the condition of the colony's children they could not have done so, for the children were under their very feet; in a settlement which still failed to muster 5,000 souls in 1800, there was no escaping one's responsibilities. This is not to say that the early governors wished to evade their responsibilities. Not only were they moved by the misery of the convicts' children (for they were essentially humane men), but they realized that the future of the colony had to be built upon these very children. In a colony where there were three times as many men as women, and where the distribution of female convicts was never properly supervised, there was, as might have been expected, a deplorably high proportion of illegitimate and abandoned children. In 1807, on Governor Bligh's testimony, there were 397 married women in the colony, 1,035 "concubines", 807 legitimate children and 1,024 illegitimate children;[11] something, as Governor King had already pointed out, had to be done to rescue these children "from the future misery to be expected from the horrible examples that they hourly witness from their parents and those they live with".[12]

However, it was one thing to have good intentions in this matter, but quite another to find the means to carry them out. Phillip, it is true, had been instructed by the Secretary of State for the Colonies that it was His Majesty's

> further Will and Pleasure that a particular spot in or as near each town as possible be set apart for the building of a church, and four hundred acres adjacent thereto allotted for the maintenance of a minister, and two hundred for a school-master,[13]

but this charming, bucolic scene had little reality in an uncleared country whose soil and climate were not understood, and whose citizens, weak from malnutrition, were huddled despondently on the coast waiting for the arrival of store ships from England to save them from starvation.[14] Phillip and his immediate successors, no matter how sincere their interest in education, could count on little more than their own ingenuity to effect any provision for schools. Occasionally a literate soldier like Corporal William Webster of the New South Wales Corps could be diverted from his military duties and ordered to keep a school; occasionally a literate convict like Thomas McQueen could be released from his penal duties and set to the same task; occasionally a missionary of the London Missionary Society, driven out of the Pacific islands by perversely pagan natives, would seek sanctuary at Port Jackson and be offered a place as a schoolmaster, but whoever the schoolmaster was, his support and accommodation were vexing problems for the governor. A ration, a grant of land, the services of an assigned convict or a small payment from funds made available by the Society for the Propagation of the Gospel were the only resources the governor had. For the rest he could only hope that the schoolmasters would attract fee-paying pupils, and though there was ample evidence that his hopes were not being realized, he could do little more than exhort settlers, magistrates and clergy to support the schools.[15] The governors themselves set a worthy example by opening subscription lists, establishing orphanages and taking a benevolent interest in the pupils' progress; Hunter, King, Bligh and Macquarie all smiled in avuncular fashion upon the processions of children which made their way to Government House each year to be examined and praised by His Majesty's representative, and in return for the governors' condescension the children dutifully returned their thanks. "We . . . beg leave to return your Excellency our humble Thanks for the kind attention you have shown towards the promotion of our Education", they assured Governor Bligh in the well-drilled words of an Address. "We are truly sensible of Your Excellency's wise and public-spirited views to support and encourage the interest of the rising Generation of this Colony. . . ."[16]

In all this the governors were not concerned to assert the supremacy of either Church or State. All their actions were matters of expediency. To finance schools they had made direct land grants, assigned convicts and issued rations; they had accepted S.P.G. funds and subscriptions from the public; they had diverted money from fines and impositions and had made grants from public revenue.[17] To staff the schools they had used soldiers, convicts, dispossessed missionaries and any other literate person they could find; to accommodate the schools they had used churches, barracks, store-houses and private buildings, and to supervise them they had used the colonial chaplains. The chaplains, in their turn, were not at first disposed to provoke any argument on the constitutional basis of colonial education. They were, they realized, officers of the Crown and bound by their commissions "to observe and follow such orders and directions . . . as you shall receive from our Governor . . . or any other of your superior officers, according to the rules and discipline of war".[18] So long as the Anglican Church in New South Wales was represented only by colonial chaplains there was little likelihood of any constitutional conflict between Church and State. The chaplain who so far forgot his position as to challenge the governor was soon reminded of his subordinate status. Twenty-five years after the settlement was founded the governor could still inform the Secretary of State that the Rev. Samuel Marsden, having refused to read a government order from the pulpit, had incurred his censure. "I have cautioned Mr. Marsden to beware of resisting my Commands in this way for the future", Macquarie reported, "as he shall answer for it at his peril", and five years later Marsden was again reminded of his position when the governor refused him permission to take leave and proceed to England.[19] Again, any attempt by the chaplains to create an organized Church could only succeed if it were sanctioned by the governor. It was

Teacher, Chaplain and Governor, 1788-1833

Governor Macquarie, and not the principal chaplain, who, in 1810, instructed the chaplains that they were

> to consider themselves at all times under the immediate control and superintendence of the principal chaplain, and were to make such occasional reports to him, respecting their clerical duties, as he might think proper to require or call for.[20]

It was, in fact, a thoroughly Erastian arrangement, and was based upon the general belief that the Church of England was the Established Church of New South Wales and was thereby entitled to the privileges, and subject to the restrictions, inherent in that relationship. Whether the Church of England was ever an Established Church in Australia has been a matter of legal dispute for over 150 years, but the essential point, as Kenneth Cable has pointed out, is that the Church of England "acted as if it were Established and it received privileges and monetary aid sufficient to justify that assumption".[21] Governor and chaplain might disagree violently upon the policy they should follow, but neither doubted the legality or correctness of the relationship in which they stood, and the privileged position of the Church they both served. Macquarie might complain of "The Frequent and long preserved in Efforts of Mr. Marsden to Embarrass my Government and to Impede my measures in every Way, Which an Under-hand, disingenuous, Caballing Disposition Could devise . . . .", but when, in the same letter, he came to ask the Secretary of State for six more schoolmasters, he begged leave "to Suggest the Propriety of all persons, sent hither for the purpose of disseminating the Principles of Education, being of the Established Church, Untainted by Methodism or Other Sectarian Opinions".[22]

If anyone in New South Wales doubted the privileged status which governor and chaplain believed the Anglican Church occupied in the field of education, his doubts should have been dispelled during the closing years of Macquarie's governorship. In 1820, for example, Macquarie was advised by the Colonial Office that his pleas for "the great work of rendering education co-extensive with the population" were to be supported by the introduction of "the System of Education, as at present established by Dr. Bell in the National Schools in this Country . . . ."; this system, Earl Bathurst declared, was

> the best adapted, not only for securing to the rising Generation in New South Wales the Advantages of all necessary Instruction, but also in bringing them up in Habits of Industry and Regularity, and for implanting in their Minds the Principles of the Established Church. . . .[23]

Bathurst hoped, no doubt, that Bell's system would serve in the colonies the purposes for which it had been established in England, where the High Church party, alarmed at the success of Joseph Lancaster's monitorial schools designed to educate children of all Christian sects, had prevailed upon the Rev. Dr Bell to establish schools upon the monitorial system he had devised at the Male Asylum in Madras. In 1811 the Anglican bishops created the National Society for the Education of the Poor in Accordance with the Principles of the Established Church which they hoped would spread Dr Bell's system and check the growth of Lancaster's schools now organized in the British and Foreign School Society. No blame can be attached to Earl Bathurst for advocating a monitorial system for, although its whole pedagogical basis was later condemned, there was almost universal agreement, in 1820, that monitorial instruction was one of the most beneficial inventions of the age—"the STEAM ENGINE of the MORAL WORLD", as Bell liked to call it, ". . . the *lever* of *Archimedes* transferred from matter to mind".[24] Nevertheless, Bathurst's decision to impose upon a community of mixed religious affiliations a monitorial system which was also exclusively Anglican can only be regarded as a glaring instance of Tory obtuseness. It accorded perfectly, however, with Macquarie's detestation of Dissent, and he extended a very warm welcome to the instrument of Bathurst's policy, the Rev. Thomas Reddall, when that gentleman arrived in Sydney late in 1820. Reddall, who had spent nearly a year at the Central National School in London, was authorized by Bathurst to introduce Bell's system in New South Wales, and to assume a general superintendence of the schools he established; Macquarie quickly established him in a school at Airds, enrolled his own son as a pupil, and showed Reddall every social favour.[25]

Emboldened by this evidence of Colonial Office support for the Established Church, Marsden seized the opportunity to consolidate the Church's position by bringing an action against a private schoolmaster, James Bradley, for "seducing" children out of the Public School at Parramatta. Before the magistrates both Marsden and the Rev. Robert Cartwright declared that it was unlawful "according to the Established Laws of the Church for any person to teach Government Public Schools without the sanction of the Resident Chaplain . . . .";[26] the magistrates refused to convict Bradley, but it was clear that both governor and chaplain had determined upon an Anglican monopoly in education.

J. T. Bigge's Commission of Inquiry

While Macquarie and the Anglican clergy were engaged upon their designs, the Colonial Office was also laying plans for the educational future of New South Wales. In 1819 Earl Bathurst issued a commission of inquiry to J. T. Bigge, who had formerly been Chief Justice of Trinidad, authorizing him

> to examine into all the Laws Regulations and Usages of the Settlements in the said Territory [of New South Wales] . . . and into every other Matter or Thing in any way connected with the Administration of the Civil Government, the Superintendance and Reform of the Convicts, the State of the Judicial, Civil and Ecclesiastical Establishments, Revenues, Trade and internal Resources thereof, and to report to Us the Information, which You shall collect together, with your opinion thereupon. . . .[27]

Bathurst, who in his fifteen years of office virtually created the nineteenth-century Colonial Office, had been concerned about the future of New South Wales for some years. He had, of course, been petitioned and waited upon by the host of enemies which Macquarie, like every other colonial governor, had made, but he was more concerned with the deeper problem of New South Wales' rapid development from a penal colony to a prosperous, pastoral settlement. "Until a recent period", he told Lord Sidmouth in 1817, "the Transportation of Offenders to New South Wales appears to have answered in a very great degree the ends, for the Attainment of which it was adopted". However, he went on, the flow of migrants and the increasing number of emancipated convicts

> has so increased the population of Free Settlers that the prosperity of the Settlement as a Colony has proportionately advanced, and hopes may reasonably be entertained of its becoming perhaps at no distant period a valuable possession of the Crown. It is this very circumstance which appears to me to render it less fit for the object of its original Institution.[28]

The future of New South Wales was thus committed to the judgment of John Thomas Bigge whose reports were tabled in the House of Commons between June 1822 and March 1823.[29] There is general agreement amongst historians that his reports, and their voluminous, unpublished appendices, constituted an invaluable source of information and effected a major change in Colonial Office policy. This may well be true as a general statement, but it is not true of his report on the state of religion and education which, in a brief ten pages, provided little more than a sketchy, and somewhat inaccurate, descriptive account of the colony's churches and schools. The relevant appendix on Ecclesiastical Establishments, Schools and Charitable Societies must have daunted Bathurst's officers for it consisted of an amorphous mass of statistical returns, importunate requests from schoolmasters and clergymen, and calumnious correspondence from practically everyone connected with the schools of the colony.[30]

Appointment of Archdeacon T. H. Scott

Bathurst, when he came to study the Bigge Report, was clearly disappointed with the section on religion and education. To a Secretary of State engaged upon a general

Teacher, Chaplain and Governor, 1788-1833

reorganization of colonial affairs, Bigge's ten pages were completely inadequate but, as the Commissioner had already left on another colonial investigation (this time to Cape Colony, Mauritius and Ceylon), Bathurst could only turn to the secretary of the Commission, Thomas Hobbes Scott, for supplementary information. This, it could be argued, was the opportunity for Scott to seize. When he went out to New South Wales with Bigge in 1819 Scott had little to recommend him beyond his family connexions with the Earl of Oxford and the Commissioner; a one-time wine merchant, he had matriculated at Oxford in 1813 (at the age of forty), and had been admitted as a Master of Arts the year before he sailed. On his return from New South Wales he took Holy Orders, and by the time Bathurst sought his advice in 1823 was vicar of Whitfield in Northumberland. Here, indeed, was opportunity, but Bathurst's request obviously found Scott unprepared. He had not, he protested, had time to arrange the notes he had made on this subject while in the colony, and therefore his reply must be regarded as a "hasty statement" which he would be happy to amplify and explain at a later date. What followed was a sorry muddle. That public education should be regarded as a government responsibility in New South Wales and that it should be controlled by a clerical Visitor who should also "be placed at the head of the Church Establishment" Scott asserted quite clearly, but he had no coherent plan for financing and organizing a system of schools. Perhaps part of the cost could be defrayed by having the parents contribute, annually, a bushel of "good clean sound wheat, or its equivalent in meat—or their value in money"? Perhaps one-eighth of the colonial imports could be diverted to education? Perhaps government should subdivide its land at Grose Farm, Emu Plains, Rooty Hill and Cabramatta into small farms and apply their rents to "the endowment of schools in general"? Or perhaps a new land reserve of some 25,000 acres should be established near Bathurst or Newcastle?[31]

Lord Bathurst, as Scott must have been quick to see, was

clearly impressed by this last suggestion. Within a few weeks of receiving Scott's letter Bathurst had sent a dispatch to Governor Brisbane instructing him to make "sufficient Reserves in every district which may in future be granted out for the maintenance of both a Clerical and a School Establishment".[32] The truth was that the policy of supporting the Anglican Church in the colonies by means of Clergy Reserves had an unwarranted attraction for Bathurst, although he had been engaged for the last five years in defending a similar system in Upper Canada against the indignant protests of the Protestant sects. Incredible as it may seem, Bathurst had apparently forgotten that in 1820 he had advised the Lieutenant-Governor of Upper Canada that the privileges enjoyed by the Anglican clergy there might have to be extended to the Presbyterian clergy; his forgetfulness is inexplicable when one remembers that, only a few months before he decided upon a system of Clergy Reserves for New South Wales, he had had to deal with yet another protest on this matter from the Canadian House of Assembly.[33]

Nevertheless the Secretary of State was clearly bent upon establishing Clergy Reserves in New South Wales if only someone would provide him with a detailed plan by which these Reserves could be administered. Scott set to work to provide these details in a second letter to the Colonial Office. Religion and education must be united, he urged, and any provision for their support must be based upon a reserve of land. If one-tenth of the land of New South Wales were set aside for this purpose and vested in a Board of Trustees, Scott argued, the Established Church would then be in a position to exercise its traditional functions. It would then only remain to create an archdeaconry in New South Wales, and name the incumbent as "Visitor of all Public Schools".[34]

Scott's part in all this is hard to determine. His detractors, seizing upon his appointment to the new archdeaconry, declared that with Bigge's connivance he had contrived the whole plan in order to provide himself with a fat living—a point of view supported by some dubious evidence from the Bigge family seventy years later.[35] It is hard to escape the impression that the appointment was a contrived piece of patronage. Scott, on his own admission, had begun to prepare his elaborate plan for the colonial Church while he was still in New South Wales,[36] and one wonders why no mention of it was made in Bigge's suspiciously sketchy Report unless it were suppressed to allow Scott time to take Orders. Admittedly Scott's father had been in Orders, but the new archdeacon seems to have shown no interest in a religious vocation until, at the somewhat advanced age of forty-nine, he presented himself for ordination. Scott's biographer, on the other hand, saw nothing strange in his subject's belated ordination, and felt that it was perfectly natural that Bathurst, when looking for an archdeacon, should have chosen the only cleric in England who had experience of the colony.[37]

Whatever the exact nature of Scott's appointment there can be no doubting the extent of his influence with Earl Bathurst. During the latter part of 1824, when the former Chief Justice of New South Wales, Barron Field, was in and out of the Colonial Office plotting the recall of Governor Brisbane and the repression of the "convict party", he quickly realized that Scott was the man through whom he should work. The archdeacon-elect, he told his correspondent in New South Wales,

> is intimate with Lord Bathurst . . . . he has great influence . . . . is at home in the office and [his] . . . representations from the colony will have great weight for they look to him to set your Governor and Secretary to rights and to reconcile all quarrels.

So confident was Scott of his influence that he had declined to take ship until he was given a guarantee that both Brisbane and his Colonial Secretary would be recalled. By December, Field could report that

> we may attribute the entire change of Government greatly to his [being] loath to go out under your present heads; for *he* is the confidential person at Downing Street, and it was while he was staying with Lord Bathurst in Glostershire that his lordship

introduced General Darling to him as the new Governor and Mr. Scott has since been down to Cheltenham to instruct the General.[38]

Creation of the Church and School Corporation

It was in this confident frame of mind that Scott finally set out in the *Hercules* bearing with him a dispatch informing Governor Brisbane that "His Majesty having been pleased to erect an Archdeaconry in the Colony of New South Wales . . . has been pleased to nominate the Rev'd Thomas Hobbes Scott to be the first Archdeacon", that he was to provide the new archdeacon with a salary of £2,000 a year, and was to provide him with an estate "comprising one seventh part in extent and value of all the lands in each county" for the "maintenance of the Church and the education of the Youth in New South Wales".[39] Brisbane, whose recall was announced in the same bundle of dispatches, must have reflected that at least he was well out of this pretty muddle. His instructions, though drafted with great legal care, were completely unrealistic. A Corporation, he discovered, was to be established and invested with the Clergy and School Estates, from the proceeds of which it should support the Anglican Church and "Schools and School Masters . . . in connection with the Established Church". The territory of New South Wales was to be divided into Counties, Hundreds and Parishes as a result of a "survey of the whole Colony" and "a general valuation of the Land throughout the Colony". The Clergy and School Estates, the dispatch went on,

> will, as nearly as may be, lie in one continuous and unbroken tract. . . . The lands thus to be set apart must be of an average quality and value in reference to the general value of the lands comprised in the County . . . and . . . must afford a reasonable and equal share of all those natural advantages of water carriage, or other internal communication which may be possessed by the lands in general. . . .

To carry out this task the colony's Surveyor-General (John Oxley) had at his disposal seven field-surveyors, of whom

Teacher, Chaplain and Governor, 1788–1833

one was an elderly invalid, another was paralysed, and another was about to depart with the government astronomer to measure an arc of the meridian; of the remaining four, two were already engaged on a survey of the lands of the Australian Agricultural Company.[40] No trigonometrical survey of the colony had ever been made, and the greater part of the land granted by the two previous governors remained unsurveyed.[41] "Mr. Oxley", Brisbane's successor remarked, "is a very clever Man", but neither Oxley's wit nor Darling's will could find a way around this problem. "I am quite puzzled what to do in the present insufficient state of the Survey Department", Darling reported lamely.[42]

Opposition to Scott and the Corporation

Nevertheless the archdeacon was not to be deterred, and the Surveyor-General's Office knew no peace. Oxley had been relatively restrained under pressure from the Corporation, but his successor, Major Thomas Mitchell, was too harassed to be polite. If the country were free of timber, he reported tartly in 1828, and if his surveyors could be released from all other duties, it might be possible, to judge from the progress of the Irish trigonometrical survey, to complete the Corporation's survey in twenty-four years. However, he added, seeing that the country was timbered he doubted whether the survey was practicable at all.[43] A year later his temper completely got the better of him. Was he, he asked the Colonial Secretary, to regard himself as a servant of the Corporation? Should he, as he proceeded, transfer his work "into the Archives of the Church Corporation?" "I am well aware", he roared,

> that . . . it would be very convenient for the corporation and the Public to have a complete Map; and . . . I am frequently occupied in furtherance of this desirable object while . . . the Church Corporation are at Tea, or at Dinner, or in Bed, or at Church.[44]

Mitchell's exasperation, which was shared by a majority of the people in New South Wales, was not provoked by the personal importunity of the archdeacon, but was an expression of revolt at the whole concept of a Church and School Corporation. Scott's background and personality certainly did not help his cause. From the outset he was an object of suspicion to the radical party because of his former association with Bigge's policy of support to the wealthy landowners, because of his close friendship with the Macarthurs, and because of his firm support of that most unpopular governor, General Ralph Darling. Before he had been very long in the colony he had also contrived to antagonize his own clergy, the Press, the members of every other sect, the judiciary, and even the governor whose authority he so steadfastly upheld. But, though everything he did aggravated a tense situation, his conduct did not cause it. Essentially, the opposition Scott faced was not directed at him as a person, but at his office and the assumptions underlying that office.

The colony he re-entered in 1825 was in a turbulent condition. The exclusive party—the "old colonial magnates" as Parkes later called them—had just won a notable victory; with the publication of the Bigge Report and the resignation of Macquarie they had every reason to believe that the colony no longer existed for the reformation of the convict and the rehabilitation of the emancipist, but for their personal and corporate advancement. The autocratic rule of the penal governor must be replaced by the forms of self-government, they argued, but only in so far as it suited their conceptions of social and political privilege. Arrayed against them was the emancipist party, not the "convict party" as the exclusives liked to call it, but a party of emancipists and free settlers led by liberals of many shades of opinion. The emancipists demanded nothing less than the exclusives—the right to manipulate the political machinery of the colony—but in order to succeed they had to assert a radical disbelief in the political and social assumptions on which the colony was being built; the satisfaction of their demands, as Professor Hartwell has pointed out, "would have meant a genuine social revolution".[45] By the time Scott returned, the emancipist Press was in full cry in its demand for more liberal political and judicial institutions, and the Church and School Corporation Charter which he brought with him constituted a symbol of the social order they were trying to overthrow.[46]

It was Scott's misfortune that the Press he encountered was fighting for its hand against Darling's attempts to suppress it, and would neither give nor take any quarter. In its more violent and irresponsible moments it could descend to personal abuse (Bigge, for example, was called a lecher, and Scott "a mere chronicler and clerk"),[47] but even Scott, while smarting under these personal attacks, realized that the real target of the emancipist Press was not himself, but the pretensions of his Church.[48] "England has miscalculated most seriously", the *Australian* declared.

> To raise a revenue for the Church, she has planted a scion which if it spring up to maturity, will overshadow and destroy every production within its reach. She has laid the foundations of a mighty power, which, if suffered to acquire strength in proportion to its substructure, will annihilate every interest and every sway in the Colony. The Clergy will reign triumphant—the tyrants alike of the people and the constituted Authorities—their possessions and their wealth will serve to crush on the one hand, enslave on the other, and New South Wales from being a prosperous and rising Colony, will sink into a Priest-ridden, nerveless Community. . . . Shame! Shame! Shame![49]

It was in vain that Scott begged the governor, the Colonial Office and the Bishop of London to silence these men. Despite endless litigation the emancipist editors continued their attacks on the "rapacity and extortion" of the Anglican Church, upon "sacerdotal dominancy" and upon the spectacle of "half the territory being clawed by spiritual teachers yet temporal tyrants". The Established Church's concern for property had emptied the churches of Britain, they declared;

> we find everywhere the same grasping avarice and ambition of the High Church party. Everywhere they are drawing, by falsehood, intrigue, and sycophancy, to themselves exclusively, the whole public funds allowed for instruction and religious worship. . . .[50]

But Scott and the Corporation had more than political opposition to contend with. Both Presbyterians and Roman Catholics were numerous in the colony, and both sects had formidable spokesmen in their leaders, Dr John Dunmore Lang and Father John Joseph Therry; neither cleric was inclined to accept Anglican domination and neither was afraid to speak his mind. Father Therry had good reason to fear Scott's arrival, for in the five years he had been in the colony Therry had learnt the extent of official opposition to his mission and the tenuous nature of any concessions which had been made to him. He and Scott greeted each other amicably enough, but as soon as Therry realized that the Corporation was to be given control of all government orphanages and was to apply its funds therein "towards the Education of Youth . . . in the Principles of the Established Church"[51] he launched an attack upon this "odious, irreligious and unjust system . . . . [this] partial and proselytising system" which was comparable only to that Irish system whose "baneful influence has withered the fairest flowers, and blasted the finest fruits in the land. . . ."[52] Darling knew only one way to deal with this sort of criticism. Therry, he informed Bathurst,

> is evidently disposed to be troublesome, and, constituted as this community is, might be dangerous, a large proportion of the Convicts being of the lowest class of Irish Catholics, ignorant in the extreme, and in proportion bigotted and under the domination of their Priest. . . . [His] immediate removal appears . . . desirable.[53]

Bathurst agreed, but though Therry was dismissed as a chaplain, he refused to leave the colony, and continued to be an implacable opponent of the Corporation.

Darling had no greater success in his attempts to silence Dr Lang who, even within the litigious, polemical society of New South Wales, had already established for himself a pre-eminent place as a dangerous controversialist. On several occasions Darling tried to avoid a clash with Lang by ignoring, or pretending to ignore, his conduct,[54] but when, late in 1830, Lang wrote directly to the Secretary of State and favoured him with his views on the Church and School Corporation, there was no longer room for diplomatic evasion. The Corporation, Lord Goderich read,

> has excited a spirit of disaffection towards His Majesty's Government among the native youth of the Colony; and I will even add, my Lord, has sown the seeds of future rebellion. In short, the Church and School Corporation . . . has lain as a dead weight on the Colony for the last five years, repressing emigration, discouraging improvement, secularizing the Episcopal Clergy, and thereby lowering the standard of morals and religion throughout the Territory.[55]

This was distasteful enough for his Lordship, but when he discovered that Lang had published this letter he found it difficult to find words to express his displeasure.[56] But a reprimand from a Secretary of State was nothing new to Lang,[57] and to show his defiance he published a further analysis of the Charter. "Mr. Scott's private character and general education were unexceptionable", he began,

> but his theological attainments were necessarily extremely meagre. . . . Viewing religion as a matter of State policy, and the colonial Episcopal clergy as a chartered body possessing the exclusive monopoly of intermeddling with its concerns, his maxim evidently was, "Let Episcopacy reign alone in the Australian colonies, and let no Presbyterian dog be permitted to bark within her ample domain." . . . . It will scarcely be believed, indeed, that so wanton an insult, as this precious document implied, could have been offered to the common sense of a whole community, even by the Tory administration of the period; or that men could have been found in the nineteenth century to perpetuate so gross an outrage on the best feelings of a numerous body of reputable men. But so it was; and the education of the colony thus appeared to have passed completely into the hands of the Church and School Corporation.[58]

Amidst all this controversy and recrimination Scott appeared to make his way unruffled and unrepentant Reddall was relieved of his office as Director-General of Schools and Scott assumed the role of King's Visitor; the emancipist editors were sued for libel; teachers were brought down to Sydney and trained in the monitorial system; the clergy were instructed to supervise the schools in their parishes, new schools were planned and begun. But at heart Scott was distraught and bitterly disappointed. The Courts refused to convict the emancipist editors and, when Scott attempted to discipline one of his schoolmasters, declared that he had no authority to act as King's Visitor.[59] Moreover, despite all his efforts, not one acre of the promised Clergy and School Estates passed into the Corporation's hands until February 1829, and he was forced to improvise and beg in order to support his schools and his churches. A few hundred pounds was accumulated from pew rents, a few thousand pounds from the sale of older clerical lands inherited by the Corporation and from debentures issued upon the security of the anticipated estates, but the bulk of his funds had to be coaxed out of the colonial Treasury—£11,600 in 1826, £19,847 in 1827 and £19,300 in 1828. Even after land was received, it was so poor in quality and so inaccessible that the Treasury had to continue its grants—£20,500 in 1829, £16,500 in 1830.[60]

The wonder is not that Scott became disheartened, but that he lost heart so quickly and completely. He was not, after all, a stranger to the rigours of colonial life, he was not a young or inexperienced man, and he most certainly had not been thrust unwillingly into the archdeaconry of New South Wales. Yet, within six months of his arrival in the colony, he had decided to resign, and within a year had actually submitted his resignation.[61] Within the colony he kept his head high, but his correspondents knew the extent of his defeat. During those wonderful months when he had been Earl Bathurst's confidant it must have seemed the easiest thing in the world to manipulate the destiny of New South Wales, but now he had to learn, as half-a-dozen governors had already learnt, that Downing Street had little time for a man who could not manage his own affairs. Scott learnt his lesson slowly and painfully. By 1827 he was still confounded by the lack of support he was receiving.

"Nothing is to be done for schools", he cried to Colonel Arthur, his only Australian friend,

> and then Lord Bathurst wonders [why] no reformation takes place; I should wonder if it did! . . . I do not expect any more Clerical or School assistance from England for we have received such an *economical concern* and such a refusal to build either Churches or Schools that I think would be highly worthy of the Revolutionary Government of Republican France when the Goddess of Reason was worshipped and the Cross trampled on![62]

To his authoritarian mind it seemed incredible that any impediments could be put in the way of an institution which had been incorporated by Royal Letters Patent, but he had apparently forgotten his days as Bigge's secretary and the thousand examples of litigation and appeal which he had seen reduce even His Majesty's representative to impotence. "The Corporation is about to meet", he told Colonel Arthur in 1826,

> but with what effect I know not—I foresee that the moment we begin to move there will be a thousand objections, especially *legal* ones and the whole will crumble to the ground, for by the time our references are made to England and the answers received we shall be all "grown grey in the service of the state" . . . . Don't have a Corporation whatever you do.[63]

By the middle of 1828 it must have been clear to Scott's correspondents that he was a broken man. The members of the Ecclesiastical Board for the Colonial Church had asked him to reconsider his resignation, he told Arthur, but they

> do not know my feelings and my sleepless nights. . . . I can do more good with my poor humble flock at home than I can do here. . . . I would rather be a curate than the Head of the Church here. . . . I shall officially announce to the Archbishop unless he can or will place more power and the means of enforcing it in the hands of my successor he may as well have no Church here at all.[64]

How could he continue, he asked the Ecclesiastical Board?

> One Clergyman makes my letter public through the channel of these papers, another in the exercise of my duty as Visitor sends

me an Attorney's letter concluding with a legal threat, another not only insults me before all the Clergy and even in the Church but sets at defiance my desire to enforce his residence, another requires from me all the advantages, and disadvantages of the District which I assign to him. . . . Many of them are too well supported by legal advisers, to oppose whom I have not a person capable of affording me any assistance or who are not even less conversant with Ecclesiastical Laws than myself.[65]

"Friend and foe are equally dissatisfied with me", he confided to Arthur in 1829,

> . . . That I have failed is clear and I have taken it much to heart. . . . I now count the days for my release. . . . I assure you it will be one of the happiest days of my life the day of my departure *even with the loss of* 2,000 *a year!*[66]

Dissolution of the Church and School Corporation

But the breaking of Archdeacon Scott did not mean the destruction of the Corporation. In 1827 the *Australian* had told its readers that the Corporation was about to be dissolved. "New Holland to a cassock", the editor had cried, "the news is true. . . . They will—they must . . . be disbanded",[67] but his elation had been premature. In a sense, however, the *Australian* had hit upon the truth, for even as the editor wrote, the Colonial Office was slowly swinging round to the opinion that a privileged position for the Anglican Church could not be maintained in the colonies. For fourteen years Bathurst had been taking the opinion of his legal adviser, James Stephen, whose ability and industry had given him a position of very great influence. Stephen was not to become Permanent Under-Secretary until 1836, but by the mid-1820s he already had more power than any other person in the Office. Paul Knaplund has pointed out that if one studies Stephen's comments on the mass of documents passing through the Office, one begins to understand the extent to which he made policy.[68] At first Stephen clearly advocated the support of the Anglican Church at the expense of other Churches, but by the late 1820s he could not ignore the distress and resentment this policy had caused. By the end of 1828, when he was asked to comment on a Nova Scotian Act, he reported:

> It is, I presume, vain to attempt to secure to the Church of England on the North American Continent, that species of monopoly of secular privileges which it enjoys in this country, nor does it seem probable that the real interest of that Church would be promoted by maintaining any such exclusive principle.[69]

A year later he pointed out that it was "evident that the exclusive privileges of the English church in Canada, cannot be supported. . . ."[70]

While Stephen was helping to create a new policy on the colonial Church, political affairs in England were moving the Colonial Office in the same direction. In 1827 the Tory control of the House at last began to weaken. In February Lord Liverpool, who had led the party since 1812, suffered a stroke and retired from office; Canning, who succeeded him, died within four months and Goderich (England's third Prime Minister in one year) scarcely held the Ministry together until the Christmas recess. In January 1828 Wellington assumed the leadership of the party, but it was clear to all that he could only hope to govern with the consent of the Whigs. Early in 1828 Lord John Russell demonstrated the Tories' untenable position by moving the repeal of the Test and Corporation Acts; in themselves these Acts were no longer important for they were nullified each year by an indemnity Act, but any formal decision to repeal them could only be regarded as a defeat for the Ultra-Tories and their policy of exclusive recognition of the Established Church. When, by a majority of forty-four, the House carried the repeal, Russell could reflect that "It is really a gratifying thing to force the enemy to give up his first line".[71]

Less than a year later the "enemy's" main defences were breached when Wellington and Peel were compelled to sponsor Catholic emancipation; to Wellington this measure of liberal reform was a tactical concession designed to preserve his decaying party in power; to Peel it was a painful sacrifice of principle which permanently warped his character.[72]

It was in this atmosphere that Wellington's Secretary of State (Sir George Murray) sat down to answer four dispatches from New South Wales dealing with the support of the clergy and the schools.[73] With Stephen at his elbow, and recent events in the House in his mind, he had no hesitation in condemning the suggestion that Van Diemen's Land should be given a Corporation similar to the one which had failed so dismally in New South Wales. "I have also thought it right", Murray added, "to counsel His Majesty to revoke His Letters Patent, by which the Corporation has been erected in the latter Colony".[74] A year later, while the King lay too near death to sign his name, his stamp was placed upon Instructions which ordered Governor Darling to replace the Corporation by a temporary Commission.[75] But these and other evidences of a prudential liberalism were not enough to save the Tories when, upon the King's death in June 1830, Parliament was dissolved and general elections were held. In November, when Wellington conceded his defeat, Grey formed a new Ministry and opened the way to a general reform of English public life.

It would be wrong, however, to credit this Ministry with any intention to reform colonial life by restricting the wealth and influence of the Anglican Church in the colonies. It is true, of course, that by 1835 Stephen's view had so far triumphed that the Secretary of State could tell the governor of New South Wales that any attempt "to select any one Church as the exclusive Object of public Endowment, even if it were advisable in every other respect, would not long be tolerated", but to argue that this point of view was acceptable to the Grey Ministry in 1830-31 would be a serious misreading of the evidence.[76] In the first place, Grey's Secretary of State for the colonies was Viscount Goderich, that same Goderich who had held office in the Tory administrations of Liverpool and Canning, and who had led his own short-lived Tory Ministry in 1827. While it was true that he was a moderate Tory (he had, for example, supported both the Test and Corporation Acts Repeal Bill and the Roman Catholic Relief Bill), he could by no stretch of the imagination be regarded as a radical reformer, and his appointment to the Colonial Office was nothing more than a reward for the part his group of Canningites had played in bringing Wellington down.[77] Such reputation as Goderich had, rested upon the monetary and commercial reforms he had introduced during his period as Chancellor of the Exchequer in the Liverpool Ministry. He now addressed himself to colonial affairs in the same mercantile spirit, and began by reconstructing colonial land regulations. It is clear that Goderich's attitude to the colonial waste lands was influenced by two circumstances. In the first place he had been, to some extent, converted to the Wakefieldian principle that colonial waste land should not be granted, but should be sold at a price sufficiently high to prevent dispersion, and that the revenue thus raised should be used to encourage the emigration of labourers who, because of the high price of land, would be compelled to remain labourers for some considerable time.[78] In the second place, he had before him the report of a House of Commons committee which condemned the Clergy and School Estates as an example of the evils which flowed from land grants which lay unworked and unproductive while settlers were forced to go further out to acquire land.[79] Early in 1831, Goderich began to formulate his new land policy. In a long dispatch to Darling he announced that he was convinced that the existing land regulations "have not had the intended effect of preventing large tracts of land from being appropriated by Persons unable to improve and cultivate them, and Secondly that they are founded upon an erroneous view of the true interests both of the Colony and of the Mother Country".[80] He went on, in words which were a paraphrase of Wakefield's, to stress the need for concentration of settlement and a flow of labour. In future, he concluded, "no land whatever shall be disposed of otherwise than by sale, a minimum price (say, five shillings an acre) being fixed. . . ."

This is the only context in which Goderich ever discussed the Church and School Corporation. Whether writing to Australian or Canadian governors he was explicit that the dissolution of such a Corporation was dictated simply by its failure to answer its purpose, and the unproductive nature of its lands. "It comes, therefore, simply to be a question, whether it is the best means of raising the sum which is required", he told Darling;

> a question on which there cannot be a doubt, when it is remembered, that, while they cause very serious inconvenience to the Settlers, these reserves, at the present moment, do not even pay the expense of management.[81]

He would not, he insisted to the Governor of Upper Canada, be drawn into any discussion on the propriety of creating or abolishing an Established Church. "It is sufficient to repeat", he went on,

> that His Majesty's Government have advised the abandonment of the Reserves, for the simple reason, that . . . they have been found not to answer the expectations entertained at the time the system was established. . . .[82]

Moreover, he made it clear to Darling, he had no intention of withdrawing, or diminishing, the aid which had traditionally been given to the Church of England in New South Wales. Because the Clergy and School Estates had not produced any revenue the Treasury had always been called on to make a large annual grant, he reminded Darling, and the "policy of the proposed change is . . . to trust for the means of meeting the future expense of the Church Establishment to the same sources from which it is at present defrayed. . . ."[83]

Archdeacon Thomas Hobbes Scott might have been driven to resignation, the Church and School Corporation might have been dissolved, but there was, as yet, no intention of modifying the Anglican monopoly of education. The most that can be said in favour of Goderich's colonial reputation as a liberal reformer is that in replacing Darling by Sir Richard Bourke he placed the future of New South

Wales in the hands of a more liberal governor than the colony had ever known,[84] and opened the way for a reappraisal of the colony's educational problems.

NOTES

[1] For an analysis of the composition of the First Fleet see Eris O'Brien, *The Foundation of Australia*, Appendix B. See also L. L. Robson, *The Convict Settlers of Australia*.

[2] By July 1790 there were forty-seven child convicts in Sydney and thirty-six at Norfolk Island, *H.R.A.*, I, i, 203. For a recent study of education in early colonial Australia see John F. Cleverley, *The First Generation*.

[3] See F. C. Hooper, 'The Point Puer Experiment', *Journal of Education* (V.I.E.R.), Vol. 3, No. 1 (Mar. 1956).

[4] Adam Smith, *An Inquiry Into the Nature and Causes of the Wealth of Nations*, p. 353.

[5] Quoted F. A. Cavanagh, 'State Intervention in English Education', *History*, Vol. 25, No. 98, p. 144 (Sept. 1940).

[6] Ibid.

[7] William Roberts, *Memoirs of the Life and Correspondence of Mrs Hannah More*, Vol. III, pp. 133-6. See also Vol. II, pp. 295-301, Vol. III, pp. 160, 256-61.

[8] Quoted Cavanagh, op. cit., 145.

[9] John Stuart Mill, *On Liberty*, p. 132. For a recent discussion of Mill's point of view see M. J. Charlesworth, 'The Liberal State and the Control of Education', *Melbourne Studies in Education, 1967*, and M. H. Stannus, 'Education and the Liberal Ideal', ibid., *1971*.

[10] Edmund Burke, *Works*, Vol. VI, p. 146. The Tories took office under the younger Pitt in 1783 and, with the exception of the months Feb. 1806 to Mar. 1807, held office until the fall of the Wellington Ministry in 1830.

[11] D. C. Griffiths, *Documents on the Establishment of Education in New South Wales, 1789-1880*, p. 19.

[12] King to Portland, 9 Sept. 1800, *H.R.A.*, I, ii, 537.

[13] Grenville to Phillip, 22 Aug. 1789, *H.R.A.*, I, i, 127.

[14] For conditions in the "starving time" see Lois Davey and others, 'The Hungry Years: 1788-1792', *Historical Studies*, Vol. 3, No. 11 (Nov. 1947).

[15] For a descriptive account of the early colonial schools see V. W. E. Goodin, 'Public Education in New South Wales before 1848', *Journal and Proceedings*, R.A.H.S., Vol. 36, Parts 1-4, 1950.

[16] *Sydney Gazette*, 7 June 1807.

[17] See Goodin, op. cit.; Instructions to Governor Bligh, 25 May 1805, *H.R.A.*, I, vi, 18-19.

[18] *H.R.N.S.W.*, I, Part 2, 27.

[19] Macquarie to Bathurst, 24 May 1814, *H.R.A.*, I, viii, 256; Macquarie to Bathurst, 15 May 1818, *H.R.A.*, I, ix, 776. As late as 1819 an Imperial Act decreed that a priest ordained for colonial service held a revocable licence and could not get a living in England without a special permit from the bishop of his diocese. The Rev. Thomas Reddall's certificate of ordination, dated 19 Dec. 1819, was endorsed "for the cure of souls in His Majesty's Foreign Possessions", but in itself did not enable him to perform his clerical duties in N.S.W.; that authority was contained in his commission as an Assistant Chaplain, dated 20 Dec. 1819. Reddall Papers. (M.L.).

[20] Report of the Commissioner of Inquiry on the State of Agriculture and Trade in the Colony of New South Wales, 1823, p. 68, *House of Commons Papers*, 1823, Vol. 10. See also Ross Border, *Church and State in Australia, 1788-1872*, Ch. 2.

[21] Kenneth C. Cable, 'The Church of England in New South Wales and its Policy towards Education prior to 1880', unpublished M.A. Thesis, University of Sydney, 1952, Appendix A. See also Ross Border, op. cit., Ch. 4.

[22] Macquarie to Bathurst, 15 May 1818, op. cit., 776-7.

[23] Macquarie to Marsden, 20 Apr. 1818, ibid., 781; Bathurst to Macquarie, 13 May 1820, *H.R.A.*, I, x, 304.

[24] Quoted J. L. and Barbara Hammond, *The Bleak Age*, p. 150; see also J. W. Adamson, *English Education, 1789-1902*, Chs. 1, 4.

[25] Macquarie to Reddall, 6 Jan. 1822. Reddall Papers. (M.L.) P. A. Mulgreave was given a similar appointment in Van Diemen's Land. Goulburn to Macquarie, 23 Nov. 1820, *H.R.A.*, I, x, 372.

[26] Appendix to Bigge Report, Bonwick Transcriptions, Box 27, p. 6434. (M.L.).

[27] Commission of John Thomas Bigge, *H.R.A.*, I, x, 3-4.

[28] Bathurst to Sidmouth, 23 Apr. 1817, ibid., 807. For a discussion of Bathurst's influence at the Colonial Office see N. D. McLachlan, 'Bathurst at the Colonial Office, 1812-27: A Reconnaissance', *Historical Studies*, Vol. 13, No. 52 (Apr. 1969).

[29] Bigge's three reports are to be found in *House of Commons Papers*. See Bibliography.

[30] The section on The State of the Ecclesiastical Establishments in New South Wales and Van Diemen's Land forms pp. 67-76 of the third Report. The Appendix on Ecclesiastical Establishments, Schools and Charitable Societies is to be found in the

P.R.O. as C.O. 201/127. For an analysis of Bigge's school statistics see Goodin, op. cit., Part 4.

[31] For a sympathetic study of Scott, see Ransome T. Wyatt, 'A Wine Merchant in Gaiters', *Journal and Proceedings*, R.A.H.S., Vol. 35, Parts 3–5 (1949). Scott's letter, dated 4 Sept. 1823, is C.O. 201/147 (P.R.O.). See also R. J. Burns, 'Archdeacon Scott and the Church and School Corporation', C. Turney (Ed.), *Pioneers of Australian Education*.

[32] Bathurst to Brisbane, 3 Oct. 1823. *H.R.A.*, I, xi, 139–40.

[33] Copies or Extracts of Correspondence respecting the Clergy Reserves in Canada: 1819 to 1840. Part I, pp. 1–24, *Great Britain and Ireland: Parliamentary Documents*, Vol. 26, 1813–40.

[34] A copy of Scott's second letter, dated 30 Mar. 1824, is in N.S.W. Governor's Despatches, Vol. 5, 1823–4 (M.L.), and is reproduced in part in A. G. Austin, *Select Documents in Australian Education, 1788–1900*, pp. 6–8.

[35] Matthew Bigge to Bonwick, 6 Sept. 1897, Bonwick Transcripts, Biography, Vol. I, p. 259. (M.L.). In this letter Bigge's nephew claimed that family legend had it that his uncle had told Scott to take Orders in preparation for the archdeaconry he would recommend.

[36] Wyatt, op. cit., p. 150. See also C.O. 201/147 (P.R.O.).

[37] Ibid., p. 151. It should also be noted that in Bigge's absence Scott was being called on for supplementary advice on matters other than religion and education. See his solicited advice of 22 Aug. 1823 on the Legislative Council in C.O. 201/147 (P.R.O.).

[38] Field to Marsden, 28 June, 31 Aug., 21 Nov. 1824, Marsden Papers, Vol. I. (M.L.); Field to Marsden, 16 Dec. 1824. Af23. (M.L.).

[39] Bathurst to Brisbane, 21, 28 Dec. 1824, 1 Jan. 1825, *H.R.A.*, I, xi, 419 et seq.

[40] Oxley to Darling, 24 June 1826, *H.R.A.*, I, xii, 456–7. The Australian Agricultural Company, established with the Colonial Office's blessing in 1824, had authority to take up 1,000,000 acres, all of which remained to be surveyed at the time of Scott's arrival.

[41] Members of the Land Board to Darling, 11 Mar. 1826, ibid., 407.

[42] Darling to Hay, 4 Sept., 10 Oct. 1826, ibid., 535, 645.

[43] Mitchell to Darling, 29 Apr. 1828, *H.R.A.*, I, xiv, 178–9.

[44] Mitchell to Colonial Secretary, 3 June 1829, *H.R.A.*, I, xvi, 203.

[45] Gordon Greenwood (Ed.), *Australia: A Social and Political History*, p. 56.

[46] The *Australian*, founded by W. C. Wentworth and Robert

Wardell, began publication in October 1824; in May 1826 it was joined by the *Monitor* (E. S. Hall), and in April 1827 by the *Gleaner* (L. H. Halloran). Although the *Gleaner*'s erratic editor was later to become one of Archdeacon Scott's most litigious critics, his paper, during its brief existence (Apr.–Sept. 1827), defended the archdeacon and his Corporation on several occasions.

[47] *Monitor*, 9 Feb. 1829. Scott was capable of retaliating in kind. The editor of the *Monitor*, he declared, "has gone through the various gradations of a profligate life", and his printer "is the keeper of one of the most notorious brothels in Sydney; but his two colleagues Robert Howe and Dr Wardell are on a par . . . ." Scott to Hamilton, Correspondence of Thomas Hobbes Scott, Vol. I, 18 Aug. 1828 (M.L.); Scott to Arthur, Papers of Sir George Arthur, Vol. XIII, 9 July 1826 (M.L.).

[48] Scott to Darling, Correspondence of Thomas Hobbes Scott, op. cit., 8 Jan. 1827; Scott to Arthur, Papers of Sir George Arthur, op. cit., 9 July 1826.

[49] *Australian*, 30 Dec. 1826.

[50] Ibid., 17 Jan. 1827, 19 Dec. 1828; *Monitor*, 30 May 1829 quoting the Glasgow *Chronicle*.

[51] Charter of the Church and School Corporation, Sec. xxxii, Austin, op. cit., p. 21.

[52] Therry to Macleay, 24 June 1826, *H.R.A.*, I, xii, 546.

[53] Darling to Bathurst, 6 Sept. 1826, ibid., 543–5. For an estimate of Therry's work see Eris O'Brien, *Life and Letters of Archpriest John Joseph Therry*.

[54] E.g. in the Wemyss case, *H.R.A.*, I, xiv, 472–5.

[55] Lindesay to Goderich, 18 Nov. 1831, *H.R.A.*, I, xvi, 454.

[56] Goderich to Bourke, 3 Apr. 1832, *H.R.A.*, I, xvi, 590. The published letter made up five pages of a twenty-seven page pamphlet which Lang published in 1831 under the title *Account of the Steps taken in England with a view to the Establishment of an Academical Institution or College in New South Wales*.

[57] Sir George Murray had reprimanded him in 1829. Twiss to Darling, 26 Sept. 1829, *H.R.A.*, I, xv, 179.

[58] J. D. Lang, *An Historical and Statistical Account of New South Wales*, Vol. II, pp. 464, 517–8.

[59] Scott to Hamilton, Correspondence of Thomas Hobbes Scott, op. cit., 18 Aug. 1828; Darling to Bathurst, 7 May 1826, *H.R.A.*, I, xii. 273 et seq.

[60] Documents and Correspondence Relating to the Establishment and Dissolution of the Corporation of Clergy and School Lands in the Colony of New South Wales, pp. 21–54, *Great Britain and Ireland: Parliamentary Documents*, Vol. 19, 1838–9.

[61] Scott arrived in Sydney 7 May 1825. According to Marsden

Scott's resignation had been sent to England before 27 Sept. 1825; according to Hassall, Scott was "determined to leave" by 7 Apr. 1826; Scott himself declared that his resignation had gone to England before 24 May 1826. Marsden to Coates, 27 Sept. 1825, Bonwick Transcripts, Missionary, Vol. 5. Box 53; Hassall to Hassall, 7 Apr. 1826, Hassall Correspondence, Vol. 2. (M.L.); Scott to Arthur, Papers of Sir George Arthur, op. cit., 24 May 1826.

[62] Scott to Arthur, Papers of Sir George Arthur, op. cit. 9, 26 Mar. 1827.

[63] Ibid., 5 Apr. 1826, 8 Jan. 1827.

[64] Ibid., 15 July, 6 Aug. 1828. An Ecclesiastical Board had been established to control the affairs of the colonial Church. Its members were the Archbishops of Canterbury and York and the Bishop of London; its secretary was Archdeacon Hamilton. Formally, the Bishop of Calcutta remained Scott's diocesan.

[65] Scott to Hamilton, Correspondence of Thomas Hobbes Scott, op. cit., 18 Aug. 1828, 1 Sept. 1829. See also Scott to Bishop of Calcutta, 31 July 1828.

[66] Scott to Arthur, Papers of Sir George Arthur, op. cit., 17 Jan., 17 Mar., 9 June 1829. On 16 Sept. 1829 Scott handed over his responsibilities to William Grant Broughton who later (1836) became Bishop of Australia.

[67] *Australian*, 17 Jan. 1827.

[68] Paul Knaplund, *James Stephen and the British Colonial System*, Chs. 2, 3. See also T. Barron and K. J. Cable, 'The Diary of James Stephen, 1846', *Historical Studies*, Vol. 13, No. 52 (Apr. 1969).

[69] Ibid., p. 138.

[70] Ibid.

[71] Quoted E. Halévy, *The Liberal Awakening*, p. 266.

[72] Ibid., pp. 306-7.

[73] Darling to Goderich, 11 Feb. 1828, *H.R.A.*, I, xiii, 771: Darling to Huskisson, 27, 30, 31 Mar. 1828, *H.R.A.*, I, xiv, 47, 76, 95.

[74] Murray to Darling, 25 May 1829, *H.R.A.*, I, xiv, 789.

[75] Murray to Darling, 19 June 1830, *H.R.A.*, I, xv, 560.

[76] Glenelg to Bourke, 30 Nov. 1835, *H.R.A.*, I, xviii, 201. S. H. Smith and G. T. Spaull, *History of Education in New South Wales*, pp. 46, 53-4, see the dissolution of the Corporation in terms of Whig reform.

[77] It is, of course, misleading to think in terms of two distinct parties in this period. Most Ministries were coalitions in which a moderate man of either party might find himself if his services were required, or his faction needed to be rewarded or placated.

Australian Education, 1788-1900

For the formation of the Grey Ministry see E. Halévy, *The Triumph of Reform*, pp. 13-14.

[78] Wakefield's theories, first published anonymously in 1829, were quickly taken up by his supporters who formed the National Colonization Society in 1830, and through this organization began the conversion of the Colonial Office. The extent to which the Colonial Office was influenced by Wakefieldian principles is discussed in Douglas Pike, 'Wilmot Horton and the National Colonization Society', *Historical Studies*, Vol. 7, No. 26 (May 1956), and June Philipp, 'Wakefieldian Influence and New South Wales, 1830-1832', ibid., Vol. 9, No. 34 (May 1960). Mrs Philipp contends that the chaotic state of land tenure in Australia determined the form of the new regulations "which owed little or nothing to Wakefield; they were, however, given a Wakefieldian gloss in the despatches which explained their general purpose." But see also Peter Burroughs, 'Wakefield and the Ripon Land Regulations of 1831', *Historical Studies*, Vol. 11, No. 44 (Apr. 1965).

[79] Third Report of the Commissioners of Colonial Inquiry into the Receipt and Expenditure of Colonial Revenue, 1830, pp. 74-7, *Great Britain and Ireland: Parliamentary Documents*, Vol. 5, 1826-38. The Commission was appointed 21 June 1830 and submitted its third report 8 Dec. 1830. Goderich makes frequent reference to this report: see *H.R.A.*, I, xvi, 848, n. 9.

[80] Goderich to Darling, 9 Jan. 1831, *H.R.A.*, I, xvi, 19. The regulations foreshadowed in this dispatch and promulgated in Goderich to Darling, 14 Feb. 1831, ibid., 80, are known as the Ripon Regulations as Goderich later took the title Earl of Ripon.

[81] Goderich to Darling, 14 Feb. 1831, op. cit., 81. By a legal oversight the Order-in-Council needed to dissolve the Corporation was not issued until 1833.

[82] Goderich to Colborne, 21 Nov. 1831, *Copies . . . of Correspondence respecting the Clergy Reserves in Canada*, op. cit., p. 40.

[83] Goderich to Darling, 14 Feb. 1831, op. cit., 81.

[84] The quality of Bourke's liberalism has been seriously debated in recent years. See A. G. L. Shaw, *Heroes and Villains in History: Governors Darling and Bourke in N.S.W.*, and Hazel King, 'Villains All', *Journal of the Royal Australian Historical Society*, Vol. 53, Part 1 (Mar. 1967). See also Hazel King, *Richard Bourke*.

2

Church, State and Common School in New South Wales, 1833-1851

THE dissolution of the Church and School Corporation in 1833 left the eighth governor of New South Wales, Sir Richard Bourke, facing a difficult educational problem. A man of better family and education than any of his predecessors (with the possible exception of Sir Thomas Brisbane), he brought to the problem a scholarly and liberal mind, but the quality of his liberalism, which in other circumstances might have been counted to him for virtue, only served to complicate this problem, for it drove him to attempt a reconstruction of colonial society along lines which were repugnant to those traditional pillars of English society, the upper class and the Established Church. Early in his Australian career, in defending his handling of the King's School, Parramatta, he had found it necessary to declare his attitude to these two, traditional forces; he denied that he had hindered the promoters of the school, but he freely admitted his objections to their plans. "I feel indeed strongly", he wrote,

> the many objections, which may be urged against the Plan, upon which this School is instituted; and I have scrupled, in addition to a life annuity of £100 payable to the Master, to lay out some thousands more in providing at the Public expense a cheaper School than might otherwise be obtained for the Sons

of the wealthy Colonists and Civil Servants of the Government, whilst the Children of the poor are educating (*sic*) in mere Hovels under Convict School Masters. . . . The exclusive nature of this Establishment, as none but Members of the Church of England are ever likely to attend it, is a further objection.[1]

Bourke and the Irish National System

His solution to the problem of providing schools for all the children of the colony involved two proposals. The first, which derived from the liberal belief that the State in dealing with religious bodies should not prefer one to another, envisaged the granting of aid to all the Christian sects in the colony. Bourke submitted to the Secretary of State for the Colonies that this proposal would be supported by a majority of the colonists, and would

> promote with the best assurance of success the religious instruction and general education of this People. . . . I would observe that, in a New Country to which Persons of all religious persuasions are invited to resort, it will be impossible to establish a dominant and endowed Church without much hostility and great improbability of its becoming permanent. The inclination of these Colonists, which keeps pace with the Spirit of the Age, is decidedly adverse to such an Institution; and I fear the interest of Religion would be prejudiced by its Establishment. If on the contrary support were given as required to every one of the three grand Divisions of Christians indifferently . . . I conceive that the Public Treasury might in time be relieved of a considerable charge, and, what is of much greater importance, the people would become more attached to their respective Churches. . . . If it should be thought proper at any future period to extend assistance to other Congregations whose Members may seem to require it, there will be nothing in the present arrangement to prevent it.[2]

It could be argued that, having secured this arrangement, Bourke might reasonably have left the provision of schools to these State-aided Churches, but he was clearly aware of the danger in letting the rival sects do just as they wished in this matter; in a thinly-scattered population of mixed religious affiliations this could only result in a multiplicity of small, rival schools. His second proposal therefore took this form:

> I am inclined to think that Schools for the general education of the Colonial Youth, supported by the Government and regulated after the manner of the Irish Schools, which since the year 1831 receive aid from Public Funds, would be well suited to the circumstances of this Country. . . . I am certain that the Colonists would be well pleased to find their funds liberally pledged to the support of Schools of this description.[3]

The schools which Bourke had in mind were those which the Secretary of State for the Colonies (Lord Stanley) had introduced in September 1831 when he was Chief Secretary for Ireland. To administer these schools a Board of Commissioners for National Education had been established, though the local administration of each school was left to the "patron", the person who originally sponsored the school and put it in connexion with the Board. The essential feature of these schools was the attempt to bring together children of all sects for a general, literary education which, while Christian in spirit, was undenominational; facilities were provided for the separate religious instruction of the children of each sect. To achieve these ends the Board of Commissioners had developed a body of literary and moral knowledge in an elaborate system of textbooks, Christian in content, but free of dogma. To satisfy all parties the free use of the Bible was forbidden within the schools, a book of *Scripture Extracts* being substituted.

Bourke introduced his plan circumspectly; there was no intention, he pointed out, of withdrawing government aid from existing Church schools, and the proposed schools modelled on the Irish National Schools were to be regarded as experimental,[4] but despite his moderation, despite the public support he believed his plan enjoyed, and despite assurances of firm support from the British government,[5] he brought down on his head a violent storm of protest from the Protestant clergy.

That there might be trouble from this quarter he had foreseen in 1833,[6] but it is unlikely that he had foreseen the intensity, or extent, of the clerical opposition which now confronted him. From pulpits all over the colony the Anglican clergy began to thunder against the governor. In June 1836, for example, the Rev. G. K. Rusden, government chaplain at Maitland, came down to Sydney to attend a protest meeting at the Pulteney Hotel, and was appointed to a committee to co-ordinate the opposition of all Protestants. Back in Maitland his enthusiasm carried him away. When he appeared before his congregation on Sunday, 14 August, he was obviously very angry; he spoke at some length about the governor's educational proposals, and told his listeners that unless they signed the petition which he would put before them at the end of the service, "the Catholics would get the upper hand". As his parishioners filed out of the church he stood by the table on which the petition lay, and practically forced several assigned convicts to sign it. Bourke, on discovering this, ordered the local Police Magistrate to conduct an inquiry, Rusden apologized, and Bishop Broughton came to his clergy's defence, offering as an excuse for Rusden's conduct that gentleman's unfamiliarity with local conditions. But Bourke was not to be mollified by such a specious excuse on behalf of an intelligent man who had been over two years in the colony. He immediately reported the whole matter to the Secretary of State, adding

> but he [Rusden] is not the only Divine of the Church of England who, under the Bishop's control, inveighs from the Pulpit against the Establishment of the proposed Schools, misrepresenting their character and aim, and connecting them with the Church of Rome in a strain of declamation, which, however deficient in argument and unfounded in fact, serves the mischievous purpose of keeping up excitement and creating anger and suspicion in the minds of Persons of different religious Creeds who have hitherto lived in perfect harmony.
> The Bishop himself, when preaching some short time ago in the Church of Parramatta which I usually attend, took occasion to attack the Schools as subversive of Protestantism. It happened that, being indisposed, I felt myself obliged to quit the Church before the Sermon commenced, and thus accidentally escaped being present at a discourse, which I understand betrayed more zeal than discretion.[7]

New South Wales, 1833-1851

As Bourke saw clearly, Broughton was the mainspring of the opposition. As archdeacon in 1833 he had given the governor full warning of his opposition to these proposed measures; as archdeacon in 1835 he had given the Secretary of State full warning of his opposition even though it might cost him a proffered bishopric; now, as Bishop of Australia, he concentrated the whole of his considerable abilities upon destroying the governor's plans.[8]

The bishop had some old scores to settle with the governor, who had curbed his ambitious plans for the King's School, but more was at stake than this. The two men represented, on this remote antipodean stage, the two major forces at work in the English society of the 1830s yet, by one of those transpositions which reveals the fluidity of nineteenth-century society, it was the younger man, of the poorer family, who stood there as the conservative cleric and the spokesman of privilege, while the older man, nurtured in the conservatism of his kinsman Edmund Burke, the heir to landed estates, the successful product of a patronage-ridden army, stood there as the liberal governor and the advocate of social change. Broughton, recently returned from England, aware of the limitations which the State was placing on his Church there,[9] and fully conscious of all that was at stake in this colonial issue, played his part boldly. To organize petitions from every Anglican parish, to inspire protesting sermons from every Anglican pulpit—these were not difficult matters; but to persuade Dissenters and Presbyterians that their interests were identical with his—this was a consummate piece of diplomacy. His address to the General Committee of Protestants at the Pulteney Hotel was masterly. Fixing upon the restrictions which the Irish National scheme would place upon the use of the Scriptures in schools, he declared:

> I lay my finger upon this principle, and I say, this is the bane and plague-spot which infects the whole system. To this, as a Protestant, I must object *in toto*. . . . What does Protestantism rest upon? Upon this principle: that Holy Scripture contains all things necessary to salvation; and that the use of it

should be free to every man who has a soul to be saved. Upon this point turned the great struggle between the Reformers and the Church of Rome. When this point was gained, the Reformation was inevitable. . . . I ask you, Gentlemen, whether any suggestion for a deviation from this rule would ever have proceeded from any Protestant of any denomination whatever. Assuredly not. We may judge from what quarter the suggestion, or rather demand, proceeded. The Rule of the Roman Catholic Church, as to the free use of the Scripture . . . is diametrically opposed to ours. . . . This appeal I make to your candid judgment; that the Church for which I make a stand is that which gave to you all the word of God in your native language; yes, to you all. In every quarter . . . of the world, wherever a congregation of Protestants assemble . . . to worship God in the English language, they are and must be indebted to the Church of England for ability to read the Scriptures in that language.[10]

It says a good deal for Broughton's tactics that the irascible, bigoted, Presbyterian leader, Dr John Dunmore Lang, joined him on the Committee; Lang was to admit later that he imperfectly understood the system he had opposed, and had blindly followed Broughton's lead,[11] but for the moment the bishop's bait had succeeded, for Lang could never resist an appeal to his bigotry, and the charge that Bourke's scheme was little better than a Romish plot was the easier to make because the Roman Catholic clergy in New South Wales, like their brethren in Ireland, were at first prepared to accept the scheme. In both countries the Catholic clergy felt that the Irish National scheme, while not what they wanted, was such an improvement on what had gone before that they should give it a fair trial.

In the face of this vehement Protestant opposition Bourke was not prepared to insist upon his scheme, though he never formally abandoned it. He took what comfort he could from the Council's vote of £3,000 towards the establishment of National schools, and from his observation that "The Dissenters . . . whom the Bishop of Australia received as allies, now begin to find how adverse to their own interests are the Exclusive views of His Lordship",[12] he defended his scheme in a circular letter sent to all Police Magistrates, he made arrangements for teachers to be sent out to establish a Normal School, and he entered into a contract for the erection of a National school at Wollongong, but as all these activities provided no actual schooling for anyone, he was forced to subsidize the denominations on a £1-for-£1 basis, the "half-and-half" scheme as it was known locally. As his successor remarked, "When I arrived in the Colony (Feby. 1838) the plans of Sir Richard Bourke were considered to be virtually abandoned".[13]

Why, it might be asked, did Bourke not persevere with his plans? After all, it could be argued, he had the support of the Colonial Office, the Legislative Council, and the general body of colonists. What other support could he require? Such an array of allies, however, is more illusory than real. Certainly the Colonial Office had given Bourke firm support (and even in the face of the Protestant opposition of 1836 Glenelg continued this support), but at the same time he warned that "His Majesty's Government can have no wish to impose on them any system which is opposed to the general wishes of the Inhabitants . . . the recent proceedings in New South Wales proved the necessity of avoiding the possibility of any misconception of the views of Government on a question of such vital importance . . . ."[14] As Bourke had every reason to know, Colonial Office policy in this matter was unstable. In 1834, for example, he had thought it necessary to arm his son with letters and send him off to London to thwart Broughton's diplomacy there. "There goes home in the same ship as this Epistle the Archdeacon of N.S.W.", he explained to his friend Spring Rice,

> a very agreeable and as I believe a very amiable person, but a Tory in politics and a determined High Churchman. . . . He opposes the introduction of liberal measures . . . and would keep the Presbyterians and R. Catholics in fetters and chains of Iron. . . .
>
> Your intercourse with the Government will enable you to learn what is going on with regard to the subjects in which I am interested and the details I have given you may enable you to afford explanations or at least to give warning to the Ministers. . . .[15]

Australian Education, 1788-1900

Again, in 1836, he had been confronted with the unpalatable evidence that Lord Stanley, the Secretary of State to whom he had suggested using the Irish (or Stanley) System of Education in New South Wales, had declared in an open letter that this system was suited only to Ireland and was "never intended, except for the peculiar case of Ireland".[16] No experienced governor would place much reliance on that sort of support.

Nor will the support of the Legislative Council stand close scrutiny. The appropriation of £3,000 was supported by only eight members and was opposed by four, three of whom were non-official members, and the fourth, the governor's Colonial Secretary, not only cast his vote against the appropriation, but spoke against it at length.[17] But the essential point here is not the number of Councillors for or against the measure, but the fact that a Legislative Council whose members were nominated by the governor could not provide him with an accurate measure of the state of public opinion; it would have mattered little if all members had supported the appropriation—they represented, one might say, nothing more than an extension of the governor's own personality. Bourke himself deplored the unrepresentative character of his Legislative Council, and worked strenuously throughout his governorship to liberalize the political institutions of the colony, but while his Council remained a nominated one he could only guess at the state of public opinion. In his own mind Bourke was probably convinced that he, and not Broughton, had made the more accurate assessment of public opinion, but the possibility remained that if the non-Catholic clergy were speaking for their congregations they were speaking for seventy per cent of the population.

One must remember too—unless one is to be accused of educational egocentricity—that throughout his governorship Bourke was deeply involved in many other pressing problems, and it is perhaps enough to recall only three of them to restore a sense of proportion. These were, one must remember, the years of the outward march of the squatters, including the massive, unauthorized dispersion into the Port

Phillip District, of the creation of a large migration programme, and of the framing of a new pattern of government as the colony changed swiftly from a penal establishment to a wealthy pastoral society. It is little wonder that Bourke hesitated to force the educational issue. As his successor soon discovered, it was one thing to deplore the failure of the 1836 plan, but it was distinctly another to establish an alternative plan.

Gipps and the British and Foreign School Society System

From the outset, Sir George Gipps saw the educational problem with perfect clarity. While government money was being wasted in subsidizing the various denominations, thus allowing them to continue a wasteful duplication of rival schools, the majority of the children in the colony were not being educated at all. In a Minute which accompanied his Estimates for 1840, Gipps defined his views concisely:

> The great dispersion of the Population of New South Wales, renders (perhaps more than in any country upon earth) a system of Education necessary, that shall be as comprehensive as possible. In large towns, or in a densely peopled country, separate Schools for each denomination of Christians may easily be established, and in a qualified manner may answer the object of their Institution; though if, as I believe, the higher interest of mankind, temporal as well as eternal, require of us to nurture the youth of any country in feelings of love and charity towards each other, irrespective of religious creeds, this can perhaps only be fully done—at least, I think it can best be effected—by accustoming them to receive, in common, the first elements of instruction. But, however opinions may differ upon this as an abstract question, to insist, in New South Wales, that each separate denomination shall have its separate School, is (let the fact be disguised as it may) in reality to say, that even in our capital a large portion of the Population shall remain uneducated; and out of Sydney, there shall, for the poorer classes of society, be scarcely any education at all.
>
> Schools are, indeed, at the present moment, springing up in most of our country towns; but their existence will, in all probability, be but ephemeral, for they will stand one in the way of another, and by competing, where they ought to combine, defeat the common object of them all.[18]

Here, even more clearly than Bourke had done, Gipps declared the liberal belief that religious differences should be resolved by compromise, but in doing this he automatically condemned himself to much the same failure as Bourke had suffered. As Gipps wrestled with the problem it must have become increasingly clear to him that eventually he would have to propose something very like Bourke's scheme—there was just not sufficient room in which to manœuvre. The most desirable aspect of Bourke's scheme, he reasoned, had been the cause of its failure—its attempt to comprehend all denominations. There could be no point in attempting that again, but perhaps something worthwhile could be achieved by a scheme which would comprehend the greatest possible number. If he could devise an acceptable plan the united Protestant and Anglican opposition which had confronted Bourke could be transformed into an equally formidable support. This, of course, would almost certainly entail the loss of Roman Catholic support, but their support had never been more than half-hearted and they made up little more than a quarter of the population; they might, in any case, be placated by a separate grant for the support of their own schools. A comprehensive scheme which was avowedly Protestant would, Gipps believed, produce the support he required, but when, acting on this line of reasoning, he proposed to establish schools based upon the system of the British and Foreign School Society, he offended many more people than he pleased.

There could be no doubting the Protestant nature of his proposal, for the British and Foreign School Society had been founded in 1808 to carry on the work of Joseph Lancaster and, while excluding denominational religious teaching, used the Bible freely in its schools, but criticism was rife on other grounds. The Secretary of State told him bluntly that he had mishandled the matter; to concede the principle of a separate grant for Roman Catholics, he pointed out, was to invite every other sect to claim a similar benefit. The Presbyterians and Dissenters, though no longer the close associates of Broughton, gave Gipps no positive support, for the "half-and-half" expedient was helping them to establish their own schools, and Bourke's former supporters in the Council, still anxious to secure his original scheme, gave the new governor's proposals only the most grudging support.[19]

On the other hand Broughton and his clergy were again uncompromising in their opposition though now, remembering the events of 1836, the bishop had to shift his ground. Then it had been enough to condemn Bourke's scheme as a Romish plot, and to that end he had been grateful for the firm support of the Protestant denominations; now, faced with a scheme which was clearly Protestant, but still inimical to his aims, he had to abandon his former allies and take his stand upon the distinctive nature of Anglican doctrine. Speaking with great emotion in the Legislative Council he said:

> To compel us to send children to Schools in which that prohibition of teaching them our proper doctrines forms the fundamental regulation, will be as contrary to our principles as to require the Roman Catholics to send their children to a School where the Scriptures are to be commonly read. . . . With us it is an established point . . . of the strictest religious obligation that every child shall be taught the Lord's Prayer and the Ten Commandments, and shall be further instructed in the Church Catechism set forth for that purpose.

Appealing directly to the governor, the bishop condemned the spirit of liberalism which had inspired this new plan.

> I am compelled to address myself thus . . . in consequence of an observation which fell from Your Excellency at our last Meeting, that the possession of any privilege, distinction or advantage, by one particular portion or class in the community, must lead to its being regarded with jealousy by all others, finally, with hatred, and so to its ruin and destruction. With the utmost respect for Your Excellency, I must think that this is virtually to abjure the principles of the projectors and conductors of the Revolution, who were distinguished by the name of Whigs, and who never did admit or act upon such a principle, with regard to the Established Church. And I must say, that if we, abandoning their principles, should ever be

induced to legislate upon the assumption, that exclusive privileges have necessarily the tendency and the termination which Your Excellency imputes to them . . . we shall find that . . . we are . . . far advanced towards the institutions of a republic; and I greatly fear also, a republic without religion. . . .

I will say a word or two upon the tendency, I think experience justifies me in calling it the necessary tendency, of this liberality of sentiment in religion, the praise of which is so much coveted. . . . In all religious declinations from that which is good there is that tendency to advance . . . to the extreme of evil, which renders it highly important to resist the beginnings of it. . . . Your Excellency I am aware may regard the views which I have taken as the mere prejudices of education and habit, by which I am still trammelled, though your more vigorous mind may have broken through and cast them off. I beseech you, Sir, do not yield to that way of thinking. . . .[20]

This, of course, was a severe blow to the governor's plans, supported as it was by a flood of petitions from every parish. Against the Dissenters' tepid support Gipps had to balance an unexpected and formidable Anglican opposition in addition to the Roman Catholic opposition he had anticipated. Even this was more fervid than he had expected.

At the outset the Catholic Press had given Gipps's scheme qualified approval for it did offer the Catholic schools a measure of support, but as Anglican and Protestant hostility to the separate Catholic grant mounted, editors and priests began to fear that Gipps, to save the main part of his scheme, would abandon them. They gave notice that their tepid support would be withdrawn,[21] and that they would exert themselves to destroy the governor's plans. When Gipps attempted to negotiate with Bishop Polding he was quickly made aware that no compromise was possible. ". . . the Governor had sent for the Bishop and myself to talk over a new scheme of education for the people", Polding's Vicar-General later recalled.

> He wished to introduce a common instead of the denominational system, there being some agitation prevailing on that subject, a system of which Bible-reading would have formed a

part. When he heard that we could not come into the scheme, in his abrupt way he said: 'The fact is, I must adhere to the strongest party, and I do not think that you are the strongest party.'

This cut the interview short. We took up our hats and retired.

Our reply was in the procession. Although the national symbols were omitted, a procession proceeded from the Cathedral of many thousand persons. Bands of music intervened at intervals of the long array. A thousand children in white dresses preceded the ecclesiastical portion of the long array which stretched a mile in front of them. The clergy, from all parts of the Colony, were in their chasubles, the Bishop followed in open carriage with cope and mitre. Nothing approaching to this demonstration had ever been witnessed in the colony. . . . As the procession returned, people were heard saying: 'Only the Catholics could do this. We must come second'. . . . This was the answer given to the remark that we were the weaker party. It proved us strong in union; and we heard no more of the new scheme of education.[22]

Gipps thus found himself in a position where, if the Roman Catholic and Anglican clergy were speaking for their adherents (and, like Bourke, he had no means of disproving this conjunction of opinion), he was sponsoring a plan which was opposed by more than three-quarters of the population —a situation against which successive Secretaries of State had warned quite clearly. After 1839 Gipps stood ready to introduce a general system of education if the public asked for it, and he remained clear in his statements that only government schools under a national system could adequately serve the country, but, as he saw it, the situation did not change.

There were those, however, who believed that by 1844 the situation had changed, and that Gipps's refusal to implement the recommendations of his Council constituted a breach of faith. In the latter half of 1844 a Select Committee of the Legislative Council inquired into the state of education in the colony and recommended the establishment of the Irish National system, a recommendation which the Council endorsed by a majority of one vote.[23] Gipps replied by reasserting his interest in the creation of a general system of education, but he went on to remind the Council of the fate of similar schemes in 1836 and 1839:

> Without the co-operation of the Ministers of Religion, it seems to me scarcely possible to establish any system of Education, with a prospect of its being extensively useful; and I need scarcely remark that the Clergy throughout the Colony are at present even less disposed to co-operate in the establishment of a general system than they were on the occasions which I have referred to.[24]

In saying this Gipps was not seeking to make mischief or to denigrate his Council. He had read the Select Committee's report thoroughly and he agreed wholeheartedly with its recommendations; but he had also read the transcript of evidence thoroughly and he knew that both the Anglican and Catholic bishops had uncompromisingly rejected the Irish system. Broughton, he found, had declared:

> . . . if I am to understand by a general system, the system of the British and Foreign School Society, the Irish, or any other that prohibits full instruction in religion, I should most decidedly object to it.[25]

Archbishop Polding, well aware that many of the Irish bishops had repudiated the Irish National system and that the Sacred Congregation of the Propaganda had advised each bishop to make his own judgment on this issue, had told the Select Committee that "the Irish system . . . is a system which I could never approve of for this colony. . . ."[26] Gipps, then, was acting in a responsible manner when he rejected the Select Committee's recommendation, but at this point the governor's enemy (though one-time supporter), the brilliant, erratic Robert Lowe, made the claim in the columns of his newspaper, the *Atlas* (7 December 1844), that the governor's refusal to go on with the scheme sprang from a secret pact between Gipps and Broughton whereby the former would leave undisturbed the existing provisions for education if the latter would support his unpopular squatting regulations. The crux of the matter,

Lowe pointed out, was the state of public opinion. "Has His Excellency looked at the last controversy", he asked, "without being fully aware that the bigoted clamour against the general system has *not* been raised by the people, but *solely* by the Clergy?" In a correct answer to Lowe's question lies the only explanation of Gipps's actions we are ever likely to get. To the Secretary of State he declared that Anglican and Roman Catholic opposition to the Select Committee's recommendations (for the latter Church had now reversed its earlier support of the Irish National system) represented an overwhelming majority against his proposals. But how genuine was Gipps in giving this opinion? By way of support for Lowe's accusation one must remember that Broughton did go out of his way to support Gipps's squatting policy, that the two men had been schoolboys together at King's School, Canterbury, and that the governor might have been expected to take the advice of his Legislative Council which, since the passage of the Act for the Government of New South Wales and Van Diemen's Land in July 1842, was partly elective.[27] On the other hand, one must remember that the squatting party for whom Lowe spoke were, in resisting Gipps's land policy, playing for very high stakes, that neither Lowe nor any later writer who repeated the charge ever advanced any evidence to support it,[28] that Broughton had enunciated a land policy similar in essence to Gipps's as early as 1842,[29] and that the Secretary of State agreed that Gipps had taken the correct action in refusing to accept his Council's recommendation on this point. It should be added that there is nothing in Broughton's or Gipps's characters to suggest that either man would bargain on a point of principle.[30]

The explanation of Gipps's actions is rather to be found in the general condition of the colony in 1844, for Gipps had seen it as his duty to reconstruct the whole basis of land tenure in Australia and thereby had antagonized practically every squatter and landowner in the colony. None of his predecessors had been able to restrain the squatters who, despite exhortation and proscription, had swept beyond the limits of settlement so neatly drawn on the governors' maps, and had rapidly occupied the pastoral lands of eastern Australia from Port Phillip to Moreton Bay. Bourke, in the mid-1830s, had appraised the problem realistically when he asked, "How may this Government turn to the best advantage a state of things which it cannot wholly interdict?",[31] but his solution, the issuing of grazing licences at a nominal £10 a year, while giving an appearance of legality to the squatting expansion in no way settled the future of the pastoral lands of Australia. As Gipps saw it, some 3,000,000 acres of land had been practically alienated for a yearly payment of £7,000, and the squatter was asserting a prescriptive right to this land through long occupation. In these circumstances he believed he must assert the rights of the Crown and secure this land for posterity, but when his policy was made public in April 1844 it provoked a violent reaction, for not only did his proposals involve the squatter in the purchase of part of the lands he now occupied so cheaply, but they came at a time when the colony, and the squatters, had scarcely recovered from a severe depression. Only a few months before Gipps's policy was announced, one of the most substantial and responsible squatters in New South Wales had written hysterically to his manager:

> Pray observe most *religiously the provision not to draw upon* me—beg, borrow, steal, do anything. . . . I never was so poor in my life as I am at this moment. . . . I can assure you the state of things throughout the Colony is frightful beyond all precedent. There is in short all but universal bankruptcy. . . . In Sydney grief and despair, or distraction, are depicted in almost every face.[32]

It was in this atmosphere that Gipps's proposals were discussed; even in a country whose short history was studded with acts of bitter opposition to governors' policies, such a sustained and vitriolic campaign as now developed had scarcely been witnessed before. Traduced and vilified in the Press, obstructed in the Council chamber, opposed in London by the importing, shipping and manufacturing interests whose fortunes were bound up in the colonial wool industry, Gipps found himself without allies of any description. It is probably true that if he had exercised a little political guile he could have organized support from other classes—from small farmers and workers perhaps —but a certain inflexibility and aloofness in his character prevented him from seeing the governor's role in these terms. And so he stood alone, while the squatters and the Colonial Office between them exhausted him, broke him in health, and contrived his dismissal. His refusal, in these circumstances, to risk a repetition of the turmoil of 1836 and 1839 seems perfectly understandable.

FitzRoy and the Dual System

How was it then, that Governor FitzRoy was able to establish a Board of National Education only two years after Gipps had left the colony? In the first place the squatter had been placated; by 1848 he had recovered from the depression, and the British Government's Order-in-Council of March 1847 had secured him in the occupancy of his run. FitzRoy, by no effort of his own, was thus able to govern in an atmosphere of comparative peace and goodwill. Secondly, as Kelvin Grose has recently demonstrated, Bishop Broughton's capacity to resist state intervention in education had been seriously reduced by the financial crisis of the early 1840s.[33] The governor, forced to take desperate measures to reduce public expenditure, had drastically cut all forms of government subsidy to the Churches and their schools; then, as bankruptcy and poverty engulfed the colony, subscriptions and offerings fell off sharply; finally, in 1845, the S.P.G. advised Broughton that his Church must stand on its own feet and learn to rely less on the Society for financial aid. Broughton stood aghast at the prospect before him. In 1836 and 1839, and even as late as 1844, he had been prepared to defy Bourke and Gipps, and accept the consequences if they had decided to withdraw all aid from Church schools. But now FitzRoy was cautiously formulating an education policy and as Church finances stood it would be folly to offer him the same challenge. A compromise must therefore be suggested before capitulation was enforced, and in May 1847 Broughton put his case to FitzRoy:

> Speaking the sentiments of such of the clergy as I have recently had an opportunity of consulting, I may state with confidence to Your Excellency that they have no more anxious desire than to co-operate steadfastly with the civil authority in carrying into effect a system of Education which shall be at once beneficial to those who are placed under it, satisfactory to the public, and not at variance with the sense which they entertain of their own duties as clergymen. . . .
>
> I trust it will appear to Your Excellency from the candid exposition of our views which I have taken the liberty to submit, that we propose nothing which can interfere with the persuasions or proceedings of others.[34]

FitzRoy must have sighed with relief; so long as he continued to support the Anglican schools Bishop Broughton would not oppose a system of National schools. Thirdly, as FitzRoy probably sensed, it was not only the Anglican bishop who had modified his opposition in the years between 1844 and 1847. The evidence and report of the 1844 Select Committee probably had some influence upon public opinion, and the well-reasoned, well-written articles which Robert Lowe and W. A. Duncan printed in almost every issue of their papers (the *Atlas* and the *Weekly Register* respectively), explaining and justifying the National system, must also have won new supporters. The newly appointed Commissioners of National Education believed they could detect this swing in public opinion; the system had, they reported,

> been gradually obtaining many advocates from the ranks even of those who were formerly opposed to it. The general feeling now seems to be that no other system can be so advisable for our vast pastoral districts where the population is . . . scattered, and of various religious persuasions.[35]

Perhaps the Commissioners had in mind the remarkable conversion and contrition of Dr Lang, who not only admitted to a complete change of heart—in itself a remarkable event in Lang's career—but publicly stated his desire "to atone as much as possible for the opposition I had given to the establishment of Sir Richard Bourke's system".[36] Perhaps, too, the Commissioners were whistling to keep up their corporate courage (for there was obviously trouble enough ahead before their system could reckon itself secure), but it is at least possible that they, like FitzRoy, had judged public opinion aright.

G. W. Rusden and the Establishment of the National System

Governor FitzRoy's compromise took the form of two Boards of Commissioners. Of these the Denominational Board took over an existing body of schools subject to a degree of clerical supervision; the Denominational Commissioners, therefore, had little to do but distribute amongst the sects the funds granted by government, and arbitrate, as best they could, on the interminable squabbles and rivalry amongst them. They had no need to promote new schools; denominational fervour ensured only too many of them. The National Board, on the other hand, was faced with the task of creating an entirely new system, and its members were conscious of the opposition they would have to face. Two of them (John Hubert Plunkett, the Attorney-General, and Charles Nicholson, Speaker of the Legislative Council) had fought for a general system of schools for years, and knew how formidable this opposition could be; they were therefore very much aware that, for all their enthusiasm, their first annual report made very sorry reading. Much of their time had, of course, been taken up with administrative matters: books had been ordered from Ireland, a secretary had been appointed, plans had been laid for a Model School and regulations had been drafted, but in the whole of New South Wales they could count only four schools under their control. This was by no means a true indication of what they might do in the future, for they had specifically announced that until the arrival from Ireland of the necessary textbooks, and the teachers to take charge of the Model School, they could not, as a general principle, entertain applications for schools, but now that they were ready to receive applications they had to face the unpleasant fact that they had no satisfactory machinery for communicating with the people for whom the schools were intended. The Commissioners were, they reported,

> unable to devise any better plan for calling the attention of gentlemen in the interior to this important subject than by suggesting that directions should be given to the several Clerks of the Benches beyond the boundaries to suspend in their offices for public inspection a printed copy of our Regulations, with a few additional remarks pointing out . . . how a School on such principles may be most conveniently established.[37]

In view of the tenuous grip the National system had on life, this was a dangerous state of affairs and needed to be set right quickly. A decision was therefore taken to appoint agents who would advertise the system throughout the colony, assist in the establishment of schools, and exercise some of the functions of an inspector. On 28 May 1849 the Commissioners appointed John Kinchela as their northern agent and George William Rusden as their southern agent; by 5 July they had briefed them, settled on terms of remuneration, given them an advance on their salaries, and dispatched them—Kinchela to Bathurst and Rusden to Yass.[38]

The system of schools which the agents were to advertise and organize was clearly set out in the Board's Regulations, and differed only in minor details from the system Lord Stanley had proposed for Ireland. The Commissioners were prepared to provide up to two-thirds of the cost of erecting and fitting out a school wherever an attendance of thirty children could be guaranteed and local patrons found to undertake the responsibility of raising the balance of the money, superintending the erection of the school and taking a share in its conduct. The appointment of teachers was to rest solely with the Commissioners, but they would pay special regard to the recommendations of patrons. The teacher, they believed,

> should be a person of Christian sentiment, of calm temper and discretion, should be imbued with a spirit of peace, of obedience to the law, and loyalty to the Sovereign; and should

not only possess the art of communicating knowledge, but be capable of moulding the mind of youth. . . ."[39]

Teachers would receive from the Board a minimum salary of £40 per annum, and would be eligible to receive gratuities if their work were commendable, as well as a supplementary amount from fees or local subscriptions.

Instruction was to be based upon the books prepared by the Irish Commissioners, books which would "be found to contain a large infusion of what all Christians agree in regarding as the most important elements of religious truth".[40] Religious instruction was to be given, at times set apart, by each minister of religion to his own adherents, but the titles of all books used in this instruction were to be notified to the Board; above all, the schools were to avoid all sectarian friction and to promote Christian charity and tolerance. The agents were clearly instructed that while they should make every endeavour to establish new schools, they were not to intrude help if it were not wanted, and they were not to criticize existing schools established by any other organization. They were to write ahead along their route arranging public meetings, they were to display the Board's regulations and books, they were to help in the selection of patrons (and advise if they were to be trusted with Board funds), they were to furnish descriptions of proposed sites, information on the practicability of industrial and boarding schools, and statistics relating to population. Each week they were to forward a report "carefully written, half margin . . . accurately dated and numbered".[41]

Within three months of setting out, John Kinchela died at Bathurst, and the Commissioners, instead of replacing him, persuaded Rusden to undertake the complete agency for the whole of eastern Australia. It was an overwhelming task for one man and involved him in 10,000 miles of arduous and dangerous travel between July 1849 and August 1851; he emerges from this tour as something of a minor hero in Australian educational history. To those who know Rusden only as the elderly, reactionary sycophant turned amateur historian, it is necessary to point out that the Rusden who rode out of Sydney in July 1849 was a vigorous, progressive young man of thirty who, by hard reading and hard thinking, had emancipated himself from the conservative and exclusive views of his father (that Rev. G. K. Rusden who had given Governor Bourke so much trouble), and who sincerely believed in the principle of bringing to every child a sound, Christian (but non-sectarian) education. Ignorance, in his belief, was

> produced by political apathy which will do nothing for the masses, or contentious bigotry which places a prohibitory price upon the education it is willing to give. By price I mean the whole of the terms on which it is offered. . . . Let us . . . educate all *well*, leaving no child who cannot read and *understand*, using indirect compulsion if need be, and then priests and parents will be called upon to do no more than direct the energies . . . of intelligent minds.[42]

During the two years of his agency Rusden undertook five separate tours: between July 1849 and February 1850 he rode from Sydney through Albury and Melbourne to Portland and back to Sydney; during March–April 1850 and between February and July 1851 he toured the Hunter Valley, between May 1850 and January 1851 the Moreton Bay and New England districts, and in August 1851 he took up, belatedly, the work which Kinchela had begun at Bathurst. In all these districts his procedure was the same: letters sent ahead some weeks earlier would stimulate local interest and enable him to call a meeting soon after he arrived in a township; before the meeting he would try to visit every person with local influence, secure a suitable chairman and make tentative proposals for patrons; at the meeting he would display the books and regulations of the National Board, speak if requested and, if the meeting resolved to erect a school, assist the patrons to make their initial application to the Commissioners.[43] If his itinerary permitted he stayed on in the district for a few days (or, the country permitting, doubled back a little later) to ensure that interest did not flag, that promised subscriptions were collected and that a building contract was let.

New South Wales, 1833-1851

It was gruelling work for both man and horse. In November 1849 as Rusden rode through Dr Learmonth's property outside Geelong his horse, attacked by another, fell and rolled on him injuring his arm and leg. A few weeks later, his horse exhausted from a sixty-mile stage, he nearly drowned in the Wimmera River when the animal sank in the muddy bank, and outside Armidale, in September 1850, he was badly injured again when another of his horses, which he was leading, fell on him. By the end of 1850 the constant travel, and drought on the New England plateau, had so impoverished his horses that, although he had increased his string to six, he was hardly able to keep going at all. Nevertheless, when Rusden resigned in August 1851 to become Chief Clerk in the Colonial Secretary's office in Victoria, he had brought twenty-two schools into operation and applications had been made from another nineteen districts.

Rusden's reports had made one point clear to the National Commissioners: the people of New South Wales, despite bitter opposition from the Anglican and Roman Catholic clergy, were willing to support the Irish National schools. The clerical opposition, particularly from the Anglican clergy, was not confined to any academic disapproval. At Portland, Rusden had found the Rev. Mr Wilson "opposed to the National system thoroughly: would sooner bring up his own children amongst the blacks as heathens than send them to the National schools",[44] and at Armidale the Rev. Mr Tingcombe had preached violent sermons against Rusden and his schools, dropped the fees at his own schools from 1s. to 6d. a week in an attempt to counteract the agent's efforts, and (as the reverend gentleman later informed the National Commissioners) "took an opportunity of telling himself that I thought such a position of hostility to a Minister of the Church a most unfortunate one for any person to be employed in. . . ."[45] Probably the incident which distressed Rusden most was the Bishop of Newcastle's refusal to see him when he visited the Hunter Valley in 1850, for not only was Rusden a devout and prominent Anglican layman, but his father was one of the bishop's own clergy.[46]

On the other hand, wherever he travelled he found strong support from the people who were to use these schools. "We'd glory in a school like that", a mother at Wagga told him. "The children are fairly wild—just like the blacks."[47] Other parents, he told the Commissioners, "with tears in their eyes have assured me . . . they would rob themselves of a meal per day to bring . . . about . . . the education of their children."[48] His over-all impression he recorded in 1853:

> I am in a position to state . . . that some forty and fifty meetings of the people were accordingly held in less than two years, that at each of these meetings the support of the National System was resolved upon and subscribed for by the people, and that the subscriptions thus pledged amounted to more than three thousand pounds. In few cases was there a dissentient voice, and in those few the dissentients were immediately outvoted.[49]

Of greater importance was the degree of support his schools received from the squatters, for although the schools were intended for the children of the working class it was useless to expect these people, generally ignorant if not illiterate, to provide either the initiative or the money to set them in motion. In the pastoral society of the 1840s this sort of leadership could only be expected from two sources —the clergy or the squatters; so long as most of the clergy were opposed to the system, leadership had to come from the squatter. What happened when working-class people alone sponsored a school was revealed in the transactions at Stanhope and Brookfield. Of the patrons at Stanhope Rusden had to report: "Patrons all unacquainted not only with forms but with writing—and therefore they have misunderstood the Board's letters."[50] In the Brookfield district one patron informed him:

Lynderst Vale
19 March

Sir my wife Informed me that you called at my house a few days ago for establishing a school and you requested me to go and see how many children there was fitt for schooling withing

three miles of Brookfield and i write to tell you no there is fifty chirldren fitt for schooling now and there Parents is willing to come forward at any time when you think propper to come up and settle about the school House
So no moore at Present
from Patrick Roach[51]

The squatters' support was obviously essential, and Rusden used his acquaintance with a great number of them (he had managed properties for Charles Nicholson for eight years before taking up his agency) to secure their interest. Some, of course, opposed the system on principle—men like Roadknight of "Gerangamete" who joined the Rev. H. B. Macartney of Geelong to pile obstacles in Rusden's way; others, like Joseph Docker of "Bontharambo", offered opposition because they feared that National schools established in townships would draw their married labourers away from the runs, but in district after district Rusden was able to persuade prominent squatters to take the initiative; at Bacchus Marsh, for example, it was Griffiths of "Glenmore" and Labillière of "Yallock Vale"; at Wangaratta, Murphy of "Tarrawingi"; at the Wannon, Riley of "Kenilworth"; at Yuroke, Mackenzie of "Glenlyon" and the Brodies of "Bulla Bulla"; at Heidelberg, the overlander Joseph Hawdon; at Wagga, Peters of "Gumly Gumly". Gipps, who would have been interested in all this, had gone to an early grave in 1847, but Bourke, if the news ever reached him in his retirement on his Irish estates, must have smiled wryly to hear of this support for his school system.

William Wilkins

While Rusden was away in the Armidale district the National Commissioners had the good fortune to secure William Wilkins as the headmaster of their Model School. The Commissioners were at first disconcerted when, instead of the married couple trained in the Irish National system whom they had asked for, they were confronted by a young widower (Mrs Wilkins had died at Adelaide on the voyage out) trained at Dr Kay's Battersea school. Fortunately the Commissioners had sufficient good sense to overlook these irregularities and Wilkins took up his duties in January 1851. By March, when he submitted a report on the Model School, the Commissioners should have been satisfied with their own good judgment. Wilkins reported critically on the state of affairs he had found in the converted Military Hospital, but the greater part of his report was constructive, and outlined his plans for a first-rate practising-school based upon the best European and English methods he had seen at Battersea.

In the public tribute which Plunkett paid to Wilkins before the end of his first year in the colony it is clear that the Commissioners felt that they had found in him the man to shoulder the executive responsibilities of the Board.[52] Already these were proving too much for the three part-time, honorary Commissioners. By the end of 1851, for example, they had thirty-five schools in operation (and had just handed over another seven to the infant colony of Victoria); they had on their books applications for schools from another forty-seven districts, and they had lost, with Rusden's departure, their only agent and inspector. In Wilkins, as events turned out, they had found exactly the resourceful, efficient man they needed, but beyond this they had found a man of imagination and vision. In the National schools of New South Wales he saw not just a handful of ill-organized, squalidly-housed schools offering a meagre elementary education to the ragged children of the poor, but the possibility of a truly national system of education extending to every child, at every level of mental development. The existing institutions, he urged, should be brought together "in one system, in which education, commencing in the primary schools shall be successively improved in the Grammar schools . . . until it receives its greatest extension and development in the University".[53]

Wilkins's concept of an articulated, national system of education was shared by very few men in mid-nineteenth-century Australia, but his former colleague, G. W. Rusden, was obviously thinking along the same lines when he asked the people of Victoria why, with

> abundance of National Primary Schools, with a few comprehensive National Industrial and Boarding Establishments, and with the early foundation of a liberal University, for matriculation in which a certain number of the most eligible scholars in each county might have claim by State endowment . . . should not Victoria hope to rival the intellectual position of the mother country?[54]

Thus far had Bourke's tentative ideas been developed in twenty years. In his 1833 dispatch he had not even been sure of the name of the scheme he was advocating; by the mid-1850s the needs of this colonial society had transformed his mild measure of State aid to primary schools into a blueprint for a national system of primary, secondary and tertiary education. All this was, of course, visionary and no one was more aware of it than Wilkins and Rusden, for both of them had spent weary months inspecting the primitive schools of New South Wales, and both had been appalled at the plight of the Australian child.[55] For those parents who could afford substantial fees there were, by the 1850s, a large number of corporate and superior private schools to which they could send their children, and a reasonable supply of tutors and governesses. To suit the pockets of those further down the social scale there was no shortage of cheaper private schools, but for the most part they were kept by irresponsible rogues who had failed at other callings and now made elaborate claims for their "academies", though here and there an honest soul like Scott of Brisbane admitted that his only reason for opening a school was his inability to do anything else. "Mr. D. Scott", ran his advertisement in the *Moreton Bay Courier* (27 June 1846),

> begs to acquaint the parents of children that, on the 1st July, he intends opening a day and Evening School, in the Room over Mr. Zillman's Store.
> Mr. Scott having but recently risen from a bed of sickness, and being unfitted for more laborious exertion, yet anxious to render himself useful to his fellow creatures, trusts that in his

endeavours to impart useful and religious knowledge to the young, he will meet with the kind support of the public."

Through varying degrees of incompetence, squalor and brutality these private-adventure schools descended to the level of the strolling teachers whom Rusden encountered in 1849. "There are no fewer than five strolling teachers between Jugiong and Gobarralong", he reported. ". . . the teachers are ignorant . . . they come ragged and needy and having obtained a decent suit of clothing make off to dupe some other family."[56]

The State of Public Education c. 1850

If, to escape this sort of incompetence, the parent decided to send his child to a State-aided school he had the choice of a National or a denominational school, though the choice was more apparent than real, for despite loudly proclaimed differences in principle, these schools presented a remarkably uniform appearance. The most remarkable aspect of this uniformity lay in the type and quality of the religious instruction given in these schools, for in spite of all that angry clerics had said in debate neither parents nor children seem to have been sufficiently aware of the fundamental religious doctrines which were supposed to divide them. Wilkins found that in all but nineteen of the 164 denominational schools he visited there were children whose parents did not profess the tenets of the denomination to which the school belonged. In Presbyterian schools the "outsiders" made up 36 per cent of the total enrolment, in Wesleyan schools 18 per cent, in Anglican schools 21 per cent and in Catholic schools 6 per cent, though Wilkins had to admit that it had not been possible "in every case to distinguish accurately between Presbyterian and Wesleyan children".[57] Within the denominational schools surprisingly little religious instruction was given at all. Wilkins reported that "the condition of the Schools generally, as regards religious knowledge, is deplorable", and both he and Rusden were convinced that the National schools, using their book of *Scripture Extracts*, gave at least as much religious education as the denominational schools.[58] Something of the same uniformity was to be found in the secular books used. Most of the Anglican schools used a series of books prepared by the Society for the Promotion of Christian Knowledge ("decidedly the worst series of School-books used in the Colony", said Wilkins),[59] and most of the Catholic schools used the Christian Brothers or the Catholic series, but the Irish National and the British and Foreign Society books were of such superior quality that they tended to find their way into all types of schools. In Victoria, those inveterate enemies of the National Board, the Denominational Board Commissioners, entered into an agreement with the National Commissioners for the purchase of the Irish books.[60] The impression should not be given, however, that there was a plentiful supply of books in these schools, or (for that matter) apparatus of any kind. W. A. Duncan, a schoolmaster turned journalist, recalled that when he first came to the colony (1839) "one thing you never failed to see, and that was the striking fact, that not one child in six, perhaps, had any book of any kind whatever";[61] apparently the next fifteen years did nothing to remedy this state of affairs, for Wilkins estimated that 84 per cent of the schools he inspected lacked sufficient apparatus, 45 per cent lacked sufficient books, and 70 per cent had insufficient furniture; a National school at Yarralumla he found "destitute of everything, without books, slates or even a desk or seat".[62]

The truth was that these schools (with very few exceptions) were squalid and inefficient beyond belief. Most of their teachers had had no professional training, were uncouth, illiterate and brutish, managed (or mismanaged) their pupils by excessive corporal punishment, and exhibited in themselves a disgraceful example of personal conduct. Wilkins summed up his general impression with the remark that the work he had seen was "deplorable in the extreme. . . . Few schools are worthy of the name".[63] A measure of their squalor can be gained by glancing at their appearance. The Commissioners of National Education had laid it down that they would "not contribute to the ornamenting of School Houses, but merely to such expenditure as may be necessary for having the children accommodated in plain substantial buildings",[64] and parsimonious as this sounds it at least suggests a certain frugal decency. In practice, removed from effective supervision, the National schools were almost as ill-found as any others. Of the 202 schools Wilkins inspected, only 44 were adapted to the purpose of schooling, 155 were on ill-chosen sites, many were in dank, unventilated cellars, and 95 were in bad repair with pupils exposed to wind and rain. "It was pitiable", he wrote, "to see the children compelled as they were, to remain in these miserable apartments after walking miles in the cold and wet".[65] In 55 of these wretched hovels there were no out-buildings and another 72 were ill-provided with them; ". . . we feel it is our duty", Wilkins wrote, "to state explicitly that at least one-half of the schools are calculated to train the children in habits of dirtiness or indelicacy".[66] The out-buildings at both the Catholic and Anglican Model Schools in Sydney were found to be filthy, at the Presbyterian Model School they were "arranged without regard to decency . . . a disgusting annoyance to the school", and the Wesleyan Model School was conducted in a cellar subjected to "the noisome odours from the neighbouring sewers".[67] How far the outer schools fell from the standards set by the Model Schools of Sydney can only be imagined.

It is not necessary to rely on Wilkins for this impression, for Rusden in his 1850 tour in the Hunter Valley, and H. C. E. Childers in his 1851 tour of the Port Phillip district reported similar conditions,[68] but Wilkins's evidence is of special significance because it was he who saw with the greatest clarity the ultimate effect of these squalid surroundings. "The wretched hovels in which the humbler classes are content to live in the country districts", he wrote,

> are of a nature to prevent their attaining common decency much less comfort or neatness in their dwellings. Their habits and their education, in the widest sense of the term, would doubtless be greatly improved, if they could be induced to build neater and more commodious residences. But when the

New South Wales, 1833-1851

school-houses present them with examples of everything to be avoided rather than imitated; when they are framed of the rudest material, and without the slightest regard for decency, comfort or convenience; when, in short, they resemble the miserable homes of the lower classes, it cannot be expected that the children will become more refined in their domestic arrangements when they grow up. The school is an evidence of what their superiors consider good enough for them. . . .[69]

Fortunately few children spent much time in these educational slums, for less than half the children attended school at all and the average length of attendance was barely two years, but for many of them the alternative was just as brutalizing. Wilkins reminded the Select Committee that hundreds of idle children spent their days about the quays and the wharves where they learned

> to use bad language, to steal, and to practise every indecency. The more wretched of these children have no homes, but sleep in the open air, or in any place where they can shelter. They are probably the children of profligate parents who exercise neither control over, nor care for them, and not a few are entirely deserted.

Hundreds more were kept from school

> during harvest, the season for ploughing, and getting in seed. . . . We have repeatedly seen with regret, girls of fifteen or sixteen years of age driving bullocks at the plough, and engaged in other unfeminine occupations. In fact, the children are almost slaves to their parents, who indulge in idleness or extravagance, while the children are kept from school to labour.[70]

There was clearly little to choose between parents and schoolmasters in the lower ranks of Australian colonial society.

The Bush Boarding Schools

Beyond the reach of any of these schools stretched the true pastoral frontier where distance and indifference combined to keep the Australian child in a state of illiteracy. Generally speaking the squatter was a man of some education and was

Australian Education, 1788–1900

not unaware that life on the frontier involved a regression in standards of living, behaviour and culture. It was one thing to accept this regression for oneself (and it is to the squatter's credit that he accepted, with fortitude, the crudity, the privation and the dangers inseparable from frontier life), but it was another thing to accept it for one's wife and children, and still another to accept it for one's servants and their children. For his own children the squatter was sometimes able to contrive an education by sending them off to England, or Sydney or Melbourne, but more often than not they stayed on the run and grew up, heirs to fortunes quite often, in conditions which were materially crude, associating with assigned convicts and almost without education. The origins of that anti-intellectual quality which has often been remarked in the Australian character are to be sought in many places, but its development in the ranks of Australia's "landed gentry" is almost certainly to be traced to the defective education of the generation which came of school-age between 1840 and 1850.[71]

For his servants' children the squatter was neither able, nor disposed, to do very much. His flocks and his outstations were spread over such vast areas that the children on his run were never sufficiently congregated to provide the minimum enrolment of thirty which the Boards insisted on in their regulations. Rusden, who met this problem from one end of eastern Australia to the other, urged upon his Commissioners:

> The formation of large Boarding or Industrial Schools is the only mode by which the Board can place the benefits of education within reach of a numerous and increasing class, viz. hired servants who, dispersed throughout the Bush, have children in deplorable need of instruction,[72]

but he was never able to bring them to the point of starting these schools. There was nothing novel or unrealistic about Rusden's idea. In 1844 William Macarthur had reported to a Select Committee of the New South Wales Legislative Council that he was running a boarding school for fifty children on his property at Camden; in 1846 the Rev.

James Forbes had urged these schools upon the readers of the *Port Phillip Christian Herald*; in 1848 the Rev. Thomas Hastie had persuaded the Learmonths to start a boarding school on their property at Buninyong, and letters praising these schools poured in upon the Boards, but none of the Commissioners could be persuaded to sponsor a bush boarding school. The squatters were scarcely more enterprising; few, if any of them, ever copied the example set by the Macarthurs and the Learmonths.[73]

It could be argued, of course, that they were deterred by the fear of sectarian strife if they encouraged the gathering together of children of several sects. Admittedly the whole period is marked by sectarian bitterness, but this, on close examination, is found to be largely a clerical rivalry; in the practical, day-to-day life of the colony the sharp cleavages which were so passionately defined in the pulpit and the Press found little place. Hastie cheerfully admitted that the call he received from the Learmonths was lacking in denominational fervour. "The Messrs. Learmonth", he recalled in later years, "were willing to take a minister from any denomination, and the circumstances that a Presbyterian clergyman was settled there arose from the fact that no other was available".[74] He found the same toleration in his school. "Although the school is entered upon the list of the Board as belonging to the Free Church", he reported, ". . . in fact parents of all denominations have children at the school, and I have never heard any object either to the mode or subjects of teaching".[75] Macarthur had the same experience at Camden. "The teacher and most of the children were of the Church of England", he told the Select Committee, "but Roman Catholics and Presbyterians attended without any difficulty being raised".[76] Parsimony rather than piety seems to have been the real reason why the squatter drew back from this venture. To create a National day school involved a locality in the raising of one-third of the total cost of the building; to judge from the figures in Rusden's reports this meant, at the most, the raising of about £50 locally—an undertaking which probably

Australian Education, 1788-1900

cost the squatter, as a leading citizen, ten guineas or so. To create a bush boarding school the initial cost, to the Learmonths, was £350 though this sum could be reduced by sharing the responsibility with other squatters, or by regarding the buildings as an investment and passing on the interest charges in the form of higher fees. (The Learmonths calculated interest on their £350 at 25 per cent.) By bringing the school under one of the Boards the squatter would be relieved of all responsibility for the teacher's salary; fees would then need to be fixed to cover the boarding expenses and interest on building costs; the Learmonths found that fees of £10 a year for boarders and £2 a year for day-pupils were not quite enough to meet expenses, the deficit for 1850 amounting to about £60. This they described as "very heavy expense"[77]—a sentiment shared by the Commissioners. In their favour it must be remembered that they were but part-time Commissioners who were already alarmed at the expansion of the school systems they had agreed to administer. Almost to a man they were Legislative Councillors who realized that the radical and expensive project of building bush boarding schools would be too much for their colleagues to stomach, and so they did nothing and neglected the opportunity to create an efficient and stable system of rural education in place of the makeshift arrangement of rural schools, provisional schools, part-time schools, subsidized schools and itinerant teachers which they eventually found necessary. At the same time they lost an opportunity to establish a realistic system of agricultural education, and the squatter lost an opportunity to escape the charge of being "the antagonists of every other class . . . the grasping and rapacious squatters".[78]

Thus at the end of this period the Australian child remained largely without the means of education. Between them, parents, schoolmasters, clerics, squatters and Legislative Councillors had so exploited the situation that an observer like Wilkins could only report that "the Colony possesses no system of education at all, in the proper sense of the word".[79] Yet Wilkins was confident that the damage already done could be repaired. "The Colonial Youth", he insisted, "are by no means dull or incapable of cultivation; on the contrary we have found them acute, apt to learn, and when properly managed, not deficient in industry and application."[80] But despite his confidence the events of the next fifty years were to show that the devising of a system of schools to meet the peculiar conditions of Australian society was a task of some difficulty. It could hardly be attempted until the rival claims of Church and State had been resolved.

NOTES

[1] Bourke to Stanley, 10 Mar. 1834, *H.R.A.*, I, xvii, 393. Bourke's concern for the oppressed classes of society is discussed in Hazel King, 'The Humanitarian Leanings of Governor Bourke', *Historical Studies*, Vol. 10, No. 37 (Nov. 1961). But see also f.n. 84 to Ch. 1.

The relationship between Church, State and public education in N.S.W. in this period has been re-examined in three recent publications: John Barrett, *That Better Country: The Religious Aspect of Life in Eastern Australia, 1833-1850*; Michael Roe, *Quest for Authority in Eastern Australia, 1835-1851*; T. L. Suttor, *Hierarchy and Democracy in Australia, 1788-1870*.

[2] Bourke to Stanley, 30 Sept. 1833, ibid., 224-9.

[3] Ibid., 231. See J. J. Auchmuty, *Irish Education*, and Donald H. Akenson, *The Irish Education Experiment*, for the origins of the Irish National System.

[4] Bourke to Glenelg, 8 Aug. 1836, *H.R.A.*, I, xviii, 466.

[5] Glenelg to Bourke, 30 Nov. 1835, ibid., 201-7.

[6] Bourke to Stanley, 30 Sept. 1833, op. cit., 232.

[7] Bourke to Glenelg, 8 Aug., 7 Oct. 1836, *H.R.A.*, I, xviii, 466-74, 565-70.

[8] Bourke to Stanley, 30 Sept. 1833, op. cit., 232; Broughton to Glenelg, 3 Dec. 1835, *H.R.A.*, I, xviii, 699-701. Broughton's background is discussed in Ross Border, *Church and State in Australia, 1788-1872*, Ch. 6. Relations between Bourke and Broughton are examined in J. F. Cleverley, 'Governor Bourke and the Introduction of the Irish National System', C. Turney (Ed.), *Pioneers of Australian Education*. See also Kelvin Grose, 'William Grant Broughton and National Education in New South Wales, 1829-1836', *Melbourne Studies in Education, 1965*.

[9] During the 1830s Parliament undertook the reform of the Church of England. In 1833 the Irish Church Act reduced the

number of dioceses in Ireland, and after the report of the Ecclesiastical Commission (1835) several Acts were passed to remove abuses in England, e.g. Bishopric of Durham Act (1836), Established Church Act (1836), Tithes Commutation Act (1836), Church Pluralities Act (1838), Church Building Act (1838), Ecclesiastical Duties and Revenues Act (1840). See Olive J. Brose, *Church and Parliament*, Parts 1-3.

[10] *A Speech Delivered at the General Committee of Protestants on Wednesday, August 3rd, 1836, by the Bishop of Australia*, pp. 6, 7, 22.

[11] J. D. Lang, *An Historical and Statistical Account of New South Wales*, Vol. II, pp. 512-13. This retraction occurs in the 1852 edition; the first edition (1840) reveals the vehemence of Lang's initial opposition to the Irish National System. See Vol. II, pp. 365-74.

[12] Bourke to Glenelg, 8 Aug. 1836, op. cit., 470.

[13] Gipps to Normanby, 9 Dec. 1839, *H.R.A.*, I, xx, 426-7.

[14] Glenelg to Bourke, 27 Feb. 1837, *H.R.A.*, I, xviii, 697.

[15] Bourke to Spring Rice, 12 Mar. 1834. Bourke Papers, Uncat. MSS, Set 403, Item 6. (M.L.).

[16] Stanley to Hodgson, 6 Aug. 1836, *Liverpool Courier*, 10 Aug. 1836. The circumstances in which this letter was written are discussed in James Murphy, *The Religious Problem in English Education*, pp. 63-6.

[17] Bourke to Glenelg, 8 Aug. 1836, op. cit., 468, 477.

[18] *V. & P.*, N.S.W. Leg. Council, 1839.

[19] Gipps to Normanby, 9 Dec. 1839, op. cit., 428; Russell to Gipps, 25 June 1840, *H.R.A.*, I, xx, 685.

[20] *The Speech of the Lord Bishop of Australia in the Legislative Council upon a System of General Education, on Tuesday 27 August 1839*, pp. 12-13.

[21] *Australasian Chronicle*, 14 Feb. 1840.

[22] Shane Leslie (Ed.), *From Cabin-Boy to Archbishop: The Autobiography of Archbishop Ullathorne*, pp. 167-8.

[23] Gipps to Stanley, 1 Feb. 1845, *H.R.A.*, I, xxiv, 232. The proceedings of this Select Committee are discussed in Ruth Knight, *Illiberal Liberal: Robert Lowe in New South Wales, 1842-1850*, Ch. 3.

[24] Introduction, *H.R.A.*, I, xxiii, p. xvii.

[25] Report from the Select Committee on Education, 1844: Minutes of Evidence, Bishop Broughton's evidence, Q. 68, *V. & P.*, N.S.W. Leg. Council, 1844.

[26] Ibid., Archbishop Polding's evidence, Q. 69. The effect of Irish and Papal opinion on Polding's views is discussed in A. G. Austin, *Select Documents in Australian Education*, pp. 38, 80-1.

[27] For Broughton's support of Gipps's squatting policy see Gipps to Stanley, 1 Feb. 1845, *H.R.A.*, I, xxiv, 780-7. Broughton

was very conscious of the Canterbury ties which should, he felt, have bound Gipps to him; to a confidant in England he once remarked: "I could not help going back five or six and thirty years or more and reflecting how little he [Gipps] and I, when sitting together in the King's School at Canterbury, expected ever to be brought into such direct opposition. . . . I was not prepared for, and therefore very acutely felt, the unkind observations which he made upon the Church of England in whose bosom he was nourished. . . ." Broughton to Coleridge, 14 Oct. 1839. Bishop Broughton Papers, Microfilm reels FM4/225-6. (M.L.) Ironically enough the two men's remains now lie a few feet apart in Canterbury Cathedral and an adulatory notice informs the visitor that these two sons of Canterbury "thought and wrought together" for the advancement of New South Wales. The word "fought" might have been more appropriate.

[28] See Lang, op. cit., Vol. II, pp. 356-7; G. W. Rusden, *National Education*, p. 173; E. R. Wyeth, *Education in Queensland*, p. 25.

[29] *Sydney Morning Herald*, 8, 10 Sept. 1842.

[30] Stanley to Gipps, 29 Aug. 1845, *H.R.A.*, I, xxiv, 492. This controversy has been thoroughly examined in John Barrett, 'The Gipps-Broughton Alliance, 1844. A Denial Based on the Letters of Broughton to Edward Coleridge', *Historical Studies*, Vol. 11, No. 41 (Nov. 1963).

[31] Bourke to Glenelg, 10 Oct. 1835, *H.R.A.*, I, xviii, 156.

[32] Nicholson to Rusden, 8 July, 3 Nov. 1843. Nicholson Correspondence in the possession of Mr P. J. Williams.

[33] See Kelvin Grose, '1847: The Educational Compromise of the Lord Bishop of Australia', *Journal of Religious History*, Vol. 1, No. 4 (Dec. 1961).

[34] Broughton to FitzRoy, 3 May 1847. N.S.W. Col. Sec.'s In Letters, Box 2/1717. (M.L.).

[35] FitzRoy to Grey, 24 Apr. 1848, *H.R.A.*, I, xxvi, 378.

[36] Lang, op. cit., Vol. II, p. 514.

[37] First Report of the Commissioners of National Education, p. 2, *V. & P.*, N.S.W. Leg. Council, 1849.

[38] For a full account of these agencies see A. G. Austin, *George William Rusden*.

[39] Regulations of the National Board of Education, p. 3, *V. & P.*, N.S.W. Leg. Council, 1849.

[40] Second Report of the Board of National Education, p. 16, *V. & P.*, N.S.W. Leg. Council, 1850.

[41] Ibid. General Instructions for the Agents in Establishing National Schools.

[42] Rusden to Denison, 3 Oct. 1835. (T.C.C.).

[43] For examples of these speeches see *Geelong Advertiser*, 22 Nov.

1849; *Moreton Bay Courier*, 25 May 1850; Austin, op. cit., pp. 129–37.

[44] G. W. Rusden, Diary, 15 Dec. 1849. (S.L.V.)

[45] Miscellaneous Letters Received by the Board of National Education, 23 Sept., 3 Oct., 21 Dec. 1850, 2 Jan. 1851. (M.L.).

[46] Rusden, Diary, op. cit., 11 Mar. 1850.

[47] Ibid., 6 Aug. 1849.

[48] Miscellaneous Letters, op. cit., 25 Jan. 1851.

[49] Rusden, *National Education*, op. cit., pp. 173–4

[50] Rusden, Diary, op. cit., 3 Apr. 1850.

[51] Roach to Rusden, 19 Mar. 1850. (T.C.C.).

[52] *Sydney Morning Herald*, 29 Nov. 1851. On Wilkins see C. Turney, 'William Wilkins—Australia's Kay-Shuttleworth', C. Turney (Ed.), *Pioneers of Australian Education*, and the same author's 'The Rise and Decline of an Australian Inspectorate', *Melbourne Studies in Education, 1970*.

[53] Final Report from the School Commissioners, p. 25, *V. & P.*, N.S.W. Leg. Council, 1856–7.

[54] Rusden, *National Education*, op. cit., p. 347.

[55] Strictly speaking, Wilkins's tour of inspection (1854–5) lies outside the chronological limits of this chapter, but there is no reason to doubt that the conditions he described had applied to the schools in 1851.

[56] Miscellaneous Letters, op. cit., 26 July 1849.

[57] Final Report from the School Commissioners, op. cit., pp. 6–7.

[58] Ibid., p. 17.

[59] Ibid., p. 11.

[60] In Tasmania Thomas Arnold rejoiced at the arrival of the "excellent Irish series"; in S.A. Governor Robe ordered £200 worth of them for his schools although he disapproved of the Irish National system.

[61] W. A. Duncan, *Lecture on National Education*, p. 16.

[62] Final Report from the School Commissioners, op. cit., p. 10.

[63] Ibid., p. 12.

[64] Regulations of the National Board of Education, op. cit., p. 2.

[65] Final Report from the School Commissioners, op. cit., p. 3.

[66] Ibid., p. 5.

[67] First Report of the Commission appointed to enquire into the State of Education, pp. 2–3, *V. & P.*, N.S.W. Leg. Council, 1855.

[68] For Rusden's reports see Miscellaneous Letters, op. cit. Childers' report is reproduced in Edward Sweetman, *The Educational Activities in Victoria of the Rt. Hon. H. C. E. Childers*, pp. 23–44.

New South Wales, 1833–1851

[69] Final Report from the School Commissioners, op. cit., p. 4.
[70] Ibid., pp. 6, 18.
[71] See Alexandra Hasluck, *Portrait With Background*, p. 127; James Clark Ross, *A Voyage of Discovery and Research, 1839–1843*, Vol. I, p. 120; E. W. Landor, *The Bushman: or Life in a New Country*, p. 114.
[72] Miscellaneous Letters, op. cit., 27 Oct. 1848.
[73] For a detailed account of these schools see A. G. Austin, 'The Bush Boarding School in the Port Phillip District', *Journal of Education* (V.I.E.R.), Vol. 3, No. 3.
[74] W. B. Withers, *The History of Ballarat*, p. 7.
[75] Inward Correspondence of the Denominational Schools Board, 21 Nov. 1850, 10 Mar. 1851. (S.L.V.).
[76] *V. & P.*, N.S.W. Leg. Council, 1844, p. 588.
[77] Inward Correspondence, op. cit., 21 Nov. 1850, 19 Feb., 10 Mar. 1851.
[78] G. F. James (Ed.), *A Homestead History*, p. 162.
[79] Final Report from the School Commissioners, op. cit., p. 25.
[80] Ibid., p. 12.

3

Church, State and Common School in Van Diemen's Land, Western Australia and South Australia, 1829–1851

For Colonel George Arthur, Lieutenant-Governor of Van Diemen's Land (as for Governor Bourke in New South Wales), the collapse of the Church and School Corporation brought serious problems. More conservative and rigid than Bourke, more attached by personal inclination to Tory and High Church principles, Arthur nevertheless saw clearly that the conditions in his colony demanded religious and educational services which his own Church could not provide. Early in his term of office he defined the task he had undertaken and, unpalatable as his views might have been to many of the free settlers, he stated bluntly:

> This Colony must be considered in the light of an extensive Gaol to the Empire—the punishment of Crimes and reformation of Criminals the grand objects, in its Penal character, to be attended to; and these, under Providence, can alone be effected by the presence of a respectable Military Force; by the erection of proper places for confinement; by an active Judicial Establishment; by a more general diffusion of knowledge; and by the powerful operation of Religion.[1]

But when Arthur looked at the calibre of his Anglican clergy he was convinced (as his successors in turn were convinced)

Australian Education, 1788-1900

that they were not equal to the task of ministering to the unusual Van Diemen's Land community. In 1826 he wrote:

> I take the liberty of suggesting to Your Lordship, whether it may not be more advisable to engage two Ministers from the Wesleyan Mission. . . . I should conceive they would be better qualified for the Office than any Gentleman who has received a liberal University education.[2]

Thus began Arthur's policy of supporting denominations other than his own and by 1836, near the end of his term, he was prepared to extend support to any sect which would assist his endeavours "to remove that Convict taint, the extinction of which, *as regards the rising generation*, cannot, I submit, be purchased by too costly a sacrifice".[3] In the same dispatch, while affirming his strong attachment to his own Church, he pointed out that he had granted aid to Roman Catholics, Wesleyans, Independents and Presbyterians, and went on, in words which recall Bourke's:

> I very fully appreciate the views entertained and expressed in his opinion before the Council by the Chief Justice, and other equally reflecting and excellent persons, who seem to dread any countenance being given to other sects, as injurious to the interests of the Established Church. I go all lengths with them in the conviction that some Establishment is necessary; but I do not think that the support of an exclusive system was at any period wise; it is not only impolitic, and defeats the end aimed at, but in the present day I conceive it would be impracticable to support it without such an opposition as would shake the Church itself.[4]

Arthur's Education Policy in Van Diemen's Land

Arthur's educational proposals also bore a general resemblance to Bourke's. Dissatisfied with the exclusive nature of the existing schools aided by government funds (all twenty-nine of them were Anglican schools), and sceptical of their efficiency, Arthur ordered his Colonial Secretary and his Chief Magistrate to report on the state of the schools and make recommendations. Armed with conflicting advice from these gentlemen (and a great deal of sound, though unsolicited, advice from the Rev. F. B. Naylor),[5] Arthur proposed to the Secretary of State, in May 1836, that four schoolmasters trained by the British and Foreign School Society should be sent out to establish a system of teacher training. There was, he believed, so little sectarian strife in the colony that "children could be induced to assemble in each parish, under one schoolmaster, regulated by one manual of instructions, applicable to all. . . ." In this way, he believed, "those violent schisms which have in other Countries rent asunder, and cast discredit upon the universal Church, may possibly be avoided".[6]

Arthur was well aware that this policy would bring him into conflict with Bishop Broughton, for it was only two years since he had been treated to a thorough-going episcopal reprimand for offering aid to all sects. After criticizing Bourke's policy in New South Wales and Arthur's in Van Diemen's Land, Broughton had gone on to affirm that

> all governments instead of being zealous for the cause of God according to their own principles, are at this moment blowing hot and cold at once. A miserable expedient into which they are betrayed by the affectation of being thought liberal. . . . This pusillanimous way of proceeding will cause them I think to fall at last, and to fall without dignity. . . . These are my opinions, which I think you will perceive are not likely to bring me into great favour with those now at the head of affairs. My reason for now stating them is that I am certain you are in danger of being led away by the specious theories now afloat.[7]

With this reprimand fresh in his mind, Arthur assured Bourke that though he considered Broughton's attitude "exclusive in the extreme", he was anxious "to go rightly to work in this matter, from circumstances which have occurred between Mr. Broughton and myself, and which render it important that every cordiality will soon exist again between us".[8] But there was little that Bourke could suggest to his lieutenant-governor, except to lament "the intolerance of the Bishop of Australia" and to express the belief that "the question of National Education is becoming better understood and gaining support daily".[9] It was probably as well for Arthur's peace of mind that before he could put his scheme into operation and bring the bishop's wrath down upon his head in greater measure, the Colonial Office had recalled him.

Franklin and the British and Foreign School Society System

Arthur's successor, Sir John Franklin, the gallant Arctic explorer, brought to the narrow, sordid society of Van Diemen's Land a breadth and quality of mind which the colony had never known before. In his warm patronage of scientists like Gould and Strzelecki, and in his establishment of the Tasmanian Society of Natural History and its renowned *Journal* he displayed all the best qualities of a cultivated man of science. His experience of life had given to his Tory principles a quality of humanitarianism and had transformed his earlier puritanical Evangelicalism into a broad and tolerant faith,[10] but he was ill-prepared for the rough and tumble of colonial politics and his first public pronouncement on education revealed the unformed state of his policy.

He began his address to the Legislative Council (10 July 1837) with the familiar gubernatorial assertion of loyalty to the Church of England, but he immediately went on, in the manner of his predecessor, to praise the missionary work of other sects, and to pledge to these people his "support and countenance and protection". The British Government, he pointed out, supported the principle that some general arrangement should be made to embrace the education of all denominations but, he concluded lamely, "I am not yet prepared to propose any specific plan for placing the establishment [of education] generally upon a footing in accordance with this principle; but it is a subject which will engage my anxious thoughts at a very early period".[11] A year later (30 June 1838), Franklin had got no further in his deliberations than the enunciation of this proposition:

> That on almost all points of practical doctrine there is, notwithstanding the diversity of their outward forms . . . a general concurrence of opinion amongst the Presbyterians, the

Van Diemen's Land, Western and S. Australia, 1829-1851

Episcopalians, the Wesleyans, the Independents. That although the dissent between Protestant denominations and the Roman Catholic community is much wider yet than even between these communities there are points on which it may perhaps be possible for them to harmonize.[12]

There would be, Franklin foresaw, strong objections to any plan of general education, but he hoped that there would be "mutual forbearance of the various denominations".

But the governor himself contributed little to the fostering of "mutual forbearance" by vacillating when he should have led, for his pronouncement of June 1838, which clearly foreshadowed a general system of education, was followed in December by the vague proposal that all schools supported by public funds should be "under the immediate control of some ecclesiastical authority . . . [and] shall be conducted in accordance with the principles of some Christian church or congregation".[13] Seeing that every one of the existing public day-schools was already Anglican, Franklin's proposal did little more, in practice, than confirm an Anglican monopoly in education, a condition of affairs which was repugnant to large sections of the community and the Press. In the early months of 1839 the *True Colonist* embarked upon a sustained attack on Archdeacon Hutchins in general, and his ecclesiastical and educational ambitions in particular; in April an incident at Sorell, where Hutchins was alleged to have refused the use of the schoolhouse to other sects who had formerly used it for worship, gave the editor fresh ammunition, and his readers were regaled with examples of "the intolerant, overbearing spirit of the Protestant Episcopal Church", of its "arrogantly assumed superiority . . . intolerant pride . . . disposition to persecute", its "grasping, overbearing, persecuting, intolerant spirit".[14] The archdeacon's conduct, the editor declared, "is founded on the assumption that he possesses territorial jurisdiction in Van Diemen's Land", and one correspondent warned that Hutchins and his clergy believed that

> the education of the youth of the colony is a matter peculiarly the province of their Church and that all Public Institutions

for Education are, and ought to be under her sole and full control. . . . The Archdeacon's late narrow-minded and wanton conduct ought to be the warning note to summon to his post each man who is opposed to a system of education, calculated to imbue the minds of the young with narrow and bigoted sectarian principles.[15]

There was, as it turned out, no need to summon the lieutenant-governor to his post, for he had already sensed the folly of his latest proposals and had determined to implement his original plans for a system of general education. By public notice dated 6 May 1839 he warned that he intended to submit amendments to his December regulations; he went on to say that as it was his

> most anxious desire that a religious education should be afforded to all classes of the community, His Excellency will consider it a fundamental condition . . . that whilst the Public Schools will henceforth be conducted as nearly as circumstances will permit, upon the principles of the British and Foreign School Society, the reading of portions of the entire Scriptures shall be daily required in each.[16]

Sentiments such as these, while as music in the ears of the *True Colonist*, were anathema to Archdeacon Hutchins and his clergy, and Franklin soon began to feel the force of the opposition he would have to withstand. The first substantial challenge came in June from the archdeacon himself. He began by deploring the secular character of the London University, and went on to affirm that "the course we are now entering upon is I fear only the first step towards a similar result; and I am not prepared to move even so much as one inch along a path likely to terminate at the entrance of such a temple of darkness". Franklin's new system, he declared, he could "neither approve nor support", and he announced his determination to "withdraw altogether from any connexion with the Government Schools in this island".[17]

It is interesting to watch Franklin's attitude hardening under these attacks. By September 1839, fortified by advice

Van Diemen's Land, Western and S. Australia, 1829–1851

from Sir John Herschel on the success of a system of general education in Cape Colony,[18] he assured his Council that his policy was in keeping with general colonial policy on education, and went on to quote a paragraph from Herschel's letter:

> So long as Christian principles are broadly laid down as the basis of all proceedings, everything calculated to perpetuate religious or civil distinctions . . . or to foster a spirit of domination on the part of any religious sect ought to be most strenuously and pointedly avoided.[19]

A month later, when the final draft of his regulations was published, he stated bluntly that "the Free Day Schools are to be conducted, as nearly as may be, on the British and Foreign School System",[20] and when, in December, eleven of Hutchins's clergy objected that these regulations would drive them out of the schools, he replied with perfect courtesy, but complete firmness, that he was persuaded that he was "consulting the general interests of the Colony, both in a moral and social point of view, as well as the wishes of a majority of its Inhabitants".[21]

It was in this tense atmosphere that the newly-appointed Board of Education occupied its offices in Liverpool Street and set about its business, but its progress was very limited. Over the years the Board made a number of conciliatory gestures (for example, it authorized the use in its schools of an Anglican publication *The Faith and Duty of a Christian*), but the Anglican clergy remained implacable and their hostility inhibited expansion. Some advances were made: British and Foreign School Society books were reprinted in Hobart, and eventually large quantities of them were obtained from England; James Bonwick, his wife, and five other married couples, all trained in the Society's methods, were brought out, but over-all the Board made little impact on the educational problems of the colony. Between 1840 and 1842 the number of its schools remained stationary at twenty-five and its pupils increased only from 1,148 to 1,460.[22]

Australian Education, 1788-1900

Anglican Opposition

In 1843 the Anglican clergy's smouldering hostility flared into open attack. Rebuffed in renewed attempts to secure government aid for their own schools, they sought to discredit the governor, the Board and its schools with the publication of John Loch's *An Account of the Introduction and Effects of the System of General Religious Education Established in Van Diemen's Land in 1839*. Loch's pamphlet was a formidable document; it ran to more than 100 pages, was carefully prepared, closely reasoned and thoroughly documented; it not only examined the whole constitutional basis of the system, but made a number of serious charges of mismanagement and proselytizing. Moreover, its publication coincided with the arrival in the colony of the impressive figure of Francis Russell Nixon, first Anglican bishop of Tasmania.[23] Nixon made it perfectly clear from the moment of his arrival that he was worthy to serve his metropolitan, Bishop Broughton; he sympathized with his clergy for the years during which they had laboured without "effectual resident Episcopal supervision", but these tribulations, he assured them, were over—"your spiritual father . . . is amongst you; your counsellor is at hand".[24] That there might be no doubt of the benefits to be derived from episcopal supervision the bishop went on to inform them that he had suspended two of their number, had taken steps to set up a Consistorial Court to ensure the maintenance of sound discipline, had quarrelled with the Secretary of State and the Archbishop of York over the appointment of Convict Chaplains, and was about to return to England to settle affairs with these two dignitaries. As a further earnest of his zeal Nixon began an acrimonious correspondence with Dr Willson, who, on behalf of the Roman Catholic Church, had assumed the title of "Bishop of Hobart Town". Willson's right to such a title Nixon categorically and strenuously denied, and despite Willson's reasonable and urbane replies Nixon continued, over several months, to make the most extravagant claims to ecclesiastical dominance.[25] One can thus understand the enthusiasm with which he supported Loch's charges. In October 1843 he petitioned to be heard in person before the Legislative Council and finally took his place before a crowded gallery on the thirty-first of the month. He came quickly to the point:

> A scheme of education has been prevalent in this colony which has not had for its end the training up of God-fearing people ... unsound in theory and unsafe in practice; a system of which I utterly disapprove as lord bishop of this diocese. ... It is a monstrous system ... as a father, I would rather see my children die than that they should be so nurtured; I would rather thus than that they should be trained up next door to infidels. The system is self-condemnatory; it is ... at positive issue with the commands of Christ.[26]

It was in vain that the governor tried to reason with the bishop, for by now he was quite beside himself; he called upon the names of "the Cranmers, the Ridleys, the Latimers of old, who shed their blood rather than violate their consciences", and called upon his audience to bear witness "that posterity shall never say that the first Lord Bishop of Tasmania was afraid to speak his mind, that he was a recreant to his trust or that he did not raise his voice ... in behalf of the church, before God and before his country".[27]

Eardley-Wilmot and Bishop Nixon

Franklin had been spared this painful scene, for he had been recalled in August, and the full weight of the bishop's attack (like so many other misfortunes which had their origins in the Arthur–Franklin period) fell upon his hapless successor, Sir John Eardley-Wilmot. Franklin's peremptory recall was, to some extent, a reflection of the political and economic tensions which were building up in the little colony, and Eardley-Wilmot, Van Diemen's Land's first civilian governor, a cultured and humane man, found himself without the administrative experience or strength of character to control events. He also found, before the end of his short, tragic governorship, how little sympathy and support a governor in difficulties could expect from the

Colonial Office. The colony which he had come to administer was already in the grip of the depression which afflicted all Australia in the early 1840s, but its troubles were aggravated by the penal policy he had inherited. As he recalled later:

> On my arrival here in August 1843, I found the Treasury empty, and the Revenue rapidly diminishing; the settlers either insolvent or kept from insolvency by the self-interest of their mortgagees . . . agricultural produce not paying the cost of production, labour unenquired for.[28]

The truth was that the little colony of Van Diemen's Land (its total population was only 61,638 in 1843) had become, as Governor Arthur had predicted, "an extensive Gaol to the Empire". From 1840 on, when transportation to New South Wales ended, convicts arrived in the island at the rate of 4,000–5,000 a year, creating not only serious moral and social problems, but further economic problems, for under the Probation system of convict discipline, to which the Colonial Office had committed Van Diemen's Land, employment had eventually to be found for every convict and the upkeep of gaols and police had to be provided from the Land Fund. The cost of gaols and police rose steadily as the convicts flooded in, while land sales fell off to a negligible figure.[29]

Little wonder then that Eardley-Wilmot had to face a determined anti-transportation movement. Both inside the Council and out-of-doors, in pamphlet and Press, he had to contend with a violent campaign against the policy he was pledged to implement and against himself as its instrument. Even Denison, his successor, who found little to praise in Eardley-Wilmot's régime, had to admit that the anti-transportation movement, though "a perfect hurricane" in his own day, had at least been "a violent gale during the time that Sir Eardley-Wilmot was Governor".[30] There seemed to be only two ways out of the colony's difficulties—to persuade the British Government to assume the responsibility for maintaining the police and gaols, or to raise extra revenue within the colony. Lord Stanley wasted no words in telling Eardley-Wilmot that the first proposal was unacceptable. "You must dismiss from your mind", he said, "all expectation that Her Majesty's government will consent to any such arrangement".[31] Thus the governor turned to the second proposal and immediately prepared the way for a first-class constitutional crisis. In the Council, Thomas George Gregson, a prominent landowner, and five other unofficial members set themselves (in Gregson's words)

> to resist the contribution of one shilling more by the people of this colony, so long as the inhabitants were taxed for British purposes, and that until the Home Government acted with justice to the colony in paying for the Police and Gaols, no Bill should pass by which any tax was levied on the people.[32]

By November 1845 the "Patriotic Six" had resigned, leaving the Council without a quorum, and the governor with the unenviable task of finding six new nominees. Within a year Eardley-Wilmot had been recalled in the most humiliating circumstances.

It must therefore have been with only part of his mind that Eardley-Wilmot turned to consider his educational problems. Loch's charges had certainly made a great stir, but the Board of Education had produced such a detailed rebuttal of the charges in its Report for 1843 that the governor believed that his administration had answered its critics. However, it was one thing to brandish the Board's Report in Nixon's face (as the governor had done during the bishop's emotional outburst before the Council),[33] but it was quite another to silence him, and Eardley-Wilmot's decision to support his Board of Education, and defy the bishop, had two far-reaching results. In the first place, it brought governor and bishop into direct collision, and confirmed the stand the Anglican clergy had taken with Franklin. From now on the governor could count on no support from this quarter, but worse, he was now exposed to the bishop's spleen, and there seems little doubt that it was Nixon's reports to Gladstone on the governor's private conduct which formed the major source of the "rumours" (as Gladstone called them) upon which he eventually dismissed Eardley-Wilmot.[34] In the second place it drove the Anglican clergy to find other ways of reaching the ear of Downing Street, and early in 1844 they produced an untitled, twenty-three page pamphlet which purported to be a reply to the Board's reply to Loch, and dispatched copies of it to England.[35] Though the pamphlet was preceded by a petition signed by Loch and six of the clergy, its authorship was never disclosed, but a number of pieces of evidence point to the Rev. R. R. Davies who, in the columns of the *Launceston Examiner* (June–August 1844), conducted a very protracted correspondence on the issues raised in the pamphlet. Although usually prolix he managed to put his point of view very succinctly in the issue of 20 July. "The board of education to be at once relieved of their . . . office", he wrote. "The secretary to wind up all the present schools by the 31st December of the present year."

It was to take a little longer than Davies had thought, but he was to live to see his hopes substantially realized. In August 1844 the Secretary of State (Stanley), thoroughly perplexed by the conflicting information reaching him on educational affairs in Van Diemen's Land, ordered the governor to set up a commission of inquiry and at the same time to report his own impressions of the existing system. By May 1845 three commissioners had completed a lengthy report and by June it was on its way to London. Meanwhile, in the Press and in the Council, there was strong criticism of the governor's handling of the matter. Not only, it transpired, had the governor halted any expansion by the Board while its future was under consideration, but he had sent the commissioners' report away without showing it to the Board and had refused to table it in the Council.[36] Moreover, the *Launceston Examiner* noted, it was surely significant that all three commissioners were Anglicans.[37] It was unfortunate that Eardley-Wilmot acted so secretively in this matter, for he and the commissioners had all reported fairly, and not unfavourably, on the system. Despite the great bulk of the commissioners' report, their decision came simply to this: that while they had no way of knowing exactly what conditions had been like when Loch made his charges, they were "quite prepared to say that the Schools in their present state do not merit the full measure of censure which was there cast upon them".[38] In forwarding the report Eardley-Wilmot, while suggesting a few administrative changes, affirmed that the existing system had "less objection and less evil attached to it, with more good than would be produced by a change to some other".[39]

In the light of these two reports one can only imagine that the governor was shocked and bewildered when he received the Secretary of State's reply, for it was a sustained indictment of Eardley-Wilmot and the system of education he had supported.[40] In eighty-odd closely written pages Gladstone (who had replaced Stanley at the Colonial Office) reprimanded the governor over and over again for failing to provide the Colonial Office with a detailed personal appreciation of the education system, and for his ready acceptance of a state of affairs which the Secretary of State obviously found deplorable. The petulance and scathing criticism which mark the whole dispatch are only understandable in retrospect, for it is clear now that Gladstone had already resolved that Eardley-Wilmot must go, though two more months were to elapse before that final, damning dispatch was written. The existing system, Gladstone declared, was expensive, inefficient, and a violation of the consciences of most of the inhabitants of the island. Clearly, he pointed out, it was completely unacceptable to all the Anglican and Catholic clergy and there was no point in discussing any supposed divergence of lay and clerical opinion, for this could not be proved; one had to suppose that the clergy spoke for their congregations—in which case they represented "a very great majority". The governor would, Gladstone went on, reconsider the whole matter at much greater length, and he would take as his starting point the necessity to aid the denominational schools in the manner then operating in New South Wales.

Denison's Dual System

The carrying out of Gladstone's orders fell not to Eardley-Wilmot, whose recall was dated 30 April 1846, but to his successor, Sir William Denison, who assumed office in January 1847. Denison began his term of office with several advantages which his predecessor had lacked, for not only had the financial depression passed its worst point when he arrived, but before sailing he had spent a considerable amount of time at the Colonial Office analysing the reasons for Eardley-Wilmot's failure and evolving an acceptable line of policy. Moreover if, as Professor Fitzpatrick has suggested, Franklin was recalled for being too much under his wife's influence, and Eardley-Wilmot for being too little so, Denison had the great advantage of being the very embodiment of the domestic virtues as the nineteenth-century middle class understood them. As the size of his family grew apace he could write ecstatically to his mother-in-law: "I love the 127th Psalm, which tells us that 'Children and the fruit of the womb are an heritage and gift that cometh of the Lord,' and 'Happy is the man who has his quiver full of them'."[41] But undoubtedly his greatest single advantage was the good work done for him in Van Diemen's Land by La Trobe, who had been given the distasteful task of leaving his Port Phillip responsibilities in order to administer the island between Eardley-Wilmot's suspension and Denison's arrival. Convict affairs, in particular, had been put on a much sounder footing by the time Denison arrived—an advantage which he was quick to appreciate. La Trobe, he wrote, "is a most invaluable public servant, and has done his duty here well and manfully . . . he has thus relieved me of an immense amount of work".[42] Starting with these advantages, Denison proved to be a successful governor of Van Diemen's Land. His term was not without its crises, and he could never be described as a popular governor, but in his commonplace, efficient way he served the colony well as it prepared for responsible government—a service for which he was eventually rewarded with the governorship of New South Wales.

Van Diemen's Land, Western and S. Australia, 1829-1851

His approach to his educational problems was as matter-of-fact as the rest of his attitude, but his opinions were based upon a considerable amount of reading, thought and experience. Even his bitterest political enemy, Gregson, admitted that no other governor had taken the same amount of interest in the Orphan School ("a day scarcely passes that you do not visit that Asylum"),[43] and a study of Denison's speeches, correspondence and publications reveals an extensive knowledge of current educational literature, and a number of shrewd opinions on educational principles and practice. There were, he insisted, two distinct questions to be settled. First, the type of education to be provided must be determined, and here he was adamant that it was essential to provide a Christian education based upon the combination, within the classroom, of the secular and the religious. "All I advocate", he told one correspondent, "is an adoption of religious *principles*, not of religious *opinions*."[44] The Church of England, he pointed out to his mother, would benefit by being disestablished; this attitude, he went on to assure her, sprang not from religious indifference, but from

> my conviction of the injury done to the cause of religion by their quarrels about matters of such secondary importance which has led me to stand completely aloof from all parties. I belong neither to High Church or Low Church, Broad Church or Narrow Church, looking upon all as equally in the wrong in placing stumbling blocks in the way of the simple believer in Christ.[45]

To a third correspondent he declared that

> the denominations insist upon the communication to the children . . . of certain dogmas, the truth of which I am not disposed either to assert or to contradict, but which I may fairly say that children could not by any possibility comprehend. I should gladly therefore see the . . . parties come to such an understanding as was done in Holland.[46]

But despite his preference for the Dutch compromise, and despite his impatience with "bigoted adherence to particular forms and opinions", Denison was too careful and shrewd a colonial governor to risk his future by forcing a compromise upon the sects. Putting his convictions aside, he was quite prepared to support any sect which could provide a Christian education.

The second question to be solved, he declared, was the method of financing education. That the money should come out of general revenue was an entirely wrong principle, involving a responsibility which government "ought never have been called upon to support". This responsibility should be thrown back on the people through the payment of fees, voluntary subscriptions, or a compulsory levy. In this way, not only would expenditure by the central government be reduced, but local interest would be quickened as parents sought to "get their pennyworth for their penny".[47]

However right in theory Denison might have been about the benefits of decentralization, local support and the payment of fees, events soon proved the impracticability of his ideas in the Van Diemen's Land of 1848, for his announcement that in future all schools (including the Board schools) would receive government aid at the rate of 1d. per child per day, coincided with the Council's rejection of his proposed levy. The schools receiving this paltry amount of government aid immediately deteriorated as teachers' salaries tumbled. The six married couples sent out by the British and Foreign School Society "were *starved out* of their situations" as Gregson told Denison; they, and other competent teachers, threw up their positions to establish private schools or quit the colony, and their places were taken by the colony's riff-raff, including a high proportion of convicts and ex-convicts.[48] At the same time the total number of schools increased, as the Anglicans took advantage of this new government aid to open more schools even if they had to be staffed by incompetents. By the end of 1849 there were fifty-nine Anglican schools receiving aid, four Catholic schools and eight former Board schools. The Board of Education, rather than be a party to this state of affairs, resigned; the inspector (Thomas Bradbury) who was appointed to take over the functions of the Board, died, and

Van Diemen's Land, Western and S. Australia, 1829-1851

by the end of 1849 Denison found himself supporting a multiplicity of schools which lacked either a guiding principle or a guiding hand.

Essentially, by 1849, Van Diemen's Land educational affairs had reached the same stage of development as New South Wales educational affairs. In both colonies clerical opposition had thwarted the attempt to create a thoroughgoing system of national schools, and had prevailed upon the government to support a dual system. But whereas in the older colony a substantial organization had been created to handle the dual system, conditions in Van Diemen's Land could only be described as chaotic. It was with evident relief that Denison announced, early in 1850, that he had secured the services of Dr Arnold's son, Thomas, as inspector of schools and anticipated his early arrival from New Zealand.

Foundation of Western Australia

While the governors of Van Diemen's Land were wrestling with the problems of their convict colony, Thomas Peel had embarked on his plan to found a settlement on the inhospitable shores of Western Australia. There are many features of this settlement which mark it out as different from the earlier settlements in the east—the absence of convicts, the predominantly middle-class composition of the settlers, the flavour of private enterprise[49]—but none is more significant than the simple fact that nearly half a century had elapsed since Phillip planted his fragment of eighteenth-century society on the shores of Sydney Cove. By the time Peel's disillusioned settlers struggled ashore in the high gales and driving rain of June 1829 many of the contentious issues of Australian colonial life had been settled for them in the convict settlements 3,000 miles to the east and, whether they liked it or not, could not effectively be reopened. Few events bring out the belated nature of the Western Australian settlement so clearly as the unhappy adventures of Archdeacon Thomas Hobbes Scott. Once he was convinced of the failure of his attempt to create an Anglican monopoly of education in New South Wales (see Chapter 1 above), Scott could not bear to remain in the colony which had spurned him, and took passage for England. When his ship was wrecked off Fremantle in November 1829 and he finally got ashore, he found himself in a colony only five months old, yet one whose religious and educational future was already largely determined by his experiment and failure in New South Wales. It was symptomatic of the new colony that it contained no place of worship and not one Anglican clergyman, and there is something symbolic in the picture of Scott employing his enforced idleness by building, largely with his own hands, the little rush church in which, on Christmas Day, he conducted the first communion service in Western Australia.[50]

After 1829 there was really no point in trying to reopen the case for a dominant Anglican Church, but some of the more obtuse newcomers to Western Australia made ineffectual protests against the settled colonial policy of impartial government aid to all sects. Shortly after his arrival in 1839 Governor Hutt was confronted with Anglican requests for additional aid, but he could only explain to his petitioners that what he gave to one sect he must give to others, and to prevent any further importunities he had his Council pass an Act to Promote the Building of Churches and Chapels (3 Vict., No. 6, 1840) in which he offered to subsidize private efforts made "towards the building of any Church or Chapel". By 1842 even the senior Anglican clergyman, the Rev. J. R. Wollaston, was beginning to accept the inevitable. "Sad indeed is the state of the Church here", he confided to his diary,

> made worse by the measures of an ungodly government. . . . Our case is this: the Home Government in its liberality supports all forms of Religion alike—(ergo, none at all)—and therefore the Colonial does the same . . . and not one penny, at present, goes out of the Colonial Treasury towards the support of any of us.[51]

But even government favour would have helped the Anglican cause but little, for its failure to flourish in the west was only part of the larger failure of the whole colony. The middle-class settlers of 1829-30 soon found that Western Australia was not an easy place in which to make a fortune —or, for that matter, a competence. In addition to the natural hazards of patchy land, dry summers, heavy timber and hostile natives, the early settlers were faced with a crippling shortage of labour. Those who had the enterprise, and the capital, quickly cut their losses and moved on to the eastern colonies; the population remained almost stationary at about 1,500 during the first four years of settlement, and only passed the 2,000 mark ten years after the colony was founded. The 4,000 mark was only reached after a further ten years of struggle.[52] Those who remained—the Molloys, the Bussells, the Hamersleys, the Lefroys—worked unceasingly just to survive, and the colony clung precariously to its existence from year to year.[53]

There were three direct results of this twenty-year long fight for existence—all of them detrimental to the educational development of the colony. In the first place, the struggling settler tended to become a complete materialist, obsessed with the sheer necessity to survive. "The twenty-four hours of the day", one Western Australian historian has written,

> proved for almost all settlers only just enough to make a bare living. These pioneering and hard economic conditions helped to intensify the materialist outlook which the colonists had brought from England. Success—financial success—came to be the standard by which a man's worth was measured. The schooling of children was often neglected in favour of their value as workers.[54]

This tendency to materialism was noted, and deplored, by nearly every visitor to the colony, but it was also felt by the settlers themselves. Some, like Georgiana Molloy, wrote broken-heartedly of their struggles to protect their children from the effects of their environment; others, like Samuel Moore, accepted the dilemma with more phlegm. "A difficulty now arises", he wrote, "my children want schooling and I want pig-feeders and shepherds."[55]

Australian Education, 1788–1900

In the second place, the impoverished, frontier conditions of the scattered settlements which made up the colony of Western Australia were unfavourable to the growth of Churches.[56] There had been no chaplain sent out with the original settlers, and although a few ministers of religion gradually straggled into the colony there were never enough, in the first twenty years, to plant the Church firmly. By 1842 there were only five Anglican clergy in the colony— four of them of doubtful zeal—and although the colony had been transferred from the diocese of Calcutta to that of Australia in 1836, they were bereft of episcopal advice and stimulation so long as the nearest bishop was 3,000 miles away in Sydney. In 1847 the colony was again transferred, and became part of Bishop Short's new diocese in Adelaide; within a year of his arrival Short found time to pay a visit to this western outpost of his See, and at last the accumulated confirmations and consecrations of the last nineteen years could be carried out, but there was little else the bishop could do for his tiny, scattered flock.[57] He was able to grant them a little financial help, and he was able to appoint the Rev. J. R. Wollaston as their archdeacon, but as that good man was to discover in the next seven, exhausting years, it was almost impossible, with the resources at his command, to maintain the minimum functions of his Church.[58] Personal religion, he observed shortly after he reached the colony, was "the mere shadow of a shade. The means of grace . . . have been so long neglected or out of reach, that our people require to be schooled into the very first elementary principles of Christianity".[59] Twelve years later, after an arduous and devoted ministry, he had to confess: "In the present unorganized state of our Church I find it impossible to keep up the decency and order I could wish".[60] Under these circumstances it is not surprising that the Church had not been able to supply its members' educational needs. "On the subject of schools", Wollaston sadly reported to the Society for the Propagation of the Gospel,

> I grieve to say I can communicate little that is satisfactory. The impracticability of boarding the children, from the expense

Van Diemen's Land, Western and S. Australia, 1829-1851

and the inconvenient distances at which settlers are placed from each other, renders the regular assemblage of scholars for a daily school almost impossible. . . . As to proper masters and mistresses, they are not to be found; and if they were I have no means of getting them paid at all adequate to the time they must give up.[61]

In the third place, the colony's prolonged struggle for existence had made it impossible for an impoverished government to do much to support education, either directly or through granting aid to the Churches. Governor Hutt's Churches and Chapels Act had only been in operation four years when a falling public revenue forced him to suspend it,[62] and all the early governors took refuge in the belief that in a predominantly middle-class society parents would somehow contrive to provide education for their children. Beyond this, Governors Stirling, Hutt and Clarke were able to do very little. Spasmodic attempts were made to maintain "Colonial Schools", but the first school collapsed in 1830, after a life of four months, when the master resigned to take up his trade of carpentry "to acquire the means of returning home", and the second school collapsed less than a year later, when the governor discovered that he was paying £48 a year to a master who had no pupils.[63] Eighteen years after the colony was founded there were only two Colonial Schools in existence, with a combined enrolment of thirteen pupils; another handful of poor children were, from time to time, educated in private schools at government expense.[64]

Irwin's Education Committee

In the mid-1840s the colonists' attitude to their educational problems began to change. There had always been some amongst them to reiterate the intellectual and moral dangers to which the colony was exposing itself (e.g. Leake in the Legislative Council, "Philomathes" in the *Inquirer*),[65] but there had never been any widespread response to their warnings. Now, three circumstances combined to put the educational problem in a fresh light. In the first place there

Australian Education, 1788-1900

was, during the 1840s, a steady increase in the population without any corresponding increase in the number of schools. In 1840 the population was only 2,311, but by 1842 it was 3,476, by 1846, 4,290 and by 1848, 4,622; to handle this increased population there were, in 1848, only the two Colonial Schools and nine private schools educating between them 240 children out of some 400 children of school age.[66] But more important to the predominantly Anglican colonists was the disquieting fact that ninety of these children were in Roman Catholic schools. While the Anglicans had been unable (or unwilling) to organize and support their own Church, they had been forced to stand by and watch the remarkable achievements of the tiny Roman Catholic community. Though the first priest (Father Brady) had not arrived in the colony until 1843, he had been created Bishop of Perth in 1845 (the first Anglican bishop was not appointed until 1856), had returned from Rome in 1846 with a number of Sisters of Mercy, catechists and priests, and had established a mission at New Norcia and a school in Perth before the year was out—yet his flock in 1848 numbered only 337 in a total population of 4,622.[67] The Anglican reaction to Brady's progress was compounded of admiration, envy and fear. They addressed appeals to England for financial help,[68] they quietly sent their children to Catholic schools until they constituted two-thirds of the pupils in them, they conducted a vicious anti-Catholic campaign in the Press, and they joined forces with the Protestant sects in the colony to prevent their common enemy from "wrenching the Bible from the hands and hearts of the youth of Australia".[69] In February 1847 the death of Governor Clarke provided the third circumstance which was to affect the colony's educational future, for it thrust into the office of acting-governor, Frederick Irwin, the most active and influential Anglican layman in the settlement. Irwin had been in the colony as Military Commandant and Lieutenant-Governor since its inception,[70] and had never wearied of doing good in the formation of missionary societies, the building of churches and the general elevation of colonial morals; now he seized his brief opportunity to legislate for the colony's welfare, and one of his first actions was to create an Education Committee, and commission it to establish an acceptable system of education.[71]

There could have been but little doubt of the Committee's recommendations. Its chairman was the colonial chaplain (the Rev. J. B. Wittenoom), the other three members were Anglican laymen, and two of them (Francis Lochee and R. W. Nash) had, as sometime editors of the *Inquirer*, been foremost in attacking the Catholics.[72] This, the Committee realized, was no time to make any concessions to the Catholics, for they had just sent a bitter petition to the Queen attacking the administration and demanding a separate grant;[73] by the same token, this was no time to divide the Protestant ranks by any claim to Anglican dominance. Left to their own devices (for they were mercifully free of episcopal promptings), these four good Anglicans met at Wittenoom's house on 31 August 1847, determined to conciliate the Catholics if they could, but equally determined to present a united Protestant front. The plan they hammered out in frequent meetings over the next few weeks was based upon the principle that the Colonial Schools should be open to all denominations of Christians, and should inculcate the general principles of Christianity by the reading of the Scriptures without note or comment; "the special doctrines of each denomination" should, they determined, be "left to Sunday schools or private teaching elsewhere".[74] There were moments when a vestigial sense of "Establishment" nearly led them astray. They were, for example, at first tempted to introduce "Morning and evening prayers in set form (if not objected to, of which no apprehension existed) from the Liturgy", and to conduct on Saturdays a class for "those not professedly belonging to any sect and who depend on the State for education in religion; such classes to be instructed in the principles of the Church of England, the Catechism, etc., by the Teacher or the Clergyman",[75] but their sense of the danger in which they stood was stronger than their sense of "Establishment", and they abandoned both proposals after remarking nostalgically that "the State, if it teaches any, can teach no other religion than its own".[76]

The Committee's common sense was rewarded by immediate support from the Protestant sects, the Wesleyans applauding their plan, promising to send the children from their own school and offering to lend their schoolhouse,[77] but the Catholic reaction, at first only faintly hostile, quickly developed into bitter antagonism when the Committee's schoolmaster at Perth, provoked by Catholic sniping in the Press, dashed off a heated and bigoted letter which the *Inquirer* published on 1 Dec. 1847. It was in vain that the Committee immediately rebuked their teacher, and made copies of their rebuke available to Catholic critics;[78] the fat was in the fire, and His Excellency Captain Charles Fitz-Gerald, arriving in the colony in August 1848, found that he had a sizeable conflagration on his hands.

FitzGerald and Catholic Opposition

FitzGerald's position was not an enviable one. He had scarcely had time to assess local feeling when the Colonial Office, belatedly answering the Catholic petition of 1846, warned him

> against doing, or permitting, so far as your influence extends, anything which might tend to increase the irritation against each other which unfortunately appears to exist in the minds of the Roman Catholics and of the Protestant members of the community. You will also watch an opportunity for making some grant from the Public Revenue in aid of the Religious Instruction of the Roman Catholics, regard being had to their relative numbers and consequent claim in common with other Colonists.[79]

That was all very well, FitzGerald must have thought, but where was the money to come from in this chronically insolvent colony? A fine state of affairs it was when a governor had to beg a loan of £1,200 from the banks to see his administration through a tight pinch, and be asked what security the government could offer![80] Best thing was to take a high hand with those banking fellows, but they probably knew how things stood at Government House. That fellow Cowan, who used to be Private Secretary, had just had £100 stopped from his salary to satisfy his creditors, and now the Secretary of State had got wind of another £100 that some wretch in London claimed was owed to him by no less a person that the governor himself.[81] But, money or no money, the governor had little opportunity to play for time, for his Colonial Secretary (R. R. Madden) was a militant Catholic layman and a political watchdog for Dr Brady.[82] At first the governor tried his hand at conciliation by presiding over an Executive Council meeting at which the Committee's secretary (R. W. Nash) was invited to discuss Dr Brady's grievances, but he was loath to repeat the experiment, for Madden, as Nash later reported to his Committee, "conducted himself in a manner so violent and offensive that only respect for His Excellency and the rest of the Council induced the Secretary to remain in the room".[83] It seemed as if nothing would go right in this affair. By the unluckiest of chances Irwin, when acting-governor, had inadvertently deprived Brady of a land grant for his native mission; ironically enough it was Madden who had signed the incorrect order, but Brady now bore down on FitzGerald with charges of malpractice and bigotry against Irwin, the instigator of this intolerable educational scheme.[84] This, FitzGerald knew, would make sorry reading in the Colonial Office, for in their files they would have an unfortunate dispatch from Irwin, full of attacks on Brady, including a particularly nasty accusation of making false representations at Rome in order to procure his bishopric.[85]

FitzGerald's Dual System

Some concession therefore had to be made. Brady had been asking for one of two things—either a system of education based upon the Irish National system (and it is a mark of Western Australia's isolation that he was unaware that his colleagues in the east had turned against this system), or a separate grant. To the first of these proposals the

Education Committee was completely opposed, though it is doubtful if its members really understood how the Irish National schools operated. "One of the eminent uses of Public Schools", they told the governor,

> consists in rearing together in habits of kindly intercourse and laudable emulation that population who are to form the future community. To commence their lives therefore by training them to regard each other as divided into conflicting sects, is to create and nourish all the vices of party spirit, personal hostilities and self-importance as arising from both, which it is the object of the school to prevent; it is to pour into the social machine sand instead of oil. This is a fatal objection to the Irish system.[86]

To the second proposal they were equally opposed,[87] so it became FitzGerald's responsibility to choose the lesser of two evils. To a harassed governor the expedient of a separate grant was not only the easier thing to do, administratively, but it also accorded more closely with his Colonial Office instructions than the establishment of a comprehensive system, which might, or might not, suit Dr Brady when it came to the test. In April 1849 the governor informed the Secretary of State that after talking to Dr Brady he was uncertain that the bishop would join any common system. "Finding it fruitless to hope for this union of youth", he reported,

> I have thought it but right and just to place on the estimates a grant for the maintenance of the R. Catholic schools in proportion to their numbers—Dr. Brady is entitled to this consideration as it is but just to say that the R.C. Schools both male and female are conducted in such a manner as to prove highly beneficial to the community and as far as I know without any efforts at Proselytism on the Protestant children, many of whom attend their Schools.[88]

The members of the Committee received this information with tight-lipped dignity. They regretted to hear that the governor had found it necessary to make a separate grant, and they entered a protest "against any *further* extension of a system which they believe to be opposed to the real progress of education",[89] but they continued to assert their belief that the way should be left open for all sects to use their schools. It says much for their sense of responsibility that they quickly rebuffed Bishop Short when he advised them that he "conceived the present occasion of the opposition of the Romanists a good opportunity for the Church of England body to obtain a grant in proportion to their numbers".[90] Fortunately for the good of Western Australian education, the bishop betook himself to Adelaide after this display of opportunism, and the Committee was left undisturbed to its task of providing a system of schools which should at least embrace all Protestants and Anglicans.

Of all the dual systems established in the Australian colonies before 1851 none was as drastic as FitzGerald's. Without realizing it, he had anticipated by over twenty years the divorce of the Catholic schools from the national system, and in doing so he had created the precedent of a separate grant to any organization which chose to reject the national system. But for the common sense of his Education Committee he would have committed the colony least able to afford it to a fragmentary, denominational system.

Foundation of South Australia

From its inception the colony of South Australia exhibited a mental climate significantly different from that prevailing in the other colonies. The colony's most recent historian has written:

> South Australia was settled in 1836 by men whose professed ideals were civil liberty, social opportunity and equality for all religions. . . . Not that these longed-for liberties were the only ends which settlers and speculators pursued in South Australia. They also pursued wealth, some with deplorable concentration and success, and no doubt other things beside. But it was their particular concern for particular liberties that distinguished them from other emigrants, governed their choice and their character.[91]

Providing the original impetus towards this fresh experiment in colonization were the "systematic colonizers", men like

Australian Education, 1788-1900

Edward Gibbon Wakefield, Sir William Molesworth and George Grote, philosophic radicals and utilitarians who drew their strength from Jeremy Bentham. From the outset their plans involved the provision of a high degree of civil and religious liberty, and naturally the practical men attracted to their scheme included a high proportion of Dissenters and radicals of all descriptions. George Fife Angas, a Baptist philanthropist, Robert Gouger, the first Colonial Secretary, an Independent and republican, John Brown, the Emigration Agent, Osmond Gilles, the Colonial Treasurer, George Kingston, the Deputy Surveyor-General, all three outright republicans, Richard Hanson, Advocate-General and a Utopian socialist—these were the sort of men who formed the National Colonization Society, the South Australian Land Company and the South Australian Association; these were the sort of men who wrote the pamphlets, petitioned successive Secretaries of State, drafted innumerable bills and circulars, and finally sailed to the "paradise of dissent". It must be remembered, however, as Pike has reminded us, that most of these men, true to their middle-class liberalism, sought wealth as well. This mixture of motives was clearly stated by Angas in one of the many circulars he prepared. "My object", he began, "is one of patriotic benevolence. . . .

> My conviction is, that immigration is adapted to meet the wants of many, and relieve much of the distress in this country which is largely owing to the circumstances that not only are trades and professions partially ruined by competition, but our population is increasing at about the rate of 822 a day. . . . The world has to be Christianized; and the machinery employed in the present day, good and effective as it is, is far from adequate to the attainment of that end. Emigration is according to the manifest design of Providence and should be made available. . . . That I am sincere in my convictions above stated I can give no stronger proof than the fact that I am a large holder of land in the Colony: as an investment it is better than any I can obtain in England.[92]

Again, it must be remembered that the promoters by no means intended that political rights in the new colony should

Van Diemen's Land, Western and S. Australia, 1829-1851

be extended to all—hence the embarrassing moment at the famous Exeter Hall meeting called by the South Australian Association on 30 June 1834, when a labourer, William Lovett, had the bad taste to ask the chairman whether political rights were to be confined to men of capital. The history of South Australia in its first twenty years was to show that despite all the brave talk in its founding days, the colony would have to tread, very closely, the same political path as any other colony. As the Secretary of State pointed out in 1842:

> I have learnt with regret that numbers of Her Majesty's subjects have been lured from their native land under a promise from the original promoters of this colony that it is not in my power to fulfil. . . . It forms no part of the system of [Her Majesty's] government to establish laws in one colony which are at variance with those in force in other British possessions.[93]

But when all the qualifications have been made, two aspirations remain sincere and constant—the desire for religious equality and an attachment to the voluntary principle; neither was to be achieved completely, but no theme runs more consistently through the colony's life than this dual aspiration. Thus, at the Exeter Hall meeting, the Methodist M.P. John Wilks was interrupted by frequent cheering as he stated:

> On being called upon to join this association there were two great principles to which he immediately directed his attention. His first interrogation was; "What is to be done in this new colony for the education of the people?" and his next—"What is to be done to secure perfect religious liberty?" . . . He felt it necessary to ascertain that nothing like religious persecution would pollute the soil of the new Australian colony; that there would be no restrictions direct or indirect, upon the rights of conscience within it. . . . In this new colony there was to be no dominant party, there was to be no sectarian principle, all men were to be brethren, there were to be no tithes or church-rates—none of those extortions which even those who benefit by them regret to make. There education and religion were to shed their cheering influence, as the sun sheds its genial warmth upon all denominations of men alike.[94]

Australian Education, 1788-1900

The South Australian School Society

It was in this spirit that the South Australian School Society was formed in London by George Fife Angas for the support of a school system in the colony. In a lengthy prospectus Angas urged upon his readers the need to free education in South Australia from government aid; he discoursed upon the benefits to be derived from the education of the poor ("habits of peace, order, industry and subordination") and announced an elaborate system beginning with infant schools, continuing through "Schools on the British system", and culminating in "Schools on Dr. Fellenberg's plan for instructing the youth in Agricultural and other Trades, combined with the higher branches of education until they reach 16 years of age". For some time past, he assured his readers, a gentleman in every respect suitable for the office of Head Teacher and Director of the Schools had been making himself acquainted with these systems, and was preparing to proceed to the colony. An annual subscription of one guinea, or a donation of £20 would enable one to become a member, he concluded, but "It is confidently expected that after a few years the whole expense of the establishment will be raised in the colony".[95]

Two circumstances prevented the fulfilment of these plans for voluntarily supported, non-sectarian education—one political and the other economic. It was one thing to plan in liberal terms for a new colony, but it was quite another to persuade any British government to give these plans the sanction of law, as the promoters discovered as the months of 1831, 1832, 1833 and 1834 dragged by, and their approaches were rebuffed by successive Secretaries of State. Meanwhile, those prepared to invest and migrate were becoming importunate, or losing interest, and some compromise was seen to be necessary if the colony were to be started at all. It was in these circumstances that the Bill to erect South Australia into a British Province was pushed through Parliament in July-August 1834; as a result of compromise it contained a number of ill-defined clauses

Van Diemen's Land, Western and S. Australia, 1829-1851

which were to prove disastrous once the colony was established, but only one of these clauses concerns us here. In order to get support for the Bill, the promoters had had to agree to the insertion of a clause empowering the Crown to appoint "Chaplains and clergymen of the Established Church of England or Scotland", and to grant them a salary. There is no doubt, as Gouger and others pointed out, that the acceptance of this clause was a matter of expediency, nor is there any doubt that the promoters were very busy giving the impression that it really had no significance and would shortly be repealed (as it was in 1838), but the immediate effect of it was to send to the colony an Anglican clergyman, the Rev. Charles Beaumont Howard, as the official Colonial Chaplain.

The second blow to the voluntary principle came from the early economic failure of the colony. In the face of economic hardship the colonists simply found that they could not, by voluntary subscription, support their churches or their schools. One by one their pastors found it necessary to take secular employment in order to supplement their meagre stipends: the Independent, Thomas Quinton Stow, turned to farming a lease along the Torrens River, the Baptist, Marcus Collisson, tried his hand as a shepherd for the South Australian Company, Father Benson became a part-time carpenter; at the same time, debts incurred in the building of churches stood unreduced, accumulating a ruinous amount of interest. In these circumstances it is not surprising that the elaborate School Society plans came to an ignominious end. The original master sent out by Angas (J. B. Shepperdson) resigned when he found that fees, subscriptions and English donations totalled only £80, and by 1843 his successor, William Oldham, found himself in desperate straits. The correspondence on his plight is illuminating. On 4 August 1843 William Giles, on behalf of the Society, wrote to Governor Grey's secretary:

> Within the last few minutes I have had poor Mr. Oldham with me to entreat the loan of one pound, saying he had not a loaf of bread in the house nor a shilling to purchase one. This

worthy man has hitherto been keeping the Colonial School in the hope that the Governor would be enabled to afford the colonists some assistance in paying him a salary. . . . I shall be grieved at heart to see the school given up, but really the colonists are getting so deplorably poor, that their subscriptions cannot be relied upon.

The governor instructed his secretary to reply in these terms:

> Will you reply that it is my intention to introduce a measure into the Legislative Council, one of the objects of which will be to provide funds to assist the poor in educating their children, and that so far as that school to which Mr. Giles refers is concerned, I have written to Mr. Edward Stephens to request him to furnish me with a short statement of their financial affairs, so that when I have received this I will see what I can do.[96]

In Giles's request and the governor's promise one can see the weakening of the voluntary principle. Argument on this issue became increasingly heated as Governor Grey, echoing Governor Gawler's earlier fears of the inadequacy of voluntaryism, tentatively approached the granting of State aid; the columns of the newspapers were increasingly filled with long, polemical letters and the voluntaryists, through their Society for the Preservation of Religious Freedom in the Province, organized a flood of petitions, while isolated congregations quietly sought their own immediate salvation by applying for allowances from the Treasury. By the end of 1844 the *Southern Australian* was saying bluntly:

> It was the Utopian idea of those who founded this colony . . . that they would make a trial of the virtues of the voluntary principle. . . . But this principle, essentially weak at the best, is worst of all adapted to a thinly scattered population. . . . Our remedy is . . . that the government should retrieve past errors by adopting some measure which shall ensure the education and instruction, not only of those who can voluntarily pay, but of all classes of the community.[97]

Robe and State Aid

However, it was left to Grey's successor, Robe, to enunciate a clear policy, for Grey was suddenly dispatched to New

Zealand in November 1845 when native disaffection there became serious. A worse choice than Robe, considering the temper of the South Australian colony, could hardly have been made; it can only be explained by his ready availability at a time when Grey's transfer was a matter of urgency. A High Churchman and Tory, Robe quickly demonstrated his obtuseness by recommending tithes levied on the Land Fund for the support of religion, and although the colonial reaction to that proposal checked him, he continued to plan for State aid. Months before he reached the colony Robe had wrestled, ineffectually, with the education problem. Aware of the disasters which had befallen Franklin's experiments in Van Diemen's Land, he turned this way and that seeking a solution, but got no further than devising a ridiculous mathematical formula by which a government inspector could calculate the amount of zeal with which a sect supported its Church and its schools.[98] Now that he was in the colony he decided to support all denominations impartially, stifling his conviction that this was an irreligious solution. In June 1846 he formally announced his plans to the Council and later in the session at his behest John Morphett moved:

> That His Excellency be requested to introduce into the Estimates for the financial year 1847 a sum of money for Religious and Educational purposes, to be apportioned among the different denominations of Christians . . . in the ratio to their numbers according to the late census returns, and to be applied by their respective bodies either in building places of public worship, the support of ministers of religion, the erection of school houses, or maintenance of school masters or school mistresses.[99]

On the governor's casting vote the resolution was carried (after several amendments had been defeated), and the opposition had to be carried on out-of-doors in a clamorous battle of petitions, meetings, articles and pamphlets aimed at erasing what the *South Australian Register* called "the foul blot which an irresponsible Legislature has inflicted on our Colonial character". In September, two ordinances (Nos.

13 and 14 of 1846) formally proclaimed grants of aid to religion and education, but this loose arrangement was so obviously unsatisfactory that in July 1847, by Ordinance No. 11, the governor established a Board of Education to superintend the schools receiving aid. This ordinance made no reference to the denominations, but simply stated the conditions upon which the promoters of a school could obtain government aid.

In all this the unfortunate Robe had been following, only too closely, the Secretary of State's instructions. In November 1845, after conferring with the departing Grey, Robe had asked Lord Stanley to appropriate £200 for the purchase of Irish National school-books, not because he intended to create that system of schools, but because he (and Grey) thought that "in this Province, wherein much diversity of religious persuasion prevails", these books would best suit whatever system was eventually established. His answer came not from Stanley, but from Gladstone (newly installed in office) who, assuming that the Irish National system was intended, warned him strongly against a general system, disclosed the reprimand he had felt compelled to administer to Eardley-Wilmot in Van Diemen's Land, and instructed him that, pending a detailed examination of the position in South Australia, he should follow the New South Wales pattern of offering assistance to all the sects. Robe hastened to assure Gladstone that it had never been his intention to establish any particular system, and gave his assurance that the aid he had granted was in accordance with Gladstone's principle. He concluded this placatory dispatch:

> I am clearly of the opinion that voluntary contributions alone are not sufficient to meet the wants of Religion and education in this colony; but whether we have applied the aid of Government in the right direction or not, will remain to be proved.[100]

His misgivings were soon found to be well warranted, for the controversy over acceptance of State aid continued unabated, congregations fighting among themselves (and sometimes with their own pastors) while tracts, pamphlets and petitions appeared almost daily. Robe, confronted by this turmoil and the gathering momentum of a campaign for self-government, found his task increasingly difficult. He asked to be relieved of his office, but before that happy release was afforded him he was treated to a taste of the opposition's temper when the non-official members of his Council (dubbed by the Press the "Patriotic Four" after the style of Van Diemen's Land's "Patriotic Six") walked out of the Chamber over his proposal to collect mineral royalties, leaving the legislature without a quorum.

The Central Board of Education

The issue of State aid to religion and education remained the single biggest issue throughout Robe's term of office and that of his successor, Sir Henry Fox Young, who presided over the colony's transition to a degree of self-government in 1850; it clearly dominated the elections of 1851, and was brought to a head within the first week of the new Council's life. By thirteen votes to ten the Council declined to renew the Church ordinance and the connexion between Church and State was entirely dissolved. Under these circumstances the existing educational ordinance was an anachronism, and in October a Select Committee began to examine its operation. Brushing aside a report made by a committee of the old Council in 1850, it took up the first report of the newly-appointed inspector of schools (William Wyatt) and finding therein (and from its own observations) sufficient evidence to justify Wyatt's opinion that the existing schools constituted a "fraud upon the public through the Government; fraud upon the parents, fraud, the worst of all, upon the rising generation",[101] recommended a Central Board of Education from which ministers of religion should be excluded, and the creation of a system of education similar in principle to the Irish National system. Translated into legislation (and amplified in regulations) their recommendations provided for the maintenance of "good secular instruction, based on the Christian religion, apart from all theological and controversial differences on discipline and doctrine and no denominational catechism shall be used"; teachers were to read a chapter from the Old and New Testaments each day.[102]

The Act was by no means universally popular. Roman Catholic clerics objected to it as a Protestant measure, and the Anglican bishop, Dr Short, described it as "most arbitrary and insulting", and agreed with one of his clergy who asserted "that no minister of religion would submit to see the school under his superintendence controlled by the Central Board of Education",[103] but it was a mark of South Australia's distinctive character that by the end of 1851 it was the only Australian colony whose revenue was not being used to support denominational schools.

NOTES

[1] Arthur to Bathurst, 21 Apr. 1826, *H.R.A.*, III, v, 152. The relationship between Church, State and public education in V.D.L. in this period has been re-examined in two recent publications: John Barrett, *That Better Country: The Religious Aspect of Life in Eastern Australia, 1833–1850*; Michael Roe, *Quest for Authority in Eastern Australia, 1835–1851*.

[2] Ibid., 151.

[3] Arthur to Glenelg, 26 Jan. 1836, *H.R.A.*, I, xviii, 487.

[4] Ibid., 490.

[5] C.S.O. 1/843/17847. (T.S.A.).

[6] Arthur to Glenelg, 4 May 1836. (T.S.A.).

[7] Broughton to Arthur, 24 Jan. 1834, Papers of Sir George Arthur (M.L.).

[8] Ibid. Arthur to Bourke, 2 Feb. 1836.

[9] Ibid. Bourke to Arthur, 15 Mar., 27 Sept. 1836.

[10] See Kathleen Fitzpatrick, *Sir John Franklin in Tasmania*, passim.

[11] *V. & P.*, V.D.L. Leg. Council, 1837–42.

[12] Ibid.

[13] *Hobart Town Gazette*, 14 Dec. 1838, p. 1164.

[14] *True Colonist*, 19 Apr., 10 May 1839.

[15] Ibid., 26 Apr., 3 May 1839.

[16] *Hobart Town Gazette*, 10 May 1839, p. 471.

[17] William Hutchins, *A Letter on the School Question*, pp. 3, 11.

[18] Sir John Herschel, perhaps the greatest British astronomer

of the nineteenth century, initiated Cape Colony's system of national education during the years of his monumental survey of the southern heavens (1834–8). He was one of Franklin's many scientific correspondents. See W. T. Ferguson and R. F. M. Immelman, *Sir John Herschel and Education at the Cape, 1834–1840*.

[19] *V. & P.*, V.D.L. Leg. Council, 1837–42.
[20] *Hobart Town Gazette*, 23 Oct. 1839, p. 1183.
[21] *Papers*, V.D.L. Leg. Council, 1840.
[22] Reports of the Board of Education, 1840–2, *Papers*, V.D.L. Leg. Council, 1840–2.
[23] Although the name Tasmania was not officially recognized in government circles until 1856 it was in common use throughout the 1840s and Nixon was enthroned in 1843 as Lord Bishop of Tasmania. See P. A. Howell, 'Bishop Nixon and Public Education in Tasmania', *Melbourne Studies in Education, 1967*.
[24] *A Charge Delivered to the Clergy of the Diocese of Tasmania at the Primary Visitation by Francis-Russell Nixon, Lord Bishop of Tasmania*, p. 4.
[25] Ibid., pp. 59–73.
[26] *Launceston Examiner*, 8 Nov. 1843.
[27] Ibid.
[28] Eardley-Wilmot to Gladstone, 26 Sept. 1846. (T.S.A.).
[29] See R. M. Hartwell, *The Economic Development of Van Diemen's Land, 1820–1850*, Ch. 13.
[30] Sir William Denison, *Varieties of Vice-Regal Life*, p. 13.
[31] Stanley to Eardley-Wilmot, 22 Sept. 1843. (T.S.A.).
[32] Eardley-Wilmot to Stanley, 24 Aug. 1845. (T.S.A.).
[33] *Launceston Examiner*, 8 Nov. 1843.
[34] See Kathleen Fitzpatrick, 'Mr Gladstone and the Governor: The recall of Sir John Eardley-Wilmot from Van Diemen's Land, 1846', *Historical Studies*, Vol. 1, No. 1 (Apr. 1940).
[35] Substantial portions of this pamphlet are to be found in the *Launceston Examiner*, 5, 12 June 1844.
[36] Eardley-Wilmot to Stanley, 17 Feb., 13 June 1845. (T.S.A.) Report of the Board of Education, 1845, p. 5, *Papers*, V.D.L. Leg. Council, 1845; *Launceston Examiner*, 13, 20 Aug. 1845.
[37] Ibid., 9 Apr. 1845. The Commissioners were W. D. Bernard, M.A., John Meyers, M.D., and W. Courtney.
[38] Report of the Commissioners for investigating the manner in which the system of Public Education in Van Diemen's Land is carried out. Appended to Eardley-Wilmot to Stanley, 13 June 1845, op. cit.
[39] Ibid.
[40] Gladstone to Eardley-Wilmot, 3 Mar. 1846. (T.S.A.).
[41] Denison, op. cit., p. 507.

Australian Education, 1788–1900

[42] Ibid., pp. 11, 17.
[43] *Speech of Thomas George Gregson Esq. in the Legislative Council on the state of Public Education in Van Diemen's Land*, p. 11.
[44] Denison to Rusden, 10 Oct. 1853. (T.C.C.).
[45] Denison, *Varieties of Vice-Regal Life*, op. cit., p. 223.
[46] Ibid., p. 224. By an education Act of 1806 dogmatic religious instruction was forbidden in Dutch schools, but pupils were supposed to be trained "in the practice of all the social and Christian virtues".
[47] Minute upon Education, 9 Mar. 1848, *V. & P.*, V.D.L. Leg. Council, 1848.
[48] *Speech of Thomas George Gregson*, op. cit., pp. 7–13.
[49] See J. S. Battye, *Western Australia: A History from its Discovery to the Inauguration of the Commonwealth*, Ch. 4; F. K. Crowley, *Australia's Western Third*.
[50] C. L. M. Hawtrey, *The Availing Struggle*, pp. 19–20.
[51] A. Burton and U. Henn (Eds.), *Wollaston's Picton Journal*, p. 58.
[52] C. M. H. Clark, *Select Documents in Australian History, 1788–1850*, p. 409.
[53] See Alexandra Hasluck, *Portrait With Background*, passim.
[54] W. A. P. Phillips, 'A Précis of Uncompleted Research on the Social History of Western Australia, 1829–70', unpublished Statement, University of Western Australia, 1951, pp. 29–30.
[55] Quoted W. A. P. Phillips, 'Education and Society in Western Australia, 1829–56', unpublished B.A. Thesis, University of Western Australia, 1951, p. 73. See also Hasluck, op. cit., pp. 127–32.
[56] The colonists were spread out over a number of settlements, e.g. Perth-Fremantle, Guildford, York, Australind, the Vasse, Augusta, Albany.
[57] In the year of Short's visitation there were 3063 Anglicans in Western Australia. See *W. A. Govt. Gazette*, 19 Dec. 1848.
[58] See Burton and Henn, op. cit., passim, and the same editors' *Wollaston's Albany Journal*, 1848–1856, passim.
[59] Burton and Henn, *Wollaston's Picton Journal*, op. cit., p. 207.
[60] Burton and Henn, *Wollaston's Albany Journal*, op. cit., p. 210.
[61] Wollaston to S.P.G., 9 Nov. 1846, *Swan River News*, July 1847, pp. 153–4.
[62] Hutt to Hawes, 9 June 1847. (J.S.B.)
[63] A Brief History of Education in Western Australia, 1829–1937. Typescript prepared by the Education Department of Western Australia, 1937, p. 4.
[64] Colonial Secretary to Cooke, 15 July 1831. (J.S.B.)
[65] *Perth Gazette*, 23 May 1840; *Inquirer*, 14, 21 July 1841, 25 Oct. 1843.

Van Diemen's Land, Western and S. Australia, 1829–1851

[66] First Report of the General Committee of Education, 1848. (J.S.B.).
[67] *W. A. Govt. Gazette*, 19 Dec. 1848.
[68] *Swan River News*, 1 Apr. 1847.
[69] *Inquirer*, 11 Mar. 1846.
[70] This was not an unbroken period of office.
[71] *Perth Gazette*, 5 June 1847.
[72] *Inquirer*, 4, 11 Mar. 1846, Aug.-Dec. 1847.
[73] A copy of the Catholic petition (22 Dec. 1846) is included in Grey to the Officer Administering the Government of Western Australia, 24 June 1847. (J.S.B.).
[74] Minutes and Correspondence of the Education Committee, 31 Aug., 4 Sept., 22 Oct. 1847. (J.S.B.).
[75] Ibid., 4 Sept. 1847.
[76] Ibid., 22 Oct. 1847.
[77] Ibid., 7 Sept. 1847.
[78] Ibid., 18 May 1848.
[79] Grey to FitzGerald, 3 July 1848. (J.S.B.).
[80] Colonial Secretary to Cashier of Western Australian Bank, 7 Mar. 1849. (J.S.B.).
[81] Colonial Secretary to Cowan, 14 Mar. 1849; Grey to FitzGerald, 12 June 1849. (J.S.B.).
[82] Minutes and Correspondence, op. cit., 18, 19 May 1848. For Maddens's own estimate of his role in this affair see Thomas More Madden (Ed.), *The Memoirs . . . of Richard Robert Madden*, p. 232, and John T. McMahon, *One Hundred Years*, pp. 51–3.
[83] Minutes and Correspondence, op. cit., 7 Nov. 1848.
[84] FitzGerald to Grey, 16 Feb. 1849. (J.S.B.).
[85] Irwin to Grey, 25 Jan. 1848. (J.S.B.) There is no doubt that Brady's report to Rome was quite unrealistic. "In his report to Rome", one Catholic historian has written, "Father Brady painted the picture of Perth and its immediate future in over-glowing colours, which soon waned under the searching rays of hard facts." McMahon, op. cit., p. 36. Brady was desperately anxious to see a bishopric established in W.A., but it is hard to believe that he was looking for personal advancement.
[86] Minutes and Correspondence, op. cit., 21 Oct. 1848. (J.S.B.).
[87] Ibid.
[88] FitzGerald to Grey, 20 Apr. 1849. (J.S.B.).
[89] Minutes and Correspondence, op. cit., 17 Apr. 1849. (J.S.B.).
[90] Ibid., 14 Nov., 12 Dec. 1848.
[91] Douglas Pike, *Paradise of Dissent*, p. 3. See also G. E.

Saunders, 'The State and Education in South Australia, 1836–1875', *Melbourne Studies in Education, 1966*.
[92] Angas Papers: S. A. Commission. No. 974. (S.A.A.).
[93] Grey to Stow, 23 Mar. 1842. (S.A.A.).
[94] Angas Papers, op. cit., No 19.
[95] Ibid., No. 445. Phillip Emanuel von Fellenberg translated the social regeneration aspect of Pestalozzi's theories into practice in an institution which he conducted at Hofwyl between 1805 and 1844. Here he successfully combined manual, agricultural and general education.
[96] Quoted T. H. Smeaton, *Education in South Australia from 1836 to 1927*, pp. 36–40.
[97] *Southern Australian*, 4, 8 Oct. 1844.
[98] Remarks on the distribution of Government aid towards the maintenance of Religion and Education, April 1845. (787/1845/71A. S.A.A.).
[99] *South Australian*, 7 June 1846.
[100] Robe to Stanley, 22 Nov. 1845; Gladstone to Robe, 15 May 1846; Robe to Gladstone, 7 Dec. 1846. (S.A.A.).
[101] *S. A. Government Gazette*, 7 Aug. 1851.
[102] *Debates*, S. A. Leg. Council, 19–23 Dec. 1851.
[103] *South Australian Register*, 10 Jan. 1852.

4

Church, State and Public School System in the Eastern Mainland Colonies 1851–1866

By 1851 that vast crescent of territory which had once been New South Wales had lost its monolithic character with the severance of the district below the Murray, and its transformation into the proud and turbulent colony of Victoria; eight years later, by another major piece of political surgery, the district north of Point Danger ("in latitude about 28 degrees 8 minutes") was detached and proclaimed the colony of Queensland. With the creation of these two new colonies (each with a measure of self-government) the historian's task becomes much more complex, for now he has to contend with three inexperienced legislatures whose members' prejudices and ambitions are a poor substitute for coherent, Colonial Office policy, and it is not easy, in the welter of bills, petitions, resolutions and counter-resolutions which they produced, to see any pattern of development. In fact it is only in recent years that anyone has attempted an explanation of these unruly colonial events, and some of this pioneering work remains unpublished.[1]

Liberalism and Education

In 1951 a Victorian scholar (J. S. Gregory), though concerned only with events below the Murray, suggested an interpretation of these events which might well be applied to all the colonies. The educational disputes of the 1850s and 1860s are only explicable, Gregory suggested, if we keep in mind the final, secular decision of the 1870s and 1880s; this, he claimed, was the direction in which society was moving, though local circumstances sometimes appeared to be deflecting it from its goal. In his own words:

> Agnosticism, with its questioning of long accepted teachings of the Church and, by implication, of its alliance with the State; voluntaryism with its attacks on the contaminating and debilitating influence of State support upon the Church; and sectarianism, with its bitterness and rancour . . . all these made their contribution to the movement towards secularism in the State. But at bottom the abolition of State aid to religion and the introduction of a secular system of public education were pieces of liberal reform not inspired by any doctrinaire rejection of the value of religion nor by any desire to persecute the Church, Protestant or Roman Catholic, but rather by a determination to make the State, in action and in law, the symbol of a common citizenship.[2]

This, we shall find, is a very useful interpretation so long as we are prepared to see the forces of agnosticism, voluntaryism and sectarianism operating at different levels of intensity as we move from colony to colony, and so long as we do not expect to find these forces triumphing in the 1860s, for this is essentially a decade of compromise before the final, secular solution is reluctantly accepted in the 1870s and 1880s. Once we make these allowances we are able to see how denominationalism, though seriously weakened by secularism, was nevertheless still powerful enough to force a compromise upon the liberal, reforming State. The education Acts of the 1860s are as secular as their framers dared make them in the face of a declining, but still-powerful, denominationalism. Above all we need to keep in mind Gregory's warning that the State which we see opposing the Church in the nineteenth century is not anti-religious—not even irreligious—but simply committed to the liberal belief that progress and perfectibility are to be achieved by human endeavour acting under the sanction of legal and parliamentary institutions. As a recent defender of the liberal creed has reminded us:

> The vision behind liberalism is the vision of a world progressively redeemed by human power from its classic ailments of poverty, disease, and ignorance. . . . It has treated religious and philosophical beliefs as private affairs, of ultimate moment, perhaps, to the individual's salvation and to his sense of the meaning of life, but without political significance as such.[3]

The Conflict in New South Wales

The whole of this process can be observed in New South Wales between 1851 and 1866; against the determination of the Churches to retain their traditional control of education, there can be seen developing a secular point of view which eventually suborns sufficient of the Churches to allow the liberal politicians to carry the day with their educational measures. The greater part of this prolonged campaign was the work of two men, William Wilkins, the quiet, tenacious pedagogue, and Henry Parkes, the flamboyant, erratic publicist and politician. Wilkins's role was to prepare the situation in which Parkes could act—to demonstrate to the public (and the Parliament) that only in a unified, State system of education could a solution to the colony's educational problems be found. Wilkins was in an excellent position to do this. Although he had only arrived in the colony in 1851 as headmaster of the National Model school, he became Inspector and Superintendent in 1854, Chief Inspector in 1860 and Secretary in 1864; in a system administered by a board of honorary, part-time commissioners (whose membership was constantly changing), the chief executive officer obviously had the future of the schools very much in his own hands. Wilkins set out to use this power to demonstrate the superiority of the National schools, and their right to be regarded as the proper foundation of a State system.

The Role of William Wilkins

Three main lines of action can be discerned in Wilkins's campaign. The first, which can be followed in the annual reports of the National Board, was an unspectacular but effective campaign for greater efficiency within the schools. With unrelenting persistence and patience Wilkins organized and standardized every teaching procedure—methods of instruction, methods of inspection, classification of teachers, classification of pupils; with a single document (the Table of Minimum Attainments) he dispensed with the teacher's individual judgment. The present-day teacher may curse the memory of the man who first imposed this uniformity and rigidity upon the Australian schools, but it is difficult to see how else Wilkins could have effected any improvement in the chaotic and squalid collection of schools he was called upon to administer.

In 1857, alarmed at the comparatively slow progress being made by the National system because of the difficulty of raising one-third of the cost of new buildings locally, he persuaded the commissioners to sanction "non-vested" schools; this type of school (common under the National system in Ireland and Victoria) was one whose property was not vested in the Board, but which, in return for a grant-in-aid for salaries and books, pursued the normal National school programme during the hours of compulsory attendance, remaining free beyond these hours to use the school building as the proprietors saw fit. This administrative device enabled the Board to double the number of schools on its books within a few years.

His third line of action was publicity. In 1854, Wilkins and two other schoolmasters (Samuel Turton and Thomas Levinge) were appointed as commissioners to assist a Select Committee on Education, and instructed "to visit personally the several Districts in which schools supported wholly or in part by public funds are situated, to examine the scholars, and to report on the state of Education and of the schools generally."[4] Enough has been said of the Commissioners' report in Chapter 2 to indicate the devastating nature of its indictment of the existing system. In almost every department of school management the Commissioners found the schools of New South Wales deficient; it was not a question of one system of schools being better or worse than another, they pointed out; all were in a deplorable condition because they were, in their opposition and duplication, wasting the public funds. The Commissioners went on:

> We take the opportunity of remarking, that all the recent Legislative measures on educational matters, appear to have no connection with each other; whence it happens, that with all the requisite materials for forming a comprehensive system, the Colony possesses no system of education at all, in the proper sense of the word. Primary education is divided into two great sections, repugnant, if not hostile, to each other in spirit, and independent of each other in every respect. . . . There should be but one system, especially adapted to the wants of the country, and controlled and administered by one managing body.[5]

The Commissioners' report created a sensation in the colony; it made clear the urgency of educational reform and, even more important, made clear the impossibility of sheltering indefinitely behind the compromise of 1848. Nothing shows Wilkins in a better light than this report; his ruthless exposure of the faults of his own schools was a risky manœuvre in the campaign he had planned, but he was obviously prepared to take that risk in order to demonstrate the need for a unified system, while relying on the ability of the National system to reform itself before the legislature made any decision on unification.

Ten years later, confident that the National system could now justify itself, and impatient of the legislature's failure to reorganize the whole educational structure, Wilkins returned to the attack. In two public lectures, which he later published, he gave a thorough exposition of the National system, stressed its "common Christianity" solution of the religious difficulties, and asserted that

> the great central fundamental principle of the National System is sound and faultless, perfectly adapted to the circumstances of this country, and capable of solving its education problem. Further, whatever changes may be introduced into our educational arrangements, I doubt not this principle must be

the foundation of every new scheme likely to meet with general acceptance.⁶

The Role of Henry Parkes

In this endeavour to persuade the colony that a unified system was needed Wilkins was not, of course, working alone. Both W. A. Duncan's pamphlet published in Brisbane in 1850 and G. W. Rusden's pamphlet published in Melbourne in 1853 circulated in New South Wales, and the anonymous *A Plea for Common Schools* was published in Sydney in 1857.⁷ Moreover, apart from the support of these publications Wilkins had the sustained support of the *Empire* which Parkes had established in 1850 and which remained under his editorship until 1858. Parkes's most recent biographer, A. W. Martin, has reminded us that in this towering political figure we have a "strange and enigmatic personality. A great gulf often separated his professions of principle from his practice, his avowed ends from his patent means."⁸ Nevertheless, as Professor Martin also reminds us, it would be unjust to write Parkes off "as a mere talented adventurer"; beneath the scheming, contriving politician there was, at least in the 1850s and 1860s, a sincere, integrated man who believed passionately that he was working in the cause of a better and nobler society than he found himself in. He had been denied a sound education—a handicap he always deplored—and the provision of an effective system of education which would enlighten and unite the colony became for him a necessary precursor of the constitutional reforms he desired; educational reform was an integral part of his middle class radicalism. In the first issue of his paper Parkes approached the topic cautiously. "In education", he wrote,

> we shall be for that system, or unity of systems which, by being most fitted to the circumstances of the colony, shall be most diffusive in its blessings, whatever its name, and by whomsoever it be originated, because we cannot conceive it justifiable for differences of doctrinal points amongst the well-informed to interfere between the light of knowledge and the utterly uninstructed.⁹

The Eastern Mainland Colonies, 1851–1866

As he came to understand the problem better, Parkes became firmer in his views. The denominational system, he decided, was not only inefficient in the outlying districts, but it was also divisive in its effect on society and represented a fundamental challenge to the right (and duty) of the State to control education. "We have held", he declared in 1854, "that . . . as education is necessary even to the physical and secular well-being of the State, it is as much within the province of the State to promote it as it is to provide police for our protection."[10] The denominations, he insisted, had their own good and necessary work to do, but it must have as its end the national good. In a burst of doctrinaire liberalism he told the Churches that they

> should confine their denominationalism to religion, and unite all their efforts in reference to that which is common, and which comes within the centralization and scope of a nation's effort. . . . All that concerns elementary, intellectual and moral training is capable of being done on a combined plan, damaging to no party. Here is the limit of state duty. That which pertains to another world belongs to the parent and pastor, with whom none will interfere.[11]

The Attitude of the Churches

However, no matter how diligently Wilkins worked, or how persuasively Parkes wrote, there was no point in preaching to the converted. Before Parkes the politician would essay what Parkes the journalist advocated he would have to be convinced of substantial public support; he (or any other politician) would have to be convinced that the electors, as churchmen, would acquiesce in any move to lessen the Church's control of education. Of Roman Catholic support there was clearly no hope. Certainly, during the 1850s and early 1860s, the Catholic hierarchy had not enunciated any common educational policy; as late as the Provincial Council of 1862 the bishops had asked themselves, "In the event of a general system . . . how far should we be prepared to acquiesce or accept?",[12] but by 1865 it should have been clear to the discerning politician that the Australian bishops had resolved their doubts. In 1862 the passing of the Victorian Common Schools Act had presented them with a clear-cut issue; in 1864 the publication of Pope Pius IX's *Syllabus of Errors* had presented them with an unequivocal denunciation of liberalism in general and State education in particular, and in South Australia the labours of Bishop Geoghegan had presented them with the means of supporting their own schools.[13] By 1865 it must have been perfectly clear to Parkes that the Roman Catholic Church would not support a unified State system of schools. This should have caused him no surprise, and certainly no pain, for one of the most consistent traits in his personality was an abiding horror of Roman Catholicism. But Parkes was too much the aspiring politician to antagonize one quarter of the electorate in order to indulge his bigotry. He had yet to lead a government, and the Catholic vote might be needed to hoist him into the premiership. He must assess the attitudes of the other Churches.

But when he turned to examine the other end of the ecclesiastical scale he found that the Presbyterians and Dissenters exhibited a bewildering range of opinion; nevertheless, here too it was possible to discern an emerging policy. To all these sects, in varying degrees, the mainspring of their policy was the voluntary principle—a principle evolved and embraced in the Old World as a protection against the persecution and interference of governments and Established Churches, but amidst the harsh realities of colonial life, scattered thinly along an inhospitable frontier, they faced the intransigent fact that they could scarcely maintain their churches, let alone their schools. But to ask for State aid was to open the door to all the evils they had known in the Old World, and so, reluctantly, they came to support a State system of education so long as it had no connexion with any particular sect. The most reluctant converts to this point of view were the Wesleyans, for they were essentially Anglican in outlook and temperament and felt little antagonism towards Establishment, but by 1855 even they could agree:

The Eastern Mainland Colonies, 1851-1866

Much as we prefer schools of a denominational character, yet considering the scattered condition of the rural population and other practical difficulties in the way of the Denominational System, we feel it to be our duty to assist, to the utmost of our power, any system of Education which may be established by the Colonial Legislatures.[14]

For the colonial Presbyterians this was, of course, a confused and bitter issue, for it was part of the larger issue of State aid to religion which had rent their Church in the Great Disruption. Nevertheless, most Presbyterians supported Dr John Dunmore Lang in his denunciation of the "thraldom of State connexion", and applauded his declaration that "fifteen months before the famous disruption of the Church of Scotland, I publicly renounced all connexion with the State . . . as a minister of religion".[15] He went on to urge his listeners "to take the sting out of the tails of the clergy . . . by simply leaving them—all communions alike without exception—to the sympathies and exertions of their people", and to abandon the denominational principle in education. "In so thinly peopled a country as the Land of the Squatters", he told them, "the Denominational System is utterly impracticable. The people are sensible of this themselves, and would therefore gladly co-operate for the establishment of a General System if the matter were only left to themselves".[16]

Of the attitude of the smaller sects—the Baptists and the Congregationalists—there could be no doubt. As early as 1844 their spokesmen had gone before a Select Committee on Education and denounced the denominational system as expensive, unnecessary, unjust "and while far less efficient in teaching the children the important branches of a good education it is far more efficient in teaching what ought to be put down—bigotry and religious partizanship".[17]

By the 1860s, therefore, it was possible to count all the non-Anglican Protestant sects on the side of a unified State system of education—though here and there, of course, a particular congregation asserted its Protestantism by opposing the decisions of its Synod or Conference. Collectively, these sects accounted for about 21 per cent of the population of New South Wales, while the Roman Catholics, the opponents of a State system, accounted for about 28 per cent of the population[18]—a sufficiently balanced state of the parties to make the Anglican attitude the key to the whole situation. It is at this point that K. C. Cable's study of Anglican educational policy throws a strong ray of light on Parkes's tactics, for Cable has traced the steps by which most of the laity, and some of the clergy, drew away from their bishops' educational policy and took up a position almost indistinguishable from that of the Protestant sects.[19] In point of fact the educational issue does not appear to have been a major issue in Anglican Church politics; it was resolved, without being extensively debated, once the Evangelical rebels amongst laymen and clergy had won their major battle on Church government. On Cable's evidence, the powerful Evangelical wing, fearing and resenting Bishop Broughton's pretensions to the Establishment of the colonial Anglican Church and his alleged sympathy with the Oxford Movement, had already challenged him on a number of occasions before he called his fellow bishops to Sydney in October 1850 to explore the confused and complicated question of the status of his Church.[20]

Broughton's situation was a delicate one. No matter how one looked at it, the colonial status of the Anglican Church was a legal problem of some complexity; an easy solution could have been found if the British Parliament had been prepared to legislate on the matter, but this it steadfastly refused to do.[21] The bishops appear to have been conscious of the danger in which they stood; they took pains to declare that their deliberations were only exploratory, but the tone of their report was distinctly authoritarian, and two of their pronouncements produced a violent reaction in the Evangelical camp. In the first place, by a majority of five to one, the bishops declared their adherence to the doctrine of Baptismal Regeneration—a serious blow to the Evangelicals who, in the celebrated Gorham judgment of 1849, had had their right to reject this doctrine upheld by the Privy

Council.²² In the second place, the bishops recommended that provincial and diocesan synods should consist only of clergy—a decision which the laity had to contest, or tamely submit to future episcopal dictation. These two decisions again drove the Evangelical clergy and the laity into an alliance, and through parish meetings, pamphlets, petitions and counter-petitions the conflict grew to serious proportions. At its height, Cable has remarked, "Archbishop Laud seemed a paschal lamb when compared with Bishop Broughton", and Governor FitzRoy, the last person to be deeply concerned with ecclesiastical matters, warned the Colonial Office that he "greatly feared that should his Lordship succeed in obtaining his object, great divisions in the Church of England will be the result".²³ As it had done before, the British Parliament again refused to legislate, and the Australian bishops were finally driven to accept the unpalatable fact that they could only determine the development and policy of their Church in consultation with their laity, and pay the price these laymen would demand.

It has seemed necessary to follow this issue in some detail, for it was out of the alliance of laity and Evangelical clergy that there developed a new Anglican viewpoint, hostile to the high pretensions and alleged Romanism of the bishops, sympathetic to the aims of the Dissenters, and capable of finding in voluntaryism the principle upon which the Anglican Church could take its place in colonial society. The extent of the Evangelical victory can be measured in the appointment of Bishop Barker, a Low Churchman, as Broughton's successor, and his decision to organize the financial support of his Church on a voluntary basis through the Sydney Diocesan Church Society.²⁴ The success of this scheme, the unstinted middle-class support which it stimulated, underlined the extent of the victory which the laity had won, and allayed the doubts which had beset colonial educational reformers ever since Bourke had challenged the Anglican clergy in 1836. Of the events surrounding the passage of the Public Schools Act of 1866 Parkes was able to affirm what Bourke had only been able to surmise thirty years earlier. "From the first", Parkes wrote, "the lay members of the English Church did not warmly sympathize with the heated feelings of their clergy; and in the course of time, the clergymen themselves, for the most part, withdrew from the conflict and accepted the new system."[25]

But if the strength of lay opinion favouring educational reform was as clear as we have supposed, why was the necessary legislation not passed until 1866? The answer to this question almost certainly lies in the unstable character of New South Wales politics in the first decade of responsible government during which the average life of a Ministry was a bare twelve months. Urgent problems of constitutional reform, land utilization and fiscal policy had to be resolved in a system of politics in which parties, as we know them, had yet to be developed; it was a politics of personalities and factions rather than parties, with groupings constantly changing, and attempts to settle the education question were largely dictated by expediency. Although almost every Ministry before 1866 made some attempt to settle the question, none was prepared to force fundamental reform, and no politician was prepared to stake his career on it.

The Public Schools Act, 1866

In January 1866 James Martin and Henry Parkes formed a coalition Ministry which, though built on many compromises, was strong enough to hold office for nearly three years;[26] aware that their differences of opinion on fiscal matters would, if exposed, bring them down, they agreed to leave this question alone, and to concentrate on urgent, social legislation. The way was thus open for Parkes to initiate the reforms which he had been advocating for so many years: the climate of public opinion was favourable and political circumstances were opportune. In September, Parkes brought down his Public Schools Bill and revealed the fundamental nature of the changes he intended to make. The two existing boards were to be replaced by a Council of Education; denominational schools assisted by State funds were to remain, but only if they had substantial enrolments,[27] placed themselves under the new Council of Education, subjected themselves to inspection, gave four hours of secular instruction each day and accepted children of other denominations. The Bill further provided that no new denominational school could receive aid unless it was within five miles of a public school which had an attendance of eighty; if the two schools were not separated by more than two miles, the public school had to have 120 pupils before the denominational school could be recognized.[28] Obviously the secularists were not yet able to dismiss the denominationalists' claims out of hand, but they had left the Churches with little to rejoice about. After 1866 the denominational schools could never hope to rival the public schools; at best they could hold their ground, but as population increased they faced an inevitable decline in relative importance.

Parkes's speech in the second reading debate is generally hailed as one of his greatest and, although to the modern ear it is marred by its excessive length and its florid character, it is nevertheless a skilful parliamentary speech designed to make its point without unnecessarily inflaming the opposition. It is not quite what one would have expected from a former editor of the *Empire*, but after twelve years of politics Parkes had learnt to subordinate the journalist in him.[29] Before the House he set out to justify his Bill on two main grounds. First, leaning heavily on Macaulay, he sought to establish the duty of the State to educate its citizens, but he quickly moved from this general consideration to the existing system in New South Wales which, he declared, was unnecessarily expensive, of inferior quality, divisive in its effect and "in an alarming degree limited in its supply."[30] The reason for this sorry state of affairs, he went on, was

> the unseemly contention amongst those members of society who ought above all others to lend their efforts to promote harmony and goodwill amongst the people, I mean the clergy of the various churches . . . the most inveterate as they are the most powerful enemies that popular education has to fear.

It was not the parents who sought this multiplicity of little,

Church schools; after studying the proportions in which the various denominations were represented in the National schools he was convinced "that there is hardly a parent in the country, belonging to whatever church he may, who, if left to himself objects to send his child to these schools". The real cause of objection was rather to be found in "the petty desire of every parish clergyman to have a school of his own", and this was a luxury which the colony could not afford, for everywhere there were

> children who, whilst ministers of religion are cavilling over a division of the spoils, are left destitute of all instruction, and often sink into the worst courses of evil as a consequence. . . . We know that some of those young natives, led step by step in crime till they forfeited their lives on the gallows, never had the slightest chance of instruction.

In was in the names of the 100,000 children whom he believed to be in this unhappy plight that Parkes finally appealed to the House. "By what you do now", he urged, "you may render a service that will be felt hereafter in the aspirations of a hundred thousand lives—of that unknown multitude arising in our midst . . . who for good or evil must connect the present with the future."

Parkes had obviously chosen his moment well. There was a great deal of clerical clamour when the Bill appeared, and Parkes found himself at the centre of an "ecclesiastical storm" in which "no limit was set by my reverend and very reverend assailants to their inventive skill in personal abuse",[31] but in the House only five out of forty-five members opposed it. It was also significant that the Anglican clergy could muster only 3,939 signatures for their petitions, while their Roman colleagues could claim to represent 8,459 petitioners.

Separation and Gold in Victoria

In Victoria, the initial progress of the National system was strongly affected by Separation and the ensuing administrative upheaval. The National Board Commissioners in New South Wales had washed their hands of their responsibilities below the Murray almost as soon as Separation was announced in 1850, and by March 1851 had handed over their files to Superintendent La Trobe although, according to their own statement, they retained the legal responsibility for these schools until June.[32] Such a transfer of authority should not have been made until a board had been incorporated in Victoria, but La Trobe, beset by many worries, deferred any action until September, and then the action he took was the extraordinary one of asking the Denominational Board Commissioners to administer the affairs of the National schools.[33] These gentlemen were not unfamiliar with the affairs of the National schools, for they had already been at work plotting their extinction—an opportunity which La Trobe had presented to them when he called for a report on the suitability of the National schools for the new colony. Their answer, presented in the form of a Proposed Plan for General Education,[34] left the National schools only an insignificant and diminishing role in Victorian education, but it is not surprising that a harassed lieutenant-governor should have handed this conveniently arranged plan to his Attorney-General for drafting in the form of an Education Bill. In fact, if the Attorney-General had not made such a sorry muddle of it, and if John Pascoe Fawkner and Francis Murphy had not opposed the Bill so forcefully in the Council, that, for all practical purposes, would have been the end of the National schools.[35] When, in despair, the Attorney-General withdrew his ill-framed Bill, the government was faced with the urgent necessity of creating some sort of legal authority in which to vest the property inherited from the National Board in New South Wales; to achieve this limited, administrative end it secured the passage of a simple Bill to incorporate a National Board. The system's enemies were well aware that this was only a "machinery" measure, and should not be allowed to commit the government to the support of National schools; as one opponent ((Sir) John O'Shanassy) protested some years later, when the National schools had continued in existence too long to suit his taste, the National Board was originally incorporated "for the purpose of receiving property, but not to make the National system a Victorian system".[36]

It was in this discouraging atmosphere that the newly-appointed National Commissioners met to begin their work, and it is probably significant that they held their early meetings in rooms procured by one of their own number after the Colonial Secretary had announced his inability to find any for them. However, the Commissioners themselves hardly inspired any confidence, for while most of them were competent men of affairs, only one of them (Hugh Childers) had any claims to being an educationist, and none of them supported the National system wholeheartedly; even Childers took his seat fresh from his duties as inspector of denominational schools. In these circumstances it is hardly surprising that within eight months the Commissioners had decided that one member should constitute a quorum for the transaction of routine business. One must remember, too, that throughout its existence (1851-62) the National Board worked under great practical difficulties brought about by the coincidence of Separation and the discovery of gold.[37] Before the government had had time to establish an adequate administration it was swamped by an influx of gold-seekers which increased its population seven-fold within a decade, and the National Board, like every other government agency, was forced to spend much of its time dealing with a migratory population whose rate of expansion was unpredictable.

Alliance of Church and State

But serious as they were, these were only administrative problems which, somehow, these competent men of affairs would have solved. What they could not solve, in Victoria where the conflict between Church and State ran deeper than in any other colony, were the rival claims of denominationalism and secularism to dictate the nature of the educational system. This is not yet the period of militant atheism and rationalism which was to distinguish Victoria from her more orthodox sister colonies in the 1860s and

1870s, but already her aggressive, radical newcomers were producing a society which was more irreligious, more anticlerical, than any other in Australia. William Westgarth's assertion that "the bulk of the people considered that religion, though excellent in itself, should be confined to proper times and proper places" could probably be matched by statements in other colonial legislatures, but it is doubtful if any other colonial parliament, in the early 1850s, would have listened without indignant protest while one of its members asserted that if "a constituency sent a man there who chose to worship an image chopped out of a gum tree, such an individual would have a perfect right to sit in that Assembly", and another asked "why children should be dogged night and day by the clergy, unless they were to be trained for monks and nuns, in which case the world would very soon come to an end?"[38]

Bold words indeed, but their immediate effect, as Gregory has pointed out,[39] was to fortify rather than to vanquish the Churches, and to provoke an unusually strong alliance between Church and State. In the early, turbulent years of the gold rushes, bishop and governor stood aghast at the lawlessness and irresponsibility which threatened to engulf them, and looked to one another for mutual support. "In such a crisis as the present", Bishop Perry declared, "it especially becomes a Christian to endeavour to strengthen, not to weaken, the hands of our rulers",[40] while Archibald Michie told the Legislative Council that if "State support to religion were denied, he trembled for the result",[41] and the *Argus* advised its readers that in "a community like this it is absolutely essential that Religion should be recognized by the State; not only so, but diligently and tenderly fostered".[42] It was in this atmosphere that State aid to religion, which stood at £6,000 in 1851, was increased to £30,000 in 1853 and, despite bitter controversy, to £50,000 in 1856—a not inconsiderable proportion of the colony's annual revenue of less than £3,000,000.[43]

In the field of education this close identification of Church and State took the form of favoured treatment for the denominational system which, on several occasions, almost succeeded in becoming the only State-supported system. Politically, its cause was sponsored by the two most powerful men in the Victorian Parliament, the Anglican William Clark Haines and the Catholic (Sir) John O'Shanassy; between them these two men shared the premiership of Victoria from the inception of responsible government to the end of the National Board's life.[44] Neither man made any secret of his opposition to the National system. Haines (to take only one example of his many pronouncements on the education question) made it perfectly clear before a Select Committee of 1852 that no man who was sincerely attached to his Church could think of supporting such a system. ". . . the State", he advised, "should discountenance a system of education based on so imperfect and dangerous a foundation. . . . I am in favour of the Denominational system as the only one calculated to combine religious and secular instruction".[45] To O'Shanassy, the political leader of Victoria's Irish-Catholics (and a one-time Denominational Board Commissioner) the National schools were nothing more than agents of proselytism. Like his Vicar-General (Dr Geoghegan) he believed that "Catholics must have separate schools, or none at all aided by the State . . . preferring rather that the child should remain in his simplicity of secular acquirements than that he should risk the loss of his faith".[46] The obvious tactics for Haines and O'Shanassy to have adopted would have been the introduction of legislation specifically designed to abolish the National schools, but the fate of three earlier Bills drafted along these lines showed them that the country, and the Parliament, were too evenly divided to guarantee success to this sort of frontal attack.[47] They therefore pursued a policy (sometimes separately, sometimes jointly as in the third O'Shanassy Ministry in which Haines served as Treasurer) of destroying the National system by executive action. By starving the National schools of funds, by restricting the granting of sites and by flagrantly interpreting regulations in favour of the Denominational Board, they almost forced the National Commissioners to close up their schools.[48] By 1856 the National Board Commissioners were deploring

> the discouragement given to educational efforts in various districts of the Colony. People who would otherwise have exerted themselves in the cause, have abandoned the attempt in despair. . . . We have been precluded from taking any steps in the matter, and have been obliged to reply to all alike, that we have "no funds". . . . We have been working under great discouragements, sufficient to have abated the ardor of the warmest supporters of the National system.[49]

Within two years they were forced to retrench drastically; their training establishment was closed, teachers' house-rent allowances were cut by one-half, salaries were reduced by five per cent, assistant teachers were replaced by pupil-teachers and promotions were suspended. Early in 1862, because they could not see their way to paying current salaries, the Commissioners were forced to give a month's notice to all teachers and, although the drastic consequences of this step were averted, salaries had to be reduced by a further five per cent in April.

G. W. Rusden and the Survival of the National Board

It was touch and go, but as events fell out Haines and O'Shanassy had made two miscalculations: they had underestimated the resilience of the National Board, and they had over-estimated the duration of the alliance between Church and State. Left to their own devices, the original National Board Commissioners would have lacked the will to resist Haines and O'Shanassy, but when in mid-1853 they were joined by G. W. Rusden, the one-time agent of the National Board in New South Wales, they acquired exactly the sort of irascible, argumentative and litigious colleague they needed. It is doubtful if any of these cautious Legislative Councillors ever liked the arrogant young civil servant who had been thrust upon them by La Trobe, but they, and their opponents, soon learned to respect his ability and his zeal. When Rusden finally resigned his seat in 1862 one of their number voiced the opinion of them all when he wrote:

". . . and now I feel, on the eve of your departure a degree of responsibility which your vigilance hitherto quite saved me."[50] His zeal in the cause of national education was well known before he joined the board; his work as an agent, his book, *National Education*, and his evidence before the Select Committee of 1852 gave unmistakable proof of his allegiance. "No country", he told the Select Committee,

> can ever be well educated under a Denominational system, which I look upon, politically, as a prostitution of principle; economically as a waste of public funds . . . by emptying the public exchequer into the lap of every greedy sectarian, a failing revenue must eventually be the result; no large expenditure can safely be entrusted to the reckless dissipation of conflicting interests.

When the chairman interposed to suggest that the witness might describe the improvements that could be made to the denominational schools he replied belligerently:

> I would not attempt to improve them, any more than I would pay five shillings for putting in a new knife blade when I could get a better knife for half the money. . . . I think them advisable nowhere. . . . I conceive that no public primary school should be founded on any other system than some such a one as the National.[51]

For nearly ten years this was the man who kept the National schools in existence. If a deputation was to wait upon the governor, or a protest was to be prepared, or the clergy were to be reprimanded for exceeding their functions in the schools, or resolutions were to be drafted, it was Rusden who was the member to do it. Rarely absent from a board meeting, sensitive to every shift in political power, and aware (in a maddening degree) of every regulation, he was in a unique position to check or circumvent his opponents' moves.[52] Thus, despite restrictions and prohibitions, the number of National schools crept up to 181, a system of training and classification was established, a limited contribution was made to the problem of education on the goldfields, and, after a false start (when the board's first inspector joined a digging party and defaulted with £93 2s. 6d.), a surprisingly good inspectorate was established. The master of ceremonies at the opening of a National school at Castlemaine might have to admit that he had had this honour thrust upon him because he was the only clergyman in the district who would support the National system, but the enthusiastic audience to whom he was speaking was more than a thousand strong.[53]

In fact the crowd which gathered in Castlemaine that day to gape at the Past Master of the Mount Alexander Lodge of Free and Accepted Masons as he poured corn, wine and oil upon the foundation stone of the National school was an indication of how badly Haines and O'Shanassy had miscalculated. While they were playing their waiting game, the climate of public opinion had been changing more rapidly than they appreciated. Society, men began to realize, had not disintegrated; Eureka notwithstanding, Victoria had not gone republican or infidel, and politicians who only a few years before had called upon the Church to save the State, now began to deprecate the alliance they had sponsored. By 1857, it was possible for Archibald Michie to introduce a Bill to abolish State aid to religion although only three years before he had thought this aid necessary "in the then peculiar state—the transition crisis of social history—through which Victoria was then passing". The situation had now changed, he maintained, and it was possible to ask "whether the social condition of the colony is not so far changed—so far favourably revolutionized—as to justify this discussion".[54]

The Common Schools Act, 1862

It was in this atmosphere that the emergency alliance between Church and State was abandoned, but as soon as the secularists moved to the offensive it became apparent that their ranks included two distinct parties—those who were prepared to exclude the clergy (and religion) from the schools, and those who believed that a State system of education could be built upon a basis of "common Christianity".

The out-and-out secularists could not yet hope for a hearing in a society which had so recently allied itself with the Church, and the initiative passed to the "common Christianity" party, and its brilliant young leader, George Higinbotham.[55] An unsuccessful education Bill sponsored by Michie in 1857 had first brought Higinbotham into the educational arena with an editorial in which he condemned the dual system and asserted that, though education should be taken out of the hands of the churches, it should be founded upon religion—"that essential religious teaching which was necessary for persons of all sects, and which could be imparted by any honest man of any sect".[56] By 1862, when Richard Heales introduced his Common Schools Bill, Higinbotham was his most powerful supporter in the House.[57] His trained, legal eye must have seen the shoddy framing of the Bill and the looseness of its phrasing, but to Higinbotham, as to Heales, it represented the limit to which the Parliament would let them push the denominationalists. There was nothing in the Bill to suggest that the denominational schools were to be driven out of existence—they were, in fact, invited to continue as "non-vested" schools—but the conditions under which they could expand, in a rapidly expanding colony, were no more encouraging than they were in the New South Wales legislation. O'Shanassy, quick to see the threat this Bill represented, brought in a rival Bill, and Haines threatened another, but Higinbotham and Heales had read the mood of the House aright, and the Common Schools Act became law on the last day of the session.

The Queensland Primary Education Act, 1860

Like Victoria, Queensland began its separate existence with a legacy of National and denominational schools inherited from New South Wales, but the compromise which eluded Victoria for a decade was achieved in Queensland within eighteen months. Most of the credit for this celerity must go to that brilliant colonial figure, Sir Charles Nicholson. Between his arrival in Australia in 1834 and his departure in 1862, Nicholson established a striking reputation in an extraordinary number of fields: whether one regards him as a physician, a squatter, a financier, a politician, an educationist, a collector, or a philanthropist, he remains an outstanding figure. Few men could match his knowledge of the issues involved in colonial educational affairs, for in his years as a National Board Commissioner in New South Wales, and as Provost of the University of Sydney, he had learnt, by bitter experience, how difficult it was to reconcile the denominationalists to the realities of colonial life. "It is terribly uphill work, this continued contest with ignorance and stupid prejudice", he told one of his friends in 1853.

> I almost feel disposed at times to abandon the efforts in which for so many years I have been engaged, in promoting that *greatest* of all God's gifts, education. . . . Our National schools are still the objects of the same misrepresentation and opposition on the part of the Church of England. The University has been made equally the subject of the same railings—night after night have I been compelled to sit and listen to declamations about *godless* institutions, and every attempt made to promote education upon sound and the only practicable principles, denounced by men who have never done the slightest thing themselves in the establishment of educational means in any shape.[58]

All this experience Nicholson now brought to bear upon Queensland's problems, for he had accepted the governor's invitation to a nominated seat in the Legislative Council and had been elected to its Presidency. He realized from the outset that circumstances were, at least temporarily, very much in his favour. Neither the Roman Catholic nor the Anglican Churches had yet appointed a bishop to the new colony, the governor (Sir George Bowen) was liberal in outlook, and the colony's main newspaper, the *Moreton Bay Courier*, was owned (on lease) and edited by Charles Lilley, an able radical, whose dedication to a national system of education was at least as fervid as Nicholson's.[59] Moreover, the colonists of Queensland, still flushed with the success of their Separation movement, were determined not to repeat the mistakes of the mother colony. When the Legislative Assembly's candidates published their election pledges in April 1860, Nicholson was quick to see that he could count on overwhelming support in that chamber for a National system;[60] but these legislators, he also realized, were quite inexperienced and could, in their ignorance, lose the advantage which he could see so clearly. Working swiftly, Nicholson secured the government's agreement to introduce an education bill as one of its first measures, prepared a bill reducing the denominational schools to the status of non-vested schools within a National system, and had the satisfaction of seeing it pass smoothly through the parliament before the denominationalists could rally their forces. By the time Governor Bowen prorogued the Parliament in September 1860, he was able to say with some complacency: "Primary education has been provided for upon the general principle of that comprehensive system, which experience has proved to be peculiarly adapted to meet the requirements of our colonial communities".[61] But Bowen's complacency was premature, for he was reckoning without the influence of Dr E. W. Tufnell, Queensland's first Anglican bishop.[62] Tufnell had arrived in the colony too late to challenge the passage of Nicholson's Primary Education Bill, but under the bishop's relentless prodding the people of Queensland were soon to discover that the "common Christianity" legislation of the 1860s by no means settled the education question.

NOTES

[1] See J. S. Gregory, 'Church and State, and Education in Victoria to 1872', E. L. French (Ed.), *Melbourne Studies in Education, 1958-59*; this article is a summary of Gregory's M.A. thesis, University of Melbourne, 1951; Bro. Ronald Fogarty, *Catholic Education in Australia, 1806-1950*, which is based on his Ph.D. thesis, University of Melbourne, 1956; Kenneth C. Cable, 'The Church of England in New South Wales and its Policy towards Education prior to 1880', unpublished M.A. Thesis, University of Sydney, 1952.

[2] Gregory, op. cit., p. 88.

[3] Charles Frankel, *The Case for Modern Man*, p. 29.
[4] Final Report from the School Commissioners, 1855, p. 1, *V. & P.*, N.S.W. Leg. Council, 1856–7.
[5] Ibid., p. 25.
[6] W. Wilkins, *National Education*, p. 58. See also C. Turney, 'William Wilkins—Australia's Kay-Shuttleworth', C. Turney (Ed.), *Pioneers of Australian Education*.
[7] W. A. Duncan, *Lecture on National Education;* G. W. Rusden, *National Education;* A Colonist, *A Plea for Common Schools*.
[8] A. W. Martin, 'Henry Parkes: Man and Politician', E. L. French (Ed.), *Melbourne Studies in Education, 1960–61*, p. 4.
[9] *Empire*, 28 Dec. 1850.
[10] Ibid., 3 June 1854.
[11] Ibid., 30 May 1853.
[12] Quoted Fogarty, op. cit., Vol. I, pp. 170–1.
[13] For a detailed account of Catholic educational policy in this period see below, Ch. 6; for an account of Geoghegan's work see below, Ch. 5.
[14] Minutes of the First Conference of the Australian Wesleyan Methodist Church, 18 Jan. 1855.
[15] J. D. Lang, *An Historical and Statistical Account of New South Wales*, Vol. II, p. 498.
[16] J. D. Lang, *Phillipsland: Its Present Condition and Prospects*, pp. 422–3.
[17] Report of the Select Committee on Education, 1844, pp. 555–66, *V. & P.*, N.S.W. Leg. Council, 1844.
[18] According to the 1861 census. See T. A. Coghlan, *General Report on the Eleventh Census*, p. 218.
[19] Cable, op. cit.
[20] Ibid., pp. 89, 94.
[21] Ibid., pp. 200 et seq.
[22] George Cornelius Gorham, vicar of Bramford Speke, was disciplined by his bishop because he held unsound views on the doctrine of baptismal regeneration. Before the Arches Court of Canterbury the bishop's action was upheld, but on appeal to the Privy Council Gorham was reinstated, the Privy Council holding that Gorham's views were consistent with adherence to the articles of the Church of England.
[23] Cable, op. cit., p. 223.
[24] Ibid., Ch. 7.
[25] Henry Parkes, *Fifty Years in the Making of Australian History*, Vol. I, p. 199.
[26] The Martin Ministry held office from 22 Jan. 1866 to 26 Oct. 1868. Its term of office was longer than that of any Ministry

before it, with the exception of the third Cowper Ministry (1861–3) which was of equal duration.

[27] Parkes proposed an enrolment of forty, which was reduced by the Assembly to thirty.

[28] Reduced by the Assembly to seventy.

[29] Parkes's parliamentary career between 1845 and 1866 was not continuous.

[30] Quotations from this speech are taken from David Blair (Ed.), *Speeches on Various Occasions . . . by Henry Parkes*, pp. 216–51.

[31] Parkes, op. cit., Vol. I, p. 167.

[32] Third Report of the Commissioners of National Education, p. 2, *V. & P.*, N.S.W. Leg. Council, 1851. The news of Separation reached Australia in Nov. 1850, but La Trobe retained the title of Superintendent until his commission as Lieutenant-Governor was received in July 1851.

[33] Denominational Boards had been created simultaneously in Sydney and Melbourne (Jan. 1848), but all National schools in the original N.S.W. had been administered from Sydney.

[34] *V. & P.*, Vic. Leg. Council, 1851–2, pp. 347–51.

[35] *Argus*, 13 Dec. 1851.

[36] Ibid., 18 Apr. 1855.

[37] The inauguration of the new colony took place on 1 July 1851; the news of gold discoveries in the Clunes district was circulating in Melbourne some weeks earlier. At the end of 1851 Victoria's population was 97,489; ten years later it had increased to 539,764.

[38] William Westgarth, *Argus*, 15 Nov. 1851; F. J. Sargood, *Victorian Hansard*, iii, 16; John Pascoe Fawkner, *Argus*, 10 Mar. 1854.

[39] Gregory, op. cit., pp. 34 et seq.

[40] Quoted G. Goodman, *The Church in Victoria during the Episcopate of the Rt. Rev. C. Perry*, p. 175.

[41] *Argus*, 1 Dec. 1852.

[42] Ibid., 13 Dec. 1852.

[43] The controversy is exhibited in the following pamphlets published in Melbourne during 1856: A. Cairns, *A Lecture on the Mutual Relations and Duties of Church and State*; T. T. A'Beckett, *A Defence of State Aid to Religion*; H. B. Macartney, *State Aid to Religion and Education*; A. M. Ramsay, *How the Money Goes*.

[44] Except for the period Oct. 1859–Nov. 1861, which was occupied by the short-lived Nicholson and Heales Ministries.

[45] Report from the Select Committee on Education, 1852, pp. 45–7, *V. & P.*, Vic. Leg. Council, 1852.

[46] Ibid., pp. 3–4. See also *Argus*, 9 July 1852, 10 Mar. 1854, 18 Apr. 1855.

The Eastern Mainland Colonies, 1851–1866

[47] Education Commission Bill, 1851; General Education Bill, 1853–4; Public Education Bill, 1854.
[48] For details of these manœuvres see A. G. Austin, *George William Rusden*, pp. 112–17.
[49] Fourth Report of the Commissioners of National Education, p. 5, *P. P.* (Vic.), 1856–7. See subsequent annual reports for the Board's difficulties 1856–62.
[50] Hervey to Rusden, 24 May 1862. (T.C.C.) For details of Rusden's activities as a Commissioner see Austin, op. cit., Ch. 10.
[51] Report from the Select Committee on Education, 1852, op. cit., pp. 95, 98–9.
[52] From 1851 to 1856 Rusden was Clerk of the Executive Council, from 1856 to 1882 Clerk of the Parliaments.
[53] *Mount Alexander Mail*, 15 Apr. 1856.
[54] *Victorian Hansard*, ii, 693–4. Michie's bill passed the Assembly by 32 votes to 20, and was defeated in the Council by 1 vote.
[55] Higinbotham arrived in Melbourne as a young migrant lawyer in 1854. He was editor of the *Argus* 1856–58, and entered politics in 1861. See below, Ch. 6. See also Gwyneth M. Dow, *George Higinbotham: Church and State*.
[56] *Argus*, 28 Dec. 1857.
[57] Heales was a private member in 1862, though he had led a short-lived Ministry during 1860–1. A man of working-class origins, Heales was especially concerned with social reform, education and temperance being amongst his chief interests.
[58] Nicholson to Rusden, 24 Sept. 1853. (T.C.C.).
[59] For Lilley's career see Allan A. Morrison, 'Charles Lilley', *Journal and Proceedings*, R.A.H.S., Vol. 45, Part I, 1959.
[60] *Moreton Bay Courier*, 26, 28 Apr. 1860.
[61] Quoted E. R. Wyeth, *Education in Queensland*, p. 83.
[62] See J. R. Lawry, 'Bishop Tufnell and Queensland Education', *Melbourne Studies in Education*, 1966.

5

Church, State and Public School System in Tasmania, Western Australia and South Australia, 1851–1871

BEHIND Thomas Arnold's acceptance of Governor Denison's invitation (see above, Chapter 3) lay a complex story of intense spiritual and mental turmoil. At Oxford he had begun to doubt the validity of his father's religion and the justice of contemporary society; in London, where he held an appointment in the Colonial Office, his religious scepticism developed into complete Pyrrhonism and his incipient social radicalism into a despairing conviction that the injustices of contemporary English society were probably irremediable. To young men seeking solitude in which to search for God again, and a new society capable, perhaps, of perfectibility, New Zealand in the mid-nineteenth century often appeared as a haven. To Arnold it was irresistible. His father had been attracted to these islands many years before—he had indeed bought land there—and everything that young Thomas Arnold read about them suggested to him that there he might help to lay the foundations of a better, a more fraternal, society. In November 1847 he took passage in the *John Wickliffe* and five months later, at the age of twenty-four, stepped ashore at Port Chalmers. His disenchantment with New Zealand life was swift and complete, and the legal difficulties put in the way of farming his father's land and his frustrated hopes of directing a projected college at Nelson were only minor, material causes of his disappointment. For to his sorrow Arnold found that colonial New Zealand was already taking on many of the forms of English society, that it was culturally barren and blatantly materialistic, and that when he tried to escape into solitude he found himself quite unfitted to pursue a life of solitary contemplation in its forbidding forests.[1]

Denison's offer, which came in August 1849, at least offered Arnold escape from the scene of his disenchantment. Beyond this it offered the opportunity of constructive intellectual work in a society desperately in need of redemption—and perhaps, now that his antipodean vision was fading, Tasmania might prove to be "one step on the road to England".[2] But when he reached Hobart Town in January 1850 he must have wondered if he could find the strength to face his prospects. The penny-a-day system, he soon discovered, was ruining the public schools; over most of the island this grant was affording the teachers "a mere starvation" pittance, and provoking them into falsifying their returns.[3] He must find, he realized, a steady supply of competent teachers, but when he announced a scheme for training youths of seventeen in a Normal School—the lads to pay the cost of their own board—not one applicant was to be found, and he had to drop the age of entry to fourteen, and agree to maintain the candidates, as well as educate them gratuitously. "In fact", he reported, "while the position of a school master remains what it is, it is hardly to be expected that aspirants should be found desirous of being trained to the duties of the profession on any other terms".[4]

Thomas Arnold's Reports

Nowhere in his inspector's reports could the governor find any comfort. The schools, he was told, had failed to act as a moral agency, and the children were growing up in "stolid ignorance and brutishness"; only a vast extension in the quantity and quality of the education being provided could hope to effect any improvement.[5] Denison was not a man to abandon a point lightly, but by 1853 even he must have doubted the wisdom of what he had done. His schools were obviously in an unsatisfactory condition, but his plans for their reorganization, expressed in his Bill for the Establishment and Maintenance of Primary and Other Schools in Van Diemen's Land, were obviously unacceptable to his Council which had rejected the Bill on four occasions and had now set up its own Select Committee to "take into consideration the question of Public Education and report thereon".[6] Denison's reply to this show of independence was to modify a proposal he had first put forward in 1851 and authorize a four-man Board of Inspection, representative of the major denominations, to collect further evidence on the state of the schools.

The Board of Inspection

The result of this decision must have startled any sober Tasmanian who, during the winter of 1853, chanced to come upon the strange and œcumenical spectacle of Archdeacon Davies acting as coachman of a wagonette and pair for Father Hall, Vicar-General of the Roman Catholic Church, the Reverend Dr Lillie of the Presbyterian Church, and Thomas Arnold, whose incipient conversion to Catholicism would make his exact theological position difficult to determine.[7] In a commendable state of amity these four inspectors visited sixty schools throughout the island with a growing conviction that Arnold had not been exaggerating the disgraceful condition into which the system had fallen. Everything they saw—buildings, equipment, teachers, methods of instruction—fell "far below what the wants of the community call for". The penny-a-day system they condemned completely; the average income of the teacher, they found, had fallen below that of a mechanic, and the "inevitable effect had been the degradation of the office of school master . . . but too frequently had recourse to as a *dernier ressort* by those who cannot succeed in anything else". Alone amongst the inspectors Arnold supported Denison's plan for a local educational levy and local supervision of schools; the majority report called for strong government action, holding that parents were "precluded by their own want of education from taking any *intelligent* interest in that of their children". Fixed incomes from public funds were essential, the majority asserted, though these incomes might be augmented by fees "as a stimulus to exertion".[8]

When they came to recommend a system, the four inspectors were surprisingly flexible in their views. They advocated the retention of the denominational system in Hobart and Launceston (the Vicar-General adding, "In Richmond, also Westbury, and any other Township where the number of Catholic children may be held sufficient to justify the formation of a separate School"), but they found this system "quite inapplicable" to the country districts. In every township, they declared, there must be an efficient school which could be attended by every child, and for "the sake of securing one efficient School in every Township, we are willing to recommend to our respective Churches the adoption of such a scheme".[9]

Roman Catholic Response to the Board of Inspection's Report

That Father Hall and Archdeacon Davies could put their signatures to this report seems, on the face of things, impossible—even allowing for a certain amount of ecclesiastical good-fellowship on their recent tour—but each man was aware, no doubt, that his bishop was now prepared to make some concessions on the education issue. Father Hall, for example, was obviously guided by the point of view which Bishop Willson had expressed in two petitions he had sponsored in 1852—a point of view substantially different from that of his brother bishops in the other colonies. In the first petition he spoke of "the inestimable blessings of a good secular education", and claimed that he was prepared to support general or mixed schools so long as none of the books used in these schools was objectionable to any sect, so long as "no one . . . shall be allowed to enter upon any subject connected with religion during the hours appointed for secular education", and so long as "the children shall be separated at certain specific periods, and left to the care of their respective pastors". In the second petition he specifically urged the legislature

> to adopt the *Denominational System* in as many Districts as possible, and the *General System* where the number of children is small; both of which systems have been sanctioned by the Legislative Council of New South Wales . . . and have been found to work harmoniously and satisfactorily, and thus . . . secure to the children the blessing of a good secular education, without the least infringement upon their religious principles.[10]

Bishop Willson's attitude is difficult to understand only if we make the mistake of assuming that the Catholic Church in Australia had a uniform policy on education by 1853, or if we assume that Geoghegan's views represented an official policy. It is true that Geoghegan's policy eventually prevailed amongst the hierarchy, but that this would happen was by no means clear in 1853. As Fogarty has pointed out:

> But if Quinn in Brisbane appeared to be temporizing, Geoghegan in Adelaide was going to the other extreme—at least, in the eyes of a great many. He was taking drastic steps, urging on the Church a complete break with the state and the establishment of an entirely independent Catholic system. Few were inclined to follow him.
> Between these two extremes . . . the remaining bishops took up their positions. In other words they had at that stage no hard and fast rules.[11]

Willson found himself in a dangerous position in 1852-3; under the existing system he was assured of government aid for his schools, but if Denison's local-control policy became law his flock, as a minority, would be consistently out-voted, and if the Select Committee recommended the British and Foreign School Society system (or some variety of it) he would have to withdraw his pupils. Not prepared, as Geoghegan was, to carry the burden of independent Catholic schools, he sought, as a second preference, a secular system with religious instruction tacked on, rather than an integration of secular and religious education. "Bishop Willson", Fogarty has commented, "was content to make the best he could out of what was not always a good thing".[12]

Anglican Response to the Board of Inspection's Report

But what of Bishop Nixon? What had transpired to mollify this bellicose figure? There seems little doubt that one of the most formative influences in Nixon's development as a colonial bishop was the response of his clergy and laity to the part he had played at the ill-starred Conference of Australasian Bishops in 1850. No sooner had word of the conference's decisions reached Tasmania than the clergy and laity set about making their bishop account for his opinions. A substantial majority of the clergy drew up an Address in which they protested strongly against the bishops' exclusion of the laity from synod, and their pronouncements on baptismal regeneration; at the same time, a large and influential body of laymen formed The Association of Members of the Church of England for Maintaining in Van Diemen's Land the Principles of the Protestant Reformation, enthusiastically endorsed the clergy's Address, and, when refused a public hearing by Nixon, ventilated the whole affair in the local Press.[13] Nixon did his best to quell the storm by private correspondence, but it had received so much publicity that only a public statement would suffice, and on 22 May 1851 he delivered a Charge to his clergy in which he sought to answer his critics, reassert his episcopal authority and close the breach. The Charge is a measure of Nixon's undoubted gifts—it is dignified, eloquent, paternal, scholarly and conciliatory; here and there it is prelatic and authoritarian, but his touches of acerbity are reserved for his clergy, and are always tempered by a declaration of pastoral concern. As the bishop developed his very lengthy case, it must have been obvious to his listeners that here was a man who was badly shaken by the challenge he had been offered: no one, under the circumstances,

could have been more placatory to an errant laity; no one could have been more understanding to a rebellious clergy.[14]
The connexion between this unnerving experience and the bishop's willingness to reconsider the education question can only be a matter of conjecture, but there can be little doubt that both Nixon and his archdeacon had begun to realize that the laity were in no mood to deny their children a secular education because their bishop objected to the type of school in which it was offered. By 1852 the editor of the Anglican paper, the *Tasmanian Church Chronicle*, was prepared to admit:

> It might be desirable to employ both systems . . . the *religious*, in towns . . . the *secular*, in those townships where . . . the ground is pretty equally divided between various religionists. . . . We are far from advocating such a system as the best possible; but we could reconcile ourselves to it without any sacrifice of principle.[15]

By 1853 Bishop Nixon, though still privately convinced that the denominational system was essential for the education of Anglican children, was aware that he could not carry his laity with him on this issue. Archdeacon Davies was therefore on safe ground when he put his signature to the inspectors' report, though some Anglicans felt that he should, like Father Hall, have insisted on maintaining the denominational system "in *all* places where there is a reasonable chance of carrying it out".[16]

The Central Board of Education

By the end of 1853 it was clear to the legislature that neither Willson nor Nixon was in a position to fight for the denominational principle; emboldened by the appearance of the Board of Inspection's report, the Council's Select Committee on Education determined to brush aside any attempt to preserve the denominational system and unanimously recommended "the adoption for Town and Country, of a system of General Schools . . . so modified and arranged that children of all Religious Denominations could attend".[17] In November Denison announced that, acting upon the advice of the Select Committee, he had established a Central Board, and had directed it to organize "a system of education of such a comprehensive character as may enlist in its favour the sympathies of all denominations of Christians".[18] Three months later the new Board published its interpretation of the governor's directive. Every school established by the Board, or assisted by government funds, would be known as a public school, they ruled, and in every public school

> the hour from 9 to 10 a.m. shall be set apart for Religious instruction. . . . If the teacher be a Protestant, he shall not require the children of Roman Catholics to be present at the religious instruction, except at the desire of their parents; and *vice versa* if the Teacher be a Roman Catholic. In imparting religious instruction the Teacher will be limited to the use of the Scriptures, or such books as have been sanctioned for the National Schools in Ireland, or may be hereafter specially approved by the Board. The Board are, however, prepared to sanction any arrangement by which the different Ministers of religion . . . may have opportunities of affording religious instruction on particular days (at the stated hour) to the children of their denomination.[19]

In devising this strange modification of the Irish National system, the Board obviously ran the risk of provoking denominational strife, but their scheme appears to have worked smoothly. One might have suspected, for instance, that the sects would circumvent the "mixed school" spirit of the new system by conspiring to congregate children, teachers and ministers of the one faith in the one school, but in only two places was this done. By 1866 the Harrington Street Public School in Hobart was generally known to be exclusively Catholic as all its pupils (368), and all its teachers (5), were Catholic; at Queenstown, 98 of the 127 pupils were Catholic and so were all the teachers, but at Margaret Street, Launceston, though 223 of the 227 pupils were Catholic, all the teachers were Anglican. In fact, it was very difficult for any sect to arrange matters to suit itself, for only in rare situations was any sect so concentrated and numerous that it could swamp a school, and the appointment of teachers rested with the Board, though it was expected "to pay regard to the recommendations of Ministers of Religion or other persons locally interested".[20] An examination of the Board's returns over a number of years shows that, with the exception of the two cases cited above, there was a thorough mixing of teachers and pupils, irrespective of religion.[21]

Charges of proselytizing were, of course, made but without much fervour. The Presbyterian and Dissenting ministers quickly agreed to instruct each other's pupils "without reference to denominational peculiarities",[22] Willson remained benign, and Nixon, now reluctantly convinced that he must make the best of a *fait accompli*, told his clergy:

> It surely is neither well nor wise to forego the advantages that are placed within our reach, solely, or mainly, on the ground, that we cannot have all which we may desire. It is because the Board of Education, as at present constituted, is somewhat more than willing, is anxious, that we should avail ourselves of the facilities which it offers for this purpose, that I invite you (at least for the present) to co-operate with it. Whatever may be our opinion, as to the errors in principle, which we conceive it tolerates, it surely does not accord with practical Christian wisdom, entirely to forego the solid advantages which it offers.[23]

Arnold's conversion in January 1856 produced another crop of Protestant charges that the Board's schools were agents of proselytism, but with his departure from the colony a few months later the "religious difficulty" in education practically ceased to disturb the citizens of Tasmania.[24] The conciliatory attitude adopted by both Willson and Nixon had so seriously weakened the denominationalists' case that there was little left for anyone to fight about. By September 1856, the editor of the *Tasmanian Church Chronicle* was warning his readers that denominational strife would have been better than the state of apathy into which Anglicans had lapsed.

> What the colony has to dread is a reign of indifferentism, in the hands of men who have as much sympathy with the pagoda as with the church, and who would entrust the training of our rising generation to a system of secular science, with the addition (perhaps) of pagan morals.[25]

Tasmania, Western and S. Australia, 1851-1871

But the secularists were too shrewd (or too indifferent) to be provoked into a declaration of their complete policy and, although two Commissions inquired into the operation of the 1854 compromise, hardly a witness could be found who criticized it. An Education Commission which took evidence in 1860 was thoroughly satisfied with everything it saw; it commended the decision, taken three years earlier, to create a Northern and a Southern Board for administrative convenience, and went on to declare:

> Your Excellency will not fail to observe the almost unanimous testimony of the witnesses upon . . . the general excellence of the elementary education imparted in the Schools under the control of the State. . . . We think we do not go too far in saying that Tasmania will bear a favourable comparison with many of the older countries, not only in the means but in the amount and character of education it affords to the rising generation.[26]

Seven years later a Royal Commission expressed itself with a similar complacency: "We consider the present system upon the whole to have worked beneficially for the country . . . any material defects in carrying out the present system can be removed, and increased benefits secured under it, by legislation."[27]

The Public Schools Act, 1868

The Tasmanian Parliament, acting upon the advice of this Royal Commission, passed the Public Schools Act in 1868; apart from effecting minor administrative improvements, it simply gave legislative sanction to the system which had been operating since 1854. But the legislature should have looked more closely at the evidence, and it should have remembered that Bishop Willson was dead, for the Vicar-General (Father Dunne) had made it clear that the days of compromise were nearly over when he testified that "the confidence of the Catholic clergy and the Catholic people in the system is completely shaken".[28] Within a year, the pronouncements of the 1869 Provincial Council of Catholic Bishops were to render the Public Schools Act of Tasmania a dead letter.

Australian Education, 1788–1900

Belated Educational Development in Western Australia

The forces of agnosticism, voluntaryism, sectarianism and liberalism, which shaped the educational development of the eastern colonies, are at first hard to discern in the Western Australian settlement of the 1850s and 1860s. It is true that this phase of educational development ends there, as elsewhere, with a compromise Act by which the State continues to give a grudging support to denominational schools (Elementary Education Act, 1871), but the steps by which the colony reached this typical compromise are not, at first glance, the same as those her distant neighbours took. One is conscious, too, that Western Australia only came into line with her neighbours at the last possible moment, for a year after Western Australia reached this stage of compromise, Victoria, by abolishing all State aid to denominational schools (Education Act, 1872; see below, Chapter 6) carried the constitutional development of education into a new phase.

Nevertheless, it is true that Western Australia was driven to this compromise by the same forces which drove her eastern neighbours; the same forces are there, but they are both distorted and obscured by the peculiar conditions in the colony. Gradually one realizes that one is looking at a familiar picture, but that one is looking at it through aberrated glass.

The essence of Western Australia's distinctive character is to be found in her poverty and isolation. While her eastern neighbours were shaking off the last traces of convictism, and adjusting themselves to political responsibility and goldfields' wealth, Western Australia, in order to save her 7,000 citizens from economic stagnation, had been forced to ask for convicts, and thus to condemn herself to Colonial Office direction for another twenty years. The 9,720 convicts who entered Western Australia between 1850 and 1868 may have saved the colony from immediate financial disaster, but they inhibited the flow of free migrants and the development of free institutions. When the first elected

Legislative Council came to debate the Elementary Education Bill of 1871 the colony consisted of only 25,000 people, politically unsophisticated and culturally isolated, for the 1,000 miles of desert which lay between Perth and Adelaide had effectively sealed Western Australia off from her neighbours. The colony had begun as an outpost of English middle-class society, and this, in essence, it remained throughout the whole of the nineteenth century. English ideas and English standards persisted in Western Australia while the patterns of thought and behaviour which were developing in the other Australian colonies were almost completely unknown. Even if the desert had not isolated Perth its location would have done so, for it was five days' journey from its port, and therefore cut off from the social and cultural intercourse which a capital should enjoy with the outside world.[29] One is at first astonished to find that the debate on the Elementary Education Bill was carried out in complete ignorance of the experiences of the older colonies, and that as late as 1894 a member of the Legislative Assembly who, as a former Victorian, was bold enough to quote from Higinbotham's Royal Commission Report of 1867, could be greeted with the cry "Who's he?" from his fellow-legislators.[30]

In these circumstances it is understandable that the personal views of governors and nominated officials should have counted for much more than they did in the eastern colonies, and one must keep looking behind the pronouncements and actions of officialdom to detect the real trend of Western Australian society.

Governor Kennedy and Retrenchment

Of the influence of personalities in this setting there can be no doubt. One cannot, for example, ignore the influence of a man like Captain Arthur Kennedy who arrived in Perth in July 1855 as successor to FitzGerald. Very masculine, very British, very conscious of the dignity of his office, Kennedy quickly took the colony's chaotic affairs into his large, capable hands. Informed within a fortnight of his arrival that the previous month's salaries and bills had not been paid, he seated himself fastidiously at his shabby desk, tried to ignore the stained walls and sagging ceilings of the hovel which Western Australia called Government House, and spread the colony's unprepossessing record in front of him.[31] One thing was immediately clear—FitzGerald's Estimates for 1856 were completely unrealistic; come what may, the colony would be nearly £15,000 in debt by the end of August and, unless the whole settlement was to drift into bankruptcy, belts would have to be tightened. A couple of years as a poor-law inspector during the Irish famine had taught Kennedy quite a lot about belt-tightening, and by September he had devised a detailed plan of retrenchment which he was sure would save the colony "if I meet the co-operation from Heads of Departments which I expect".[32]

Unfortunately the members of the Education Committee were not disposed to co-operate. Just before Kennedy's arrival they had published an ambitious plan for the development of public education which, however commendable in principle, could hardly have been more ill-timed. To a governor bent upon reducing expenditure the Committee's plan must have seemed perversely prodigal. "The Education given at Government Schools", Kennedy read,

> should ultimately be limited only by our means of obtaining instructors; and secondly, the fixing as a present limit, an Education for Boys equal to that obtainable at a good English Grammar School, and, for girls, such a one as a respectable middle-class person would endeavour to secure for his daughter in England.[33]

This, Kennedy decided, was sheer folly. In September he stopped payment of £10 for the hire of a piano for the Perth Girls' School, and in November sent the Committee a detailed criticism of their plan.[34] Two changes were essential, he insisted: the education provided in the government schools must be confined to "a plain and practical education" intended only for those whose parents were unable to pay private fees, and the separate grant to Catholic schools must cease.

The opposition provoked by his first directive caused Kennedy little worry. That the Committee would protest he could not doubt, but their well-meant and high-principled objections weighed little with a governor who had drastic administrative decisions to make; when three of their number resigned he immediately installed his Colonial Secretary as chairman, appointed a compliant schoolmaster to fill one of the other vacancies, and ignored further protests. The out-going members at once declared that the Committee had become "a mere branch of the Colonial Secretary's office", but this was exactly what Kennedy intended it should be,[35] and although clergymen and editors attacked his decisions[36] the governor knew that the bulk of public opinion was on his side. In May 1856 the former chairman (Rev. G. P. Pownall) resumed his seat on the Committee, and the crisis was over.[37] Kennedy's limited view of the function of public education is, of course, open to criticism,[38] but there is little doubt that he had made a shrewd estimate of the public demand for education. Even his predecessor, FitzGerald, had had doubts about the Committee's ambitious plans,[39] and the general tone of public opinion was clearly opposed to anything but the plainest of instruction. Not only in Kennedy's time, but for years afterwards, public opinion resisted any extension of the curriculum for fear that advanced studies for the colonial youth "would unfit them for becoming successful farmers and sheep-owners—where practical experience and shrewdness go much further than booklore".[40] "Our community are [sic] an industrious, hard-working, striving community", one citizen urged,

> and it is those rules which will enable a man to perform his own business and keep his own accounts which are most to be desired. . . . In nine cases out of ten, a classical or scientific education would be about as useful to the scholars as the diamond was to the cock who found it on the dunghill.[41]

Few Australian governors (or governments) have had to

Australian Education, 1788-1900

worry because they restricted public education, but most have learned to fear the consequences of opposing Catholic educational opinion. Governor Kennedy's experience was no exception to this generalization. He lost not a moment's sleep over his first educational directive, but his second—the abolition of FitzGerald's separate grant to Catholic schools—provoked a campaign which harried him, his successors, and the Colonial Office for the next fifteen years. Here, again, events must be explained partly in terms of personalities, though one needs to resist the tendency to explain them wholly in these terms—as some Western Australian historians have done.[42] It is at least probable that any governor, confronted with the truth about Western Australia's finances in 1855, would have considered cancelling the Catholic education grant; the fact that Kennedy did cancel it is not unconnected with the fact that he detested the Catholic bishop, Dr Serra, and believed him to be estranged from his flock. There was, moreover, good reason why Kennedy should have believed that he could play off the bishop against his flock, for strange things had been happening in the diocese of Perth since FitzGerald made his separate grant to the Catholic Church. That grant had been made to a Church already crippled with debt, and to a bishop whose mind was already affected by the privations and failures he had suffered, for Brady's zeal had not only led him to a bishopric, but to bankruptcy. The ridiculously large number of priests he had brought back with him from Rome in 1846 could not be sustained by a Catholic population of less than 400, and although Brady and many of his priests sold everything they possessed, and lived with an austerity that was little short of starvation, the Church was soon faced with a debt of £10,000, and pressing creditors. In desperation, Brady applied for a coadjutor to administer the temporalities of his diocese, and was granted the services of one of his Spanish priests, Dr Serra, who had recently been enthroned as bishop of Port Victoria (Darwin). In the circumstances, a more unfortunate choice than Serra could hardly have been made. Vain, punctilious and stubborn, he handled Brady and his problems without understanding or compassion, and the two prelates were soon involved in public recriminations, civil litigation, and appeals to Rome. Finally, Brady's incapacity was so manifest that he was suspended from his office by Papal instruction, and persuaded by his Metropolitan to retire. Serra had triumphed, but in doing so he had lost the sympathy of most of his laity, whose hearts were with their muddling, but warm-hearted countryman, Brady.[43]

These were the circumstances in which Kennedy sat down to consider the wisdom of continuing the separate grant to Catholic schools. He was by no means a bigot; his affection for the Sisters of Mercy, and his sympathy for their work were well known in Perth, and a prominent English Catholic (W. Monsell), remembering Kennedy's conduct during the Irish famine, could only tell Serra:

> I hear with astonishment that Governor Kennedy does not act fairly towards us. I knew him well. I saw him under most trying circumstances, and he behaved towards Catholics with great and signal fairness. . . . I am sure some misunderstanding must cause the present difficulties. . . .[44]

As Monsell probably guessed, it was not bigotry, but intense personal dislike of Serra, which was influencing the governor. It seems doubtful if anyone in Perth really liked Serra, but few can have disliked him as much as Kennedy did. To this bluff, extroverted, Irish soldier the diplomatic, intriguing, over-sensitive Spaniard personified all that he detested in foreigners and priests. Serra and his priests he thought of as "miserable, attenuated Spanish monks having a very imperfect knowledge of the English language which his Lordship himself scarcely speaks intelligibly"; to understand the true springs of action in Serra one had only to remember that he was "a Spanish subject and his remarks are indicative of his loyalty to the Sovereign of his adopted country"; all who had had dealings with him (including his own flock and the Sisters of Mercy) knew him to be unreasonable and untrustworthy; "harmony of action between the Government of a British Colony and a bigoted and very unreasonable Spaniard can hardly be accomplished".[45] But all this vituperation, it must be remembered, took place *after* Kennedy had made his decision to stop the Catholic grant. It would probably have been made no matter how attractive Serra's personality, for Kennedy's decision was based upon a resolution to use the scanty public revenue in the least wasteful fashion—to maintain schools which could be attended by all children. To achieve this, Kennedy believed that all he had to do was substitute the *Scripture Extracts* of the Irish National system for the Bible, authorize ministers of religion to instruct children of their own communion at certain times of the school day, and offer the Catholic bishop a seat on the Education Committee. Serra's refusal to participate in a general scheme certainly struck Kennedy as being an unnecessary act of priestly defiance, but Kennedy, like most Irish Protestants, had an exaggerated opinion of the virtues of the Irish National system, and he was clearly unaware of the objections which had been made to it by Catholic bishops in the eastern Australian colonies. Again, Serra's insistence on denominational education must have seemed exceedingly exclusive in a colony where no other sect was anxious to assert a similar claim. The Anglicans, if they had had episcopal direction, might have made a similar claim (as they had in the other colonies), but without a bishop to state their case they continued, as they had since 1847, to join with the Protestants in accepting a general system. At this point Kennedy would, almost certainly, have rejected the Catholic claim, no matter who had made it, but Serra's obvious unpopularity with most of his laity may have led Kennedy to assume, as Protestant administrators have frequently been prone to assume, that bishop and flock could be played off against each other. There is no doubt that he contrived to give the Colonial Office the impression that his decision would meet with little opposition.[46]

There, for a time, the matter rested. In order to balance his books Governor Kennedy had given Western Australia a system of education which the older colonies were only to accept, after a great deal of turmoil, two decades later. By a simple, autocratic decision the governor had abolished all aid to non-government schools, and had reduced the role of religion in the government schools to mere lip service to the principles of common Christianity, but this fortuitous decision happened to coincide with the mood of the majority, and, but for determined Catholic agitation, would have remained the fixed educational policy of the colony.[47] There was, of course, some non-Catholic opposition to Kennedy's decision; occasionally one finds an Anglican editor deploring his Church's participation in the general system, asserting that Anglican children were thereby becoming "undutiful, rationalistic and sceptical", and arguing the case for denominational action,[48] but these arguments were always met by the voluntaryist arguments of the Dissenters,[49] and found very little response in official Anglican circles. Mathew Hale, first Anglican bishop of Western Australia, was too well aware of his Church's poverty and diminishing influence to indulge any tastes he may have had for denominational education.[50] As early as 1847, when he was Bishop Short's archdeacon, he had travelled the dreary miles which separated one impoverished settlement from the next, and he was unlikely to have forgotten the experience, for his wife was a daughter of John and Georgiana Molloy, and had been reared in the crushing poverty and hardship of the Vasse. For years Bishop Hale served contentedly on the Board of Education which was formed to administer Kennedy's system, and in 1870 he admitted that neither he, nor any of his clergy, had ever given religious education in the schools lest "the habitual use of this liberty by us might possibly give rise to suspicions and mis-apprehensions . . . and that in the long run harm might be done to the interests of Public Education".[51] Hale's concern for the public good, for the welfare of the State before that of his own Church, gives a distinctive quality to Church–State relations in Western Australia. Whereas the other colonial bishops of the Anglican Church had to be driven to this position by their laity, Hale, coming to his diocese after the issue had been settled in the eastern colonies, adopted the credo of liberalism from the outset. When, in 1871, Catholic pressure for denominational grants could no longer be ignored, Hale published an open letter in which he made a frank statement of his attitude. "The Protestants have indeed acquiesced in the system", he wrote,

> and have helped to carry it out; and through their co-operation the Government has been able to do what it has done in planting its schools throughout the length and breadth of the land. But the Protestants have done this in the interests of the Government and in the interests of the country at large, not to please themselves, or to serve any ends of their own.[52]

On the other hand, there were a few who urged the government to carry the secularization of the schools even further. There was, for example, David Eedle who told his constituents that he "would have the Board of Education as secular as the Board of Works",[53] but it was not a sophisticated community, and although it cared little for its Churches it never dreamed of doubting the Christian basis of society. David Eedle was not elected, and the majority of Western Australians would undoubtedly have given their assent to the resolution passed at a public meeting in July 1871: "That the maintenance of the present system of education in its integrity would be preferable either to making separate grants to dissentients from that system, or to having recourse to a general denominational system."[54]

Governor Weld and the Restoration of State Aid

But if agnosticism played no part in fashioning the educational system of Western Australia, sectarianism, here as elsewhere, played a very large part, for Catholic opposition to Kennedy's system became more and more vociferous as the years passed and their ranks were swollen by Irish convicts. When FitzGerald made his separate grant in 1849 Catholics represented some 8 per cent of the population;

Tasmania, Western and S. Australia, 1851–1871

when Kennedy abolished the grant in 1855 this figure had risen to 21 per cent; by 1871 it was nearly 30 per cent.[55] Protest as they might, however, they could not move Kennedy or his successor, Dr Hampton, but their prospects suddenly brightened when word reached the colony that Hampton was to be succeeded by a Catholic, Frederick Aloysius Weld. The appointment of a Catholic governor at this point in the colony's development has assumed too sinister an aspect in Western Australian folklore; Weld was not, as many Western Australians assert, the first Catholic governor of an Australian colony, for his co-religionist, Sir Dominick Daly, had been appointed governor of South Australia in 1861, had given years of distinguished service, and was dead and buried before Weld was appointed to Western Australia. Nor was there any deep-laid Catholic plot to foist a Catholic upon the Colonial Office. Hampton's successor was publicly announced (both in London and Perth) as Sir Benjamin Pine, a typical (and Protestant) colonial governor, and he was already engaged to come out on the mail steamer of September 1868 when he chose to resign his appointment to secure a better post in Antigua.[56] The Colonial Office's only concern, when Pine resigned, was to find a person who was immediately available and who was capable of presiding over the risky experiment of granting a measure of self-government to this exasperatingly backward colony.[57] Weld, who had been a very successful premier of New Zealand and was living in retirement in England, must have seemed a happy choice to the Secretary of State, who probably hoped that the appointment might also have the effect of placating the aggrieved Catholics of Western Australia; there is, however, no direct evidence that Weld was given any specific instructions to concede the Catholics' demands.[58] Again, there is nothing sinister in the Catholic decision (July 1869) to petition the new governor through the nominated Legislative Council; this they had also done when Hampton arrived. Now, as on the previous occasion, no one could be found to second the motion that their petition be received, so, as they had done before, they forwarded their petition to England, whereupon the Secretary of State immediately referred it back to the governor and left the initiative with him.[59]

Weld's position was not an enviable one. There may have been nothing sinister in his appointment, but his religious views could not help but influence his policy. It must be remembered that he was no nominal Catholic—his piety was recognized by the rare Papal decision to allow him the privilege of a private oratory at Government House[60]—and he was clearly anxious to help his Church, but his freedom of action was limited by the measure of self-government he had been sent out to introduce. In April 1870 he outlined, for the information of the Secretary of State, a plan whereby he might hand over the existing government schools to the Protestants, and thereafter divide the education grant between them and the Catholics, though there was, he admitted, some difficulty in explaining how such a scheme would satisfy religious consciences in small country districts which could support only one school.[61] However, before he and the Colonial Office could do anything about this proposition, the first Legislative Council elections were upon him; education, he could not help but notice, was almost the main election issue, and though few of the candidates could be said to be well informed on the issue, most of them were clearly opposed to any alteration of the existing system. There was now little hope of pursuing the plan he had put forward in April; something much more modest was all he could now hope to secure for his co-religionists, but whatever was to be done had to be done immediately, before the new Councillors had found their feet and learnt to organize an opposition. Weld, it would appear, approached his young Council with polite contempt;[62] only such an attitude could have led him to expect that the proposition which he, his Colonial Secretary (F. P. Barlee), and Dr Gibney propounded in November 1871 could succeed in passing through the Council.[63] Barlee, who had come out with Kennedy in 1855, and had succeeded in holding on to his office under Hampton and Weld, was quite prepared to trim if his office were at stake; although he had derided the Catholic petition before the old Council, he now agreed, in order to please Weld, to support it in the new. To put the matter in a respectable form, he composed a memorandum to the governor stating that, although he (Barlee) and the public were opposed to any change in the system of education, he was so anxious to prevent a repetition of the turmoil the question had caused at the recent election that he advised the placing of a sum of £500 on the Estimates as a grant-in-aid to the Catholic schools. Weld continued the farce by solemnly asking Bishop Gibney for his opinion of Barlee's memorandum, and the bishop, with equal solemnity, replied that, as the majority of electors had shown themselves averse to any change, he was

> unwilling to raise or continue an agitation which might not be justified by results, and which, therefore, may be avoided without sacrifice of principle. On these grounds, still retaining my opinions and principles regarding Education, and what is due to minorities, and trusting that at some future time such views may be those of the Colony generally, irrespective of creed, I feel myself justified in accepting the proposition contained in Mr. Barlee's Memo, in the conciliating spirit in which it is made; and I trust the Legislature will see, in such frank acceptance, an earnest of my desire to obviate difficulties and to promote the public interest.[64]

But when Barlee placed the proposition before the Legislature (January 1871) both Weld and Gibney learnt that they had under-estimated the intelligence and common sense of the new Councillors. A motion to pay the £500 was thrown out by eleven votes to six, the governor's motives were impugned, and Barlee was openly condemned as a trimmer, a toady, and a traitor to the cause of Protestantism.[65] Weld protested his astonishment at the Council's action, and Gibney asked, "could any man have gone further without sacrifice of principle than I did . . . for the sake of peace?",[66] but it was clear to both of them that they would never get a separate grant past the Council if it were intended specifically for Catholic schools. Four days after

Barlee's humiliation Weld prorogued the Council, and sat back to plan his next move.

For a while there appeared to be no hope of any compromise. With every fresh move taken by the Catholic Education Committee, Protestant opposition hardened; bitter public meetings were convened by both parties, Councillors were urged to declare themselves, and the Press (almost unanimously opposed to Barlee's proposition) kept up an unremitting attack on the Catholic cause.[67] When Weld sought the advice of the South Australian governor (Sir James Ferguson), he was reminded that "recent events at Rome" had aroused so much anti-Catholic feeling that he would need to move with the utmost caution.[68] Then, in June, the situation was suddenly changed by Bishop Hale. No one had been more forthright than the Anglican bishop in condemning the Barlee manœuvre, but he had been watching, in distress, the mounting religious turmoil in the colony, and he believed that before the Legislature reassembled someone must break the deadlock. In a letter addressed to the Perth representatives in the Council, Hale declared:

> As matters now stand it appears to me to be quite certain that the question can be settled only upon the great principle of dealing with every religious body alike. If we are to have the denominational system let it be the denominational system for all. If we are to have the mixed system let it be the mixed system for all. If we are to have a system partly denominational and partly mixed let this also be for all alike; not after the fashion of the late proposition under which the liberty of the denominational system would have been assigned to one party and the restrictions of the mixed system to all the rest.[69]

In many ways this was a strange proposal for Hale to have made. He had never been under any misapprehension as to the ability of his flock to support Anglican schools, and his proposal for all-round denominationalism could, in practice, only benefit the Catholic Church. It could be argued that he hoped that the Anglicans would respond to the challenge he proposed,[70] but it is more likely that he only wished to indicate that the Anglican Church was prepared to negotiate, so long as a privilege was not, in principle, conferred on the Catholic Church. Moreover there can be no doubt that Hale was influenced by the compromise which had just been effected in England by Forster's Elementary Education Act of 1870. Nothing reveals the un-Australian character of Western Australian thought so clearly as its response to the news of this English Act. In the parliamentary debates, or the Press, scarcely a word can be found of the education Acts of the eastern colonies, but from the moment the terms of Forster's Act reached the colony, they were quoted interminably and became the catch-cries of hitherto uninformed legislators and editors.[71]

The Elementary Education Act, 1871

Forster's Act gave Weld the opportunity he had been waiting for. Now he had an unimpeachable English precedent for proposing aid to all voluntary schools while leaving the government schools undisturbed, and Bishop Hale's pronouncement cleared away most of the local difficulties. As soon as the Council reassembled, Barlee introduced an Elementary Education Bill which provided that a Central Board should supervise two classes of schools, Government and Assisted. The former were to be supported by a grant of £2 15s. per pupil, and were to provide four hours of secular instruction each day, with one hour set aside for voluntary, segregated religious instruction by ministers of religion; secular instruction was held to include general religious teaching "as distinguished from dogmatic or polemical theology". The latter schools, if they could muster twenty pupils, were to receive government aid at the rate of £1 7s. 6d. per pupil.[72] But if Weld knew his Forster's Act, so did his Councillors, and as soon as the Bill went into the committee stage the elected members insisted that the time-table clause which applied to the Voluntary schools in England must be applied to the Assisted schools in Western Australia, i.e. dogmatic religious instruction must be confined to a period at the beginning, or the end, of the school day.[73]

This was a severe blow to Weld's plans, for it ruled out the possibility of full denominational action in the Catholic schools, but there was nothing he could do to defeat this amendment; his only hope of getting the Bill through at all rested on the goodwill of those Protestant Councillors who had accepted Bishop Hale's advice. Any suggestion that the Bill was intended to confer a special privilege on the Catholic schools would have sent every Protestant member into the opposition camp. The governor accepted the amendment, and saved his Bill.

It had been a long and bitter struggle. The governor had not got all he had wanted, but he had succeeded in pulling Western Australian society back, against its wishes, to a position which it had abandoned sixteen years earlier. The real direction of society in the west, as in the east, was secular, but the conjunction of a Catholic governor and an immature community which had not yet learnt to question English precedents had succeeded in diverting Western Australian society from its goal. It was to take another twenty years before the community was free to pursue its own course.

The South Australian Select Committee Report, 1861

South Australia's insistence, in 1851, that government aid would be available only to those schools which gave "good secular instruction, based on the Christian religion, apart from all theological and controversial differences on discipline and doctrine"[74] meant that the colony had achieved, at least in legislation, what the eastern colonies were still trying to achieve in the 1860s—a sound secular education based upon a common Christianity. How well this policy suited the temper of South Australian society was revealed in the evidence and report of a Select Committee of the House of Assembly which inquired into the state of public education in 1861. The Committee reported that

> although particular defects have been pointed out in the working of the existing system, the general result of the evidence given has been to show that its effects have upon the whole been

Tasmania, Western and S. Australia, 1851-1871

satisfactory—that it has increased the amount and raised the character of the education imparted within the Colony, and that any improvement to be effected is rather to be sought in greater attention to details . . . than in the adoption of any other system. . . . The evidence shows that there is no ground for supposing that any attempt has been made to introduce sectarian teaching into any school assisted by Government. . . . The ground of objection on the part of the Roman Catholics is not on account of anything which the present system permits but on account of what it excludes; not that it allows a certain amount of unsectarian religious instruction but that it does not place the entire control of the religious and secular instruction imparted at schools attended by the children of Roman Catholic parents in the hands of the Roman Catholic clergy. . . . It is only on the part of the Roman Catholics as a body that this objection is made. Your Committee do not conceive that any necessity exists for immediate legislation upon the subject.[75]

Now this statement is too optimistic in tone and it is naïve for it ignores Lutheran objections to the system (for they, fearful of State interference, refused to accept aid until 1870), and it asserts that no attempt had been made to introduce sectarian teaching;[76] nevertheless it expresses the prevailing mood of the colony.

Protestant Acceptance of the Report

This mood was epitomized in the evidence of the Methodist spokesman, the Rev. Mr Butters:

I believe there is no dissatisfaction with the system as it exists. It amounts to about this—if we could have education as we wish, we would have it very different; but the case is so surrounded with difficulties, that we do not care to raise objections. . . . The conclusion I have come to is that we must be prepared for a compromise.[77]

One would, of course, hardly expect to find a South Australian Methodist objecting to the 1851 system, but one is, at first sight, surprised to find an Anglican bishop approving of it. In 1852 Bishop Short had declared the 1851 Act to be "a most arbitrary and insulting one", but by 1861, in answer to the question "And, as head of the Church of

England in this Colony, you are satisfied with the religious teaching imparted?" he could reply in these terms:

> Yes; believing that it is impossible, or at least impracticable, to establish what is called the denominational system. . . . If I understand the rules of the Board of Education, the system is a combination of that of the British and Foreign School Society . . . and Irish systems. I do not think, with a mixed population, such as ours, that a better system could be devised.[78]

The fact was that Dr Augustus Short had modified his views a great deal since his arrival in the colony in 1847. Then, his Tractarian leanings, the close ties he maintained with the government, and his strong sense of episcopal dignity not only led his opponents to charge him with seeking dominance for his Church, but antagonized many of his followers. By 1861 he had a better understanding of the role of an Anglican bishop in a "paradise of dissent". Like Bishop Nixon in Tasmania he had been taught a sharp lesson when he returned from that ill-fated conference of Australasian bishops in 1850. On a formal, social occasion, and in the presence of the governor, he had been sharply questioned on his part in the conference, and forced to agree to the calling of a general assembly of laymen to discuss the problem of church government.[79] At this assembly he had been compelled to witness the passing of a series of resolutions in which the laymen present protested that they "heard with regret and alarm that the Australian Bishops . . . have attempted to narrow the terms of communion . . . by their formal, gratuitous and unnecessarily dogmatical declaration on the subject of Baptismal Regeneration", and that they

> totally and absolutely repudiate any assumption of ecclesiastical authority of the Church in this province . . . and invite the Clergy to meet and express publicly, their opinion on the ecclesiastical character and authority of the Minutes and Proceedings of the Bishops in Sydney.[80]

This, and a hundred minor incidents, had shaped the bishop's mind during his years in South Australia.

Catholic Rejection of the Report

But if the Select Committee's report reflected the prevailing mood in the colony, it also reflected the unequivocal nature of the contrary mood which had been expressed by the Vicar-General of the Roman Catholic Church, the Very Rev. Michael Ryan. "The present system we condemn", Father Ryan had told the Committee, "for in its nature it is Protestant", and he had gone on to state and defend the Catholic view of education in terms very similar to those which Dr Geoghegan had used before the 1852 Select Committee in Victoria.[81] This same Dr Geoghegan was now bishop of South Australia, and it was obviously his uncompromising view which Father Ryan was expressing, for Geoghegan, earlier than any other bishop in Australia, had seen the realities of this phase of common Christianity. In 1852 he had declared: "We wish religion to be introduced into almost every act which comes under the notice of the child during education. . . . We Catholics must have separate schools or none at all aided by the State";[82] now that he had been translated to the See of Adelaide, he realized that it was idle to hope that the State would ever allow him to develop satisfactory Catholic schools with public money. It was true that his predecessor had persuaded the Board to permit the reading of the Bible in either the Protestant or the Douay version, but this, to Geoghegan, was almost irrelevant in the light of his conception of Catholic education. He had no illusions about the size of the task he had set himself, for his flock was desperately poor, and many were indifferent, but within a few months of his succession he exhorted them to reject all connexion with the government schools, and to set about establishing independent Catholic schools "wherever there was a pastor and a flock".[83] To further the cause he undertook to conduct an educational mission, he urged his clergy to do likewise, and he established a central School Fund to compensate schools for the loss of the government grant. All this, no doubt, was in Father Ryan's mind when he appeared before the Select Committee, and he must have known, too, that Geoghegan, in ironical mood, was about to petition the Legislative Council urging a total abolition of State aid so that all sects might be left to savour the effects of the voluntary principle.[84] Geoghegan could not hope, of course, to create the stir he had created in Victoria, for whereas he then spoke for some 23 per cent of the population he now spoke for some 10 per cent, and there was no South Australian O'Shanassy to support him in the legislature, but in throwing down his challenge Geoghegan warned the colonists of South Australia, and through them the people of Australia, that in developing comprehensive schools upon the basis of a common Christianity, they were inevitably creating a rival system of Catholic schools.

The South Australian colonists were not, however, perturbed. The most Protestant of all the communities in Australia, they could afford to be uncompromising in their view of the relationship which should exist between Church and State. As their governor remarked drily, when asked to comment on Weld's plan to grant aid to all denominational schools in Western Australia: "I don't think we should have the least chance of carrying it here, and expect to find irreligious education a *sine qua non* of any bill that is accepted."[85]

NOTES

[1] Thomas Arnold's autobiography, *Passages in a Wandering Life*, was published in 1900 and is therefore not always accurate in recalling the events and emotions of his early manhood. W. T. Arnold's 'Thomas Arnold the Younger', *The Century Magazine*, Vol. LXVI, No. 1, May 1903, reproduces valuable excerpts from Thomas's letters in the 1840s. See also Kenneth Allott, 'Thomas Arnold the Younger, New Zealand, and the "Old Democratic Fervour" ', *Landfall*, Vol. 15, No. 3 (Sept. 1961), and P. A. Howell, *Thomas Arnold the Younger in Van Diemen's Land*.

Throughout this chapter I have used the name "Tasmania" which was in common use by the early 1850s, though the official change from "Van Diemen's Land" was not made until 1856.

[2] Thomas Arnold to his mother, 5 Nov. 1849, quoted Howell, op cit., p. 48.

Tasmania, Western and S. Australia, 1851–1871

[3] Thomas Arnold, op. cit., pp. 126–7.

[4] Report upon the Public Day Schools of Van Diemen's Land for 1850–51, p. 2, *V. & P. & P.*, V.D.L. Leg. Council, 1852. See also *Hobart Town Gazette*, 12 Nov. 1850.

[5] The Annual Report of the Inspector of Schools for 1852, pp. 4–5, *V. & P. & P.*, V.D.L. Leg. Council, 1853.

[6] Paper No. 72, *V. & P. & P.*, V.D.L. Leg. Council, 1853.

[7] Thomas Arnold, op. cit., p. 128.

[8] Report of the Board of Inspection of the Public Schools of the Island, pp. 4–6, *V. & P. & P.*, V.D.L. Leg. Council, 1853.

[9] Ibid., pp. 5–6.

[10] Schools' Bill: Petition of the Right Reverend Bishop Willson, 3 Aug. 1852; Schools' Bill: Petition of Roman Catholic Clergy and Laity against the Schools' Bill, 15 Sept. 1852, *V. & P. & P.*, V.D.L. Leg. Council, 1852.

[11] Bro. Ronald Fogarty, *Catholic Education in Australia, 1806–1950*, I, 172.

[12] Ibid., I, 221, n. 84. Note also Arnold's comment (p. 155): "Old age, if it had 'abated' somewhat his 'natural force', had not dimmed the look of central peace which reigned in his benevolent countenance."

[13] Francis Russell Nixon, *A Charge Delivered to the Clergy of Tasmania . . . on Thursday, 22nd May, 1851*, pp. 75 et seq. See also P. A. Howell, 'Bishop Nixon and Public Education in Tasmania', *Melbourne Studies in Education, 1967*.

[14] Ibid., passim.

[15] *Tasmanian Church Chronicle*, 7 Feb. 1852.

[16] Ibid., 1 Oct. 1853. At the end of 1853 Nixon and a majority of his clergy petitioned against the abolition of aid to denominational schools. Ibid., 1 Dec. 1853.

[17] Report from the Select Committee appointed to take into consideration the Question of Public Education, 1853, p. 3, *V. & P. & P.*, V.D.L. Leg. Council, 1853.

[18] *Hobart Town Gazette*, 1 Nov. 1853.

[19] Ibid., 7 Feb. 1854.

[20] Ibid.

[21] Report of the Royal Commission on Public Education, 1867, pp. 53–9, Tas. H. of A. *Journals*, 1867.

[22] *Tasmanian Church Chronicle*, 1 Sept. 1856.

[23] Francis Russell Nixon, *A Charge Delivered to the Clergy of the Diocese of Tasmania . . . on Tuesday, 22nd May, 1855*, p. 32.

[24] *Hobart Town Daily Courier*, 18, 26 Jan. 1856; *Colonial Times*, 22 Jan. 1856; *Tasmanian Church Chronicle*, 1 Feb. 1856.

[25] Ibid., 1 Sept. 1856.

[26] Report of Commissioners appointed . . . to enquire into the state of . . . Education in Tasmania, 1860, pp. 3, 7, Tas. H. of A. *Journals*, 1860.

[27] Report of the Royal Commission on Public Education, 1867, op. cit., pp. xxviii–xxix.

[28] Ibid., p. 29.

[29] The modern port of Fremantle, 12 miles from Perth, was not developed until the 1890s; throughout the nineteenth century Perth was served by the port of Albany, 200 miles to the south.

[30] *Parl. Deb.* (W.A.), New Series, vii, 955.

[31] Kennedy to Secretary of State for the Colonies, 17 Aug. 1855, 28 Nov. 1856. (J.S.B.).

[32] Kennedy to Secretary of State for the Colonies, 17 Aug., 5 Sept. 1855. (J.S.B.).

[33] *W. A. Govt. Gazette*, 20 Mar. 1855.

[34] Secretary of the Education Committee to Colonial Secretary, 29 Sept. 1855; Colonial Secretary to Pownall, 23 Nov. 1855. (J.S.B.).

[35] Secretary of the Education Committee to Colonial Secretary, 30 Nov., 5 Dec. 1855; Minutes of the Education Committee, 12, 26 Jan. 1856. (J.S.B.)

[36] A. Burton and U. Henn (Eds.), *Wollaston's Albany Journal*, 1 Feb. 1856; *Inquirer*, 13 Feb. 1856.

[37] Minutes of the Education Committee, 31 May 1856. (J.S.B.).

[38] See J. K. Ewers, 'Governor Kennedy and the Board of Education', *Journal of the Western Australian Historical Society*, 1947.

[39] Minutes of the Education Committee, 12 Nov., 4 Dec. 1849. (J.S.B.).

[40] *Fremantle Herald*, 19 Dec. 1868.

[41] Ibid., 5 Oct. 1867.

[42] See Donald H. Rankin, *The History of the Development of Education in Western Australia*, p. 37; John T. McMahon, *One Hundred Years*, p. 69.

[43] Strictly speaking, Serra was never Bishop of Perth, for Brady, though living in retirement until 1871, never resigned his See. For details of the Brady–Serra conflict see McMahon, op. cit.; P. McCarthy, 'The Foundations of Catholicism in Western Australia', *University Studies in History and Economics* (University of W.A.), Vol. 2, No. 4 (July 1956).

[44] Monsell to Serra, 7 Nov. 1856, quoted McCarthy, op. cit., p. 39.

[45] Kennedy to Secretary of State for the Colonies, 2, 4 Aug. 1856, 13 Aug. 1857. (J.S.B.).

[46] Secretary of State for the Colonies to Kennedy, 20 Jan. 1857. (J.S.B.)
[47] Western Australia returned to this policy in the 1890s. See below, Ch. 6.
[48] *Fremantle Herald*, 29 June 1867.
[49] Ibid., 6 July 1867.
[50] Anglicans represented 68·8 per cent of the population in 1848, 58·98 per cent in 1870. See Malcolm A. C. Fraser, *Seventh Census of Western Australia*, p. 135.
[51] Papers Relative to Public Education in Western Australia, 1870, p. 11, V. & P., W.A. Leg. Council, 1870–1.
[52] Mathew Hale, *A Letter . . . on the Education Question*, pp. 3, 7. See also Bruce to the Secretary of State for the Colonies, 4 Aug. 1865. (J.S.B.).
[53] *Fremantle Herald*, 20 Aug. 1870.
[54] Ibid., 8 July 1871.
[55] Fraser, loc. cit.
[56] Buckingham to Hampton, 1 July 1868; Granville to Bruce, 22 Feb. 1869. (J.S.B.) For many years Pine had been trying to convince the Colonial Office that the Leeward Islands (where he had once been governor of St. Christophers) should be federated and brought under a governor-in-chief at Antigua. The Colonial Office adopted his views just as he was about to set out for Australia. See *D.N.B.*, Vol. XLV, p. 312.
[57] The Colonial Office had been studying the problem of self-government for Western Australia since 1865, i.e. since the decision had been taken to discontinue transportation. See J. S. Battye, *Western Australia: A History from its Discovery to the Inauguration of the Commonwealth*, pp. 275–9.
[58] However, J. T. Reilly in *Reminiscences of Fifty Years' Residence in Western Australia*, p. 87, claims that it "was an open secret . . . that His Excellency had received instructions in England . . . to concede the demands of the Catholic body."
[59] Ibid., p. 43; *Fremantle Herald*, 10 July 1869.
[60] McCarthy, op. cit., p. 57. In tracing the steps by which he was converted to Roman Catholicism Thomas Arnold records the strong impression which Weld made on him when they met in New Zealand; he reports: "One of his books which he had brought with him from Fribourg was a history of philosophy by the Jesuit professor Freudenfelt. This book seemed to me to be more genially and lucidly written than any similar work that had been put into my hands at Oxford." Arnold, op. cit. p. 99.
[61] Papers Relative to Public Education in Western Australia, 1870, op. cit., pp. 4–5.
[62] Alice, Lady Lovat, *The Life of Sir Frederick Weld*, pp. 196–7.

[63] Serra returned to Spain in 1862 and was succeeded by Dr Martin Griver who, however, did not technically become Bishop of Perth until 1873—see above, Note 43. Dr Gibney, who succeeded Griver in 1886, had been in the colony since 1863, and acted as administrator whenever Griver was absent from his See.

[64] Aid From Public Funds to Roman Catholic Schools in Western Australia, pp. 3-4, *V. & P.*, W.A. Leg. Council, 1870-1.

[65] *Fremantle Herald*, 25 Feb., 2, 18, 30 Mar., 27 May 1871. The new Council consisted of six nominated and twelve elected members; two nominees and two elected members crossed the floor during this debate, but the vote was essentially a division into nominated and elected members.

[66] Lovat, op. cit. p. 197; *Fremantle Herald*, 28 Jan. 1871.

[67] See the Perth–Fremantle Press, Mar.–July, 1871.

[68] Lovat, op. cit., pp. 199-200. Ferguson is referring to the declaration of the doctrine of Papal Infallibility; see below, Ch. 6.

[69] Hale, op. cit., p. 7.

[70] A hope that was not realized. At no time after 1871 did the Anglicans have more than two elementary schools, apart from the schools in their two orphanages. By 1889 they had only the school in the Perth Orphanage. Report of the Central Board of Education, 1889, *M. & V. & P.*, W.A. Parlt., 1890-1.

[71] *Fremantle Herald*, 5 Aug. 1871. Forster's Act gave aid to Voluntary Schools which fulfilled certain minima of instruction, and gave religious instruction only at the beginning or end of the school day so that pupils whose parents so desired could withdraw them from religious instruction without forfeiting the benefits of secular instruction. In any district where Voluntary Schools were found to be inadequate an elected School Board was empowered to establish Board (i.e. Government) Schools in which no religious catechism or formulary distinctive of any denomination was to be used.

[72] In Committee Barlee tried unsuccessfully to make the grant to Assisted Schools the same as that for Government Schools. *Fremantle Herald*, 5 Aug. 1871.

[73] Ibid.

[74] See above, Ch. 3.

[75] Report of the Select Committee of the House of Assembly appointed to report upon a system of Education, 1861, pp. 1-2, *Proc. Parlt.*, S.A., 1861.

[76] For accusations of sectarian teaching see James Bickford, *An Autobiography of Christian Labour, 1838-88*, p. 298; *Adelaide Observer*, 25 May 1867.

[77] Report of the Select Committee . . . 1861, op. cit., p. 21.

[78] Ibid., p. 18.

Tasmania, Western and S. Australia, 1851-1871

[79] *An Account of the Proceedings of the Laity and Clergy of the Church of England in South Australia, occasioned by the publication of certain Minutes of a Meeting held at Sydney by the Australasian Bishops in October, 1850*, pp. 16-22.

[80] Ibid.

[81] Report of the Select Committee . . . 1861, op. cit., p. 24.

[82] Report of the Select Committee on Education, 1852, p. 3, *V. & P.*, Vic. Leg. Council, 1852.

[83] P. B. Geoghegan, *Pastoral Letter to the Clergy and Laity of the Diocese on the Education of Catholic Children*, p. 15.

[84] Petition from the Clergy and Laity of the Roman Catholic Church, 4 Sept. 1861, *Proc. Parlt.*, S.A., 1861.

[85] Lovat, op. cit., p. 199.

6

Defining the Constitutional Code of Public Education 1872–1895

BETWEEN 1872 and 1895 the six Australian colonies passed education Acts which committed them to the establishment of national systems of education entirely supported by central government funds, and under Ministerial control.[1] As education remained a State responsibility after Federation these colonial Acts (popularly known as the "free, compulsory and secular" Acts) still constitute the legal bases of the centralized, State systems of education in this country, and therefore determine the type of education given to eight out of ten Australian children. It is obvious that anyone who would understand the character of Australian society in the last quarter of the nineteenth century must come to grips with this surprisingly uniform body of legislation, but most Australian historians, hurrying across the historiographical desert of the 1870s and 1880s, have had their eyes too desperately fixed on the landmarks of the 1890s to notice this phenomenon. The few who have taken notice have generally been satisfied to seize upon the alleged secular nature of the legislation, and explain it away as the product of sectarian conflict.[2]

Defining the Code of Public Education, 1872-1895

The Religious Nature of the "Secular" Education Acts

It has already been argued (see above, Chapters 4 and 5) that this explanation is too crude. It ignores the long-term influence of agnosticism, voluntaryism and liberalism which helped to produce the state of mind which found this "secular" legislation acceptable. These, it will be remembered, were the terms in which Gregory explained events in Victoria between 1851 and 1872; some years later Fogarty advanced a similar interpretation of the relationship between Church and State in all the Australian colonies,[3] and in 1957 Professor C. M. H. Clark restated Gregory's argument in his own provocative phrases. "By 1791", he wrote,

> convict ships had brought to Australia men and women with three quite different views of the world—the Protestant, the Catholic and the Enlightenment .... these are main themes in the history of that civilization in Australia. ... In the debate on the abolition of State aid one has the same grouping of interests and arguments which led to the secularization of State education. In all the colonies the marriage of the Rights of Man with Calvinism and the fear of Catholic domination provided the main opposition to State aid .... the secular liberals tempted into their camp the supporters of the Voluntary principle, and the men afraid of the "Satanic delusion." Thus the men of 1789, the Calvinists and the low churchmen united to drive religion out of State-subsidized education.[4]

However, in his search for the provocative phrase, Clark has gone too far; in asserting that certain groups united in order to drive religion out of the State schools (or succeeded in driving it out—his words will bear either meaning) he has been misled by too great a concern with the Victorian scene.[5] Gregory's interpretation, one must repeat, was only meant to apply to the Victorian scene, but the conclusive quality of his argument has been a standing temptation to others to apply his findings too readily to the other colonies. Nevertheless Clark's assertion has the virtue of forcing on us a close examination of the terms of the "secular" Acts. When we do this we are at once confronted by the awkward fact that these Acts did not drive religion out of the State schools. In New South Wales, Tasmania, Queensland and Western Australia the legislatures made specific provision for religious education, South Australia provided for voluntary attendance at Bible reading, and Victoria left the way open for local Boards of Advice to arrange for religious education if they desired it. Admittedly the new Acts insisted that dogmatic religious instruction could only be given to voluntary, segregated groups outside the normal school hours, and admittedly any religious instruction given within the school hours had to be of a non-denominational nature, but in saying this the legislatures had done nothing more than repeat what they had said many years before. In the "compromise" Acts discussed in Chapters 4 and 5, South Australia (1851), Queensland (1860), Victoria (1862), New South Wales (1866), Tasmania (1868) and Western Australia (1871) had all insisted that only undenominational religious education would be allowed in the public schools, unless pastors and pupils wished to meet, voluntarily, before or after the school day.

Anyone who cares to place the "compromise" and the "secular" Acts side by side will see at once that there had been a decline in the importance attached to religious instruction. In four colonies (South Australia, Queensland, Victoria and Tasmania) the legislatures had obviously decided that religious instruction in public schools was essentially a matter for pastor and parent to determine; clearly this decision represents a weakening of the Christian basis of education, but it does not constitute a decision to drive religion out of the schools. Moreover, this decision must be considered in conjunction with the decision taken in New South Wales and Western Australia where the new Acts retained the provisions of the old. The relevant sections of the New South Wales Acts made the provisions which are set out on p. 176; the two Western Australian Acts show a similar degree of identity. Both provide for general religious teaching as part of the secular instruction, and a period of voluntary, segregated, religious instruction. One must also remember that the critics who have seen in these "secular"

Defining the Code of Public Education, 1872–1895

Public Schools Act, 1866

Sect. 19. In every public school four hours during each school-day shall be devoted to secular instruction exclusively . . . and a portion of each day not less than one hour shall be set apart when the children of any one religious persuasion may be instructed by the clergyman or other religious teacher of such persuasion. . . .

Sect. 30. In the construction of this Act the words "secular instruction" shall be held to include general religious teaching as distinct from dogmatical or polemical theology.

Public Instruction Act, 1880

Sect. 7. In all Schools under the Act the teaching shall be strictly non-sectarian, but the words "secular instruction" shall be held to include general religious teaching as distinct from dogmatical or polemical theology.

Sect. 17. In every Public School four hours during each day shall be devoted to secular instruction exclusively and a portion of each day not more than one hour shall be set apart when the children of any religious persuasion may be instructed by the clergyman or other religious teacher of such persuasion. . . .

Acts the ungodly handiwork of a pagan, colonial society have apparently forgotten that two years before any Australian colony passed a "secular" education Act the British Parliament, in the Elementary Education Act of 1870 (Forster's Act), had insisted that public elementary schools could only provide religious instruction at the beginning or end of the school day so that parents who objected to this instruction could withdraw their children without interference to their secular education.

The novel aspect of these Acts is not to be found in any provision to drive religion out of the schools, but a serious and novel provision is to be found in the decision, common to all these Acts, to abolish State aid to denominational schools—a decision which does not appear in any earlier Act.[6] When this point is appreciated, one starts to wonder whether the "secular" Acts can be satisfactorily explained as logical extensions of the "compromise" Acts. The great merit of the Gregory–Fogarty–Clark thesis is its capacity to present the educational development of the colonies as a continuous and evolutionary process culminating in the "secular" Acts, but this interpretation obscures the fact that between the "compromise" and "secular" Acts there had taken place a significant (and even revolutionary) change in

Australian Education, 1788-1900

public opinion. "Agnosticism . . . voluntaryism . . . sectarianism . . . liberalism" were the terms of Gregory's interpretation, but to explain the spirit of the "secular" Acts we have to ask ourselves whether these terms had been augmented or diminished since the passage of the "compromise" Acts, or whether there had been a more subtle mutation in which all four terms remained, but suffered unequal growth.

The Argument for National Education

To answer this question (and to allow for the possibility that Clark only intended to say that certain forces combined *in order* to drive religion out of the State schools), we must examine in detail the attitude of the colonial legislatures to the principle of universal, elementary education, and here one is immediately impressed by the fervour with which the overwhelming majority of colonial politicians asserted that the State had a clear responsibility to provide (and if necessary conduct) an efficient system of schools. One is also impressed by the number of strands which had gone into this pattern of thought, even though one is aware that the whole pattern is derivative. Whether he knew it or not the colonial politician was heavily indebted to Macaulay, Mill, Kay-Shuttleworth, Huxley and Matthew Arnold, and the majority of colonial speeches on education are little more than earnest restatements of views long held in England. Thus, as in England, the central strand in this pattern of thought remained that liberalism which we have already discussed—that liberalism which, while not antireligious, was hostile to the claims of the Churches, and opposed the intervention of any authoritarian institutionalism between the State and the individual. The Churches were entitled to tolerance and respect so long as they did not attempt to disturb this social relationship, and by the 1870s there was little doubt in the liberal mind that it was the State, and not the Church, which should assume the responsibility for education.

Around this central strand a number of reinforcing strands

Defining the Code of Public Education, 1872–1895

were woven. The first of these was the "police" view of education. There was, of course, nothing novel in this point of view, for it had a very long history in English educational thought, going back at least as far as Francis Bacon who, along with Adam Smith, was frequently to be heard on the lips of the colonial politician in the 1870s. But it was Macaulay's famous speech on education, delivered in the House of Commons on the eve of the year of revolutions, which was most frequently used to bolster the colonial argument. Macaulay had begun with a highly-coloured account of the Gordon Riots, sixty-seven years earlier. "I do not know", he had asserted

> that I could find in all history a stronger proof of the proposition, that the ignorance of the common people makes the property, the limbs, the lives of all classes insecure. Without the shadow of a grievance, at the summons of a madman, a hundred thousand people rise in insurrection. During a whole week, there is anarchy in the greatest and wealthiest of European cities. The parliament is besieged. Your predecessor sits trembling in his chair. . . . The peers are pulled out of their coaches. The bishops in their lawn are forced to fly over the tiles. . . . The house of the Chief Justice is demolished. The little children of the Prime Minister are taken out of their beds and laid in their night clothes on the table of the Horse Guards, the only safe asylum from the fury of the rabble.[7]

All this the colonial politician loved to recount, but it was Macaulay's conclusion that he hammered home with the greatest fervour:

> Could such things have been done in a country in which the mind of the labourer had been opened by education, in which he had been taught to find pleasure in the exercise of his intellect, taught to revere his Maker, taught to respect legitimate authority, and taught at the same time to seek the redress of real wrongs by peaceful and constitutional means?
> This then is my argument. It is the duty of Government to protect our persons and property from danger. The gross ignorance of the common people is a principal cause of danger to our persons and property. Therefore, it is the duty of the Government to take care that the common people shall not be grossly ignorant.[8]

Australian Education, 1788-1900

But the most important aspect of this point of view was not its antiquity, but its power to convince men who would have otherwise denied it, that there was a need for State action. Thus T. H. Fellows admitted to his Victorian colleagues:

> Abstractedly I contend that the State has no right at all to interfere with education, any more than with a man's religion, or his food, or his clothing. Practically, I will admit the right, but only, I wish it to be understood when the matter is regarded as one of police, pure and simple. That ignorance is a prolific source of crime is an axiom nobody can be more fully inclined to accept than I am, and it appears to me that only to that extent has the State a right to interfere with the question of education.[9]

Crime, of course, was a matter of great moment to these respectable, middle-class men, and by an interminable quoting of statistics designed to show the connexion between ignorance and crime they succeeded in making one another's flesh creep at the thought of the lawlessness which lay all around them. With a pathetic confidence in the efficacy of the three R's to transform men's natures, they were prepared for the government to take up this burden of education, trusting that Adam Smith had been right when he assured them that "An instructed and intelligent people . . . are always more decent and orderly than an ignorant and stupid one".[10]

A second reinforcing strand was spun around Robert Lowe's jibe: "We must educate our masters". It is possible that by 1867 Lowe had all but forgotten his few turbulent years in New South Wales, and he would probably have been sardonically amused to hear that his *bon mot*, tossed off in Westminster, had reached the ears of the rough colonial democrats who now debated in those chambers where he had once stung governors with his mordant wit. But so it was, and up and down the land one heard the voice of the politician declaring that to put political power "into the hands of uneducated men, means that it shall be controlled by the cunning, crafty, and designing. . . . Our future political prosperity depends upon the educated insight and forethought of the people".[11]

Defining the Code of Public Education, 1872-1895

A third, and powerful, strand entered the pattern as men began to see a connexion between education and national prosperity. England's industrial leadership, so gloriously attested at the Great Exhibition, had, they affirmed, been overtaken as France, Germany and Switzerland, through the superior education of their workers, expanded their production. "Had England", the colonial observers declared,

> with the material at her disposal, been as free in giving technical education as other countries, she must have held first place in the list of nations. . . . No greater mistake can be made than for us not to take warning from her omissions. . . . Let the Legislature take a broad view of the matter; let us lay down the foundation of future greatness . . . by affording such facilities to every youthful citizen as will enable him, early in life, to cultivate his talents. . . . There is no time to be lost. Great attention is being paid to education in England, France, Germany and the United States of America . . . and we must fully enter into the race, in order that Victoria may attain the position which she ought to occupy.[12]

"This is a practical age", wrote the Vice-Chairman of the Technological Commission of Victoria, "and our education, from first to last, must be practical. Schiller observed, '*Ernst ist das Leben*'; and surely in this age of steam-engines and electric telegraphs our daily life *is* one of earnestness".[13]

Occasionally one can detect a finer strand as an Edward Cohen or a William Zeal proclaimed the role that education might play in the building of a national sentiment,[14] but it is rare to find any public figure who could think beyond the national interest to the cultural enrichment of the individual. If one were not aware that T. H. Huxley's biting comment on the State's reasons for wanting to educate its people had been made in South London in 1868, one would be fully justified in assuming that it had been made in an Australian colony in the 1870s or 1880s. "The politicians tell us, 'You must educate the masses because they are going to be masters' ", he informed his audience.

The clergy join in the cry for education, for they affirm that the people are drifting away from church and chapel into the broadest infidelity. The manufacturers and the capitalists swell the chorus lustily. They declare that ignorance makes bad workmen; that England will soon be unable to turn out cotton goods, or steam engines, cheaper than other people; and then, Ichabod! Ichabod! the glory will be departed from us. And a few voices are lifted up in favour of the doctrine that the masses should be educated because they are men and women with unlimited capacities of being, doing and suffering, and that it is as true now as ever it was, that the people perish for lack of knowledge.[15]

The Australian Need for National Education

Whatever their motives, the colonial politicians accorded well with Huxley's description of a "chorus of voices, almost distressing in their harmony, raised in favour of the doctrine that . . . if the country is not shortly to go to the dogs, everybody must be educated",[16] but very few of them were anxious to risk their careers by meddling with the dangerous problem of educational reform. Unfortunately for their peace of mind (and tenure of office) developments within the colonial society of the 1870s and 1880s soon turned a theoretical problem into a very practical one, and confronted the legislatures with a situation which, whatever its attendant difficulties, could not be ignored. The essence of the problem lay in the steady increase in population which went on throughout the third and fourth quarters of the nineteenth century. If, for each colony, we consider the increase in population—set out in tabular form at the top of p. 182—which occurred between the passage of the "secular" Act and the previous piece of educational legislation, we shall start to see the legislators' problem.

But this was only part of the problem. Not only was the population growing in each colony, but by its dispersion it was revealing the complete inadequacy of the school system. The land selection legislation of the 1860s and 1870s, while failing by and large to break the squatters' monopoly, did result in a large number of farmers (and their families) moving into the interior. When every allowance has been

Defining the Code of Public Education, 1872–1895

Colony	Date of "secular" Act, and population at that date	Date of previous educational legislation, and population at that date	Increase in population	Percentage increase in population
Victoria	1872 759,428	1862 551,388	208,040	38
South Australia	1875 210,076	1851 66,538	143,538	216
Queensland	1875 169,105	1860 28,056	141,049	503
New South Wales	1880 741,142	1866 428,167	312,975	73
Tasmania	1885 128,860	1868 98,738	30,122	30
Western Australia	1893 64,923	1871 25,447	39,476	155

Figures from C. M. H. Clark, *Select Documents in Australian History, 1851–1900*, pp. 664–5.

made for the obstructive tactics of the banks and their squatter clients, and when every allowance has been made for the inefficiency and failure of the selector, the fact remains that the Robertson, Duffy, Grant, Herbert, Mackenzie and Strangways Acts did create a new class of farmers. The exact number of farmers who were effectively settled by the selection Acts is almost impossible to determine, but there is little doubt that in New South Wales alone Robertson's Crown Lands Alienation Act put 21,000 farmers on the land between 1861 and 1882.[17] And not only the land drew men into the inaccessible corners of each colony. From coast to coast, long after the first frenzied decade of gold, the mineral wealth of Australia continued to create pockets of population far from the established cities and towns. There were still 52,965 gold miners in Victoria when the Education Act was passed in 1872; there were enough men in the mines of New South Wales to produce 2,000,000 tons of coal in the year the Public Instruction Act was passed; there were 18,651 people on the gold-fields in Queensland when the State Education Act was passed in 1875, and in the same year, when South Australia passed its Education Act, there were 20,000 people on the Wallaroo and Moonta copperfields. By the time Tasmania passed its Education Act (1885) "Philosopher" Smith's tin mine at Mt Bischoff was recognized as one of the richest in the world, other tin

Australian Education, 1788–1900

deposits were being worked at Mt Cameron and Thomas's Plains, the Dalley brothers' gold mine at Brandy Creek was yielding a heavy return, and Mt Lyell, not yet identified as one of the world's greatest copper-fields, was being worked profitably for gold. In Western Australia, when the Education Act of 1893 was passed, Flannigan and Hannah had just discovered the Kalgoorlie field, but Bayley and Ford's announcement of the fortune they had found by the native well at Coolgardie had already started a rush, and the lesser-known fields—Kimberley, Southern Cross, Yilgarn, Pilbara—had been thoroughly worked since the 1880s.

These, and a hundred smaller fields half-hidden in remote, scrubby gullies, were drawing men (and their families) away from the settled areas to create the thinly-scattered pattern of Australian settlement. And as they went to till the land, or dig the mines, or fell the timber, they drew after them coach roads and railway tracks and telegraph lines, with drivers to man the coaches, fettlers to lay the rails and linesmen to string the wires. By 1870 Cobb and Co. in Australia were harnessing 6,000 horses a day, driving 28,000 miles a week, and paying £100,000 a year in wages. By the time the last of the "secular" Acts had been passed the fettlers had laid over 10,000 miles of rail, and by 1870 all the capital cities had been linked by telegraph.[18]

All this lends force to Fitzpatrick's interpretation of the Australian scene after 1860. An industrialized Europe, he maintains, was now compelled to invest in the "new" countries to ensure a dependable food supply. Here, he says,

is a simple situation—the origin of a diversified economy in the circumstances of a population streaming away from the mines over an unfarmed land which could help to meet the needs of the trading and producing world, after the application to it of capital, skill and labour.[19]

But, as Fitzpatrick goes on to point out, it was one thing to have a greatly expanded labour force, "unprecedented millions" of overseas capital pouring in, and a vast new market waiting, but it was another thing to make a reality of these opportunities in a country whose distribution of rainfall and natural resources would allow only sparse and scattered settlement. The Australian answer to this challenge was found in central government control, subsidy and support, though it has taken years of patient writing by our historians to convince our American critics that the pattern of resources in Australia demanded State intervention if we were to seize our opportunities in the late nineteenth century. *Le socialisme sans doctrines*, as Sir Keith Hancock has reminded us, is an apt description of a government policy which, having put men on the land by legislation, could only keep them there by doing for them many things which, in America, they could have done for themselves as individuals, a community or a corporation. It was in this fashion that the colonial governments of Australia found themselves directly responsible for the provision of roads, railways, telegraph, water—and schools.[20]

This is the essential aspect of the "secular" Acts, the terms "free, compulsory and secular" are not, despite their popular appeal, the essential features of this legislation. They are provocative and important terms, and must be examined carefully, but they are not the essence of the decisions taken by the colonial Parliaments after 1870. In every colony, theoretical and practical considerations combined to convince the legislatures that the State should see to the education of its children, and that the State alone was capable of doing this, for neither the local communities, nor the Churches, nor the existing boards of education appeared to be capable of discharging this national duty; even in the two most populous colonies, where these boards were most efficient, it was clear that honorary, part-time commissioners authorized to subsidize the provision of schools lacked both the legislative authority and the financial resources to provide an adequate school system. Despite the brave (and equivocal) statements in their annual reports it is obvious that they were, at best, educating half the children of school age, and that the denominational schools to whom they were distributing aid were diminishing in number and contracting upon the cities almost as rapidly as the population was increasing and moving into the interior.[21] It is little wonder that the constitutional basis of each "secular" Act was a decision to place education in the hands of a department of State under a Minister of the Crown.

Such a decision did not, of course, go unchallenged. There were many, no doubt, who supported the witness who told a Royal Commission in Tasmania that "It is as much beyond the function of Government to interfere with the education of a people as it is to interfere with their religion. . . . It is opposed to all the principles of free trade".[22] There were many, no doubt, like the hard-headed wheat farmers of South Australia who were opposed to any government extension of education as a waste of money, and an interference with the right of a man to work his children as hard as he pleased,[23] but fortunately for the future of Australia these were not the dominant voices of the late nineteenth century. Nor were the legislatures prepared to trust groups like these with any real responsibility for education; provision for local Boards of Advice there might have to be under the new Acts, but their powers would be negligible.[24]

The Argument for Compulsory Education

However, it was little use establishing an elaborate and costly system of national education if parents could please themselves whether their children attended school. Logically, this should have meant unqualified compulsion, but at this point the sponsors of the Acts found themselves hoist upon their own (liberal) petard. They might argue, as C. H. Pearson argued in his report as a Royal Commissioner, that "the State is the natural guardian of children against their parents", and assert that it was therefore the State's duty to insist that the child should be given "at least that minimum of instruction . . . which is generally required to make its labour remunerative",[25] but this argument could not silence the cry that the civil liberties of the subject were being infringed. The sponsors of the compulsory clauses were forced to modify their proposals, and politicians as experienced as J. W. Stephen, the Victorian Attorney-General who was to become that colony's first Minister of Public Instruction, realized that they must qualify their demands and appear content to affirm that "compulsory education is introduced in a very mild and gradual form". "I trust", Stephen went on,

> it will be admitted that it is not a tyrannical interference with private rights. . . . I hope that as soon as the law is passed it will be obeyed, so that . . . the compulsory principle, though it will continue on the statute book, will be a dead letter, troubling no one.[26]

There are minor differences between the six colonial Acts, but the Victorian legislation on this point can be taken as typical. Although parents and guardians were obliged to send their children to school between the ages of six and fifteen, they could satisfy the law so long as their charges attended sixty days in each half-year, and they could obtain an exemption if their children were "under efficient instruction in some other manner", if they had been prevented from attending "by sickness, fear of infection, temporary or permanent infirmity, or any unavoidable cause," if they lived more than two miles from a school, or if they were certified as having been educated "up to the standard required"—a feat which the average child could perform at about twelve years of age.[27] In practice, opposition to the compulsory clauses was so strong, especially in country districts, and the machinery for enforcing them so weak (see below, Chapter 7), that no colony could be said to have an effective, compulsory system until the twentieth century.

The Argument for Free Education

On another major point the sponsors of these Acts were also forced to compromise. To a man like J. W. Stephen it seemed that education

> being made compulsory, *a fortiori*, it would be sheer tyranny to fine a man who cannot . . . pay the school fees. . . . Once

Australian Education, 1788–1900

admit that all children, whether rich or poor, ought to be educated, and it seems to me to follow, as a matter of course, that the State must pay for the education of the children.[28]

But the prospect of free education was too much for many a liberal to face. Not only would such a scheme throw a heavy burden of taxation upon men of property, but it would surely sap the moral fibre of those who accepted this charity. Would they not, they asked themselves, "be opening a door . . . to the introduction of communistic principles"?[29] And so each colony continued for some years to charge small fees, either (as in Victoria) for "extras" beyond a stipulated schedule of subjects, or (as in New South Wales) for the ordinary course of instruction.[30]

The Religious Difficulty

Thus, each in its own fashion, and in its own time, the six Australian colonies determined that the State should compel its children to submit themselves to a course of elementary education. Parents could, if they wished, satisfy the law by educating their children privately, but the real concern of the legislatures was with the mass of children whose parents could not afford private tuition, or could not avail themselves of it because of their isolation. For these children the State proposed to erect a vast system of national schools supported from general revenue, and open to all. But how, in the face of the "religious difficulty", were these schools to be open to all? If one were willing to assume that all citizens were Christians, and that they were agreed upon a common Christianity, the matter might well be resolved in the way the supporters of the old Irish National system had advocated, and therefore the systems existing in most of the colonies might be retained, but by the 1870s the falsity of this assumption was so obvious that it was hypocritical to pretend that it fitted the facts. Nowhere were the implications of the "religious difficulty" so clearly, and ironically, manifest as in Victoria, where one member of the Francis Ministry which sponsored the "secular" Act was Edward

Defining the Code of Public Education, 1872–1895

Cohen, a leading member of the Jewish community. "This being a new and free country", he argued,

> let us leave behind us all the superstitious nonsense of the old world. Let us meet here on common ground. Let us send our children to the same schools, irrespective of creed or country; and let them there be brought up in that creed of kindliness and friendliness which will make them forget that their other creeds divide them,[31]

and his presence on the floor of the Legislative Assembly was a warning that even a school system based upon common Christianity would be too exclusive.

As the debate on national education continued the community was seen to be seriously divided on the issues involved. One student of this period (P. J. Pledger) has distinguished four main groups in this debate:

1. Those secularists who claimed for the State the right to control education, and wished to exclude religious instruction.

2. Those secularists who insisted upon the State's right to control education, but wished to retain non-sectarian religious instruction.

3. Those denominationalists who preferred the denominational system as a matter of principle, or interest, but accepted the compromise of non-sectarian religious instruction.

4. Those denominationalists who rejected the secularists' claims as a matter of principle.[32]

There is a clear danger in imagining that all the contestants in this debate can be fitted neatly into one or another of these categories; the issues (and the men) were much too complex to allow any simple and static pattern to emerge, but if this warning is kept in mind Pledger's classification can help us to an understanding of this last phase in the struggle between Church and State over the control of education.

Australian Education, 1788-1900

The Secularists

The secularists who sought to exclude religious instruction from the State schools were a small but heterogeneous group. Devout as he was, Edward Cohen must be reckoned in this group; the dogmas of his own faith, he realized, made impossible any universal declaration of a common religion—therefore if it were important that all children should be educated together, as he earnestly believed, religion must be excluded from the curriculum of the nation's schools. But Cohen is not the typical figure of this group; that is the role played by the colonial rationalist. Cable, in discussing the conflict between religion and science, traces its development in English thought through Lyell, Darwin, Huxley and Spencer, and goes on to assert that "The transmission of these strands of thought to Australia was not rapid. . . . Only in the 'seventies did the controversy reach the Antipodes".[33] This is a misleading statement which can only be explained by Cable's concentration upon events in New South Wales, for controversy on this issue was very lively in Victoria in the 1860s; to postpone its arrival until the 1870s is to miss the point of many of the arguments which preceded the passage of the Victorian Education Act of 1872.

This becomes clear if one looks at the spate of lectures and sermons which were delivered on this topic towards the end of the 1860s. The most comprehensive of the attempts to defend religion from scientific criticism was that made by Professor Frederick M'Coy before a large audience in the Princess Theatre, Melbourne, on 28 June 1869. In his introductory remarks M'Coy admitted that his previous attempts to show that "the highest scientific authorities with whom he was personally acquainted were amongst the most humble-minded believers of the great religious truths" had not gone unchallenged, but he felt confident that he could substantiate his earlier claim. Warming to his subject, M'Coy then set-to briskly for nearly three hours, berating Huxley and his supporters and declaring that there "was no

Defining the Code of Public Education, 1872–1895

authority either in Scripture or science for the belief in the gradual transmutation from one species into another"—a point which he developed in a subsequent lecture devoted exclusively to an attack on "the errors of progressive development, but also those of the somewhat modified theory advocated more recently by Mr. Darwin".[34] While Professor M'Coy was resting from his labours the Rev. Dr J. E. Bromby, in the same theatre, attempted another reconciliation of science and religion, with unhappy results, for his bishop (Dr Perry), who was the chairman of his meeting, found that "he did not agree with all the inferences he (Dr Bromby) had drawn from his scientific research".[35] In fact, so disturbed was Bishop Perry that he took to the same platform a few weeks later, and dealt with Dr Bromby, Huxley and Darwin in a two-hour oration based upon his belief that "the Bible has nothing to fear from Science".[36] The general relief of the clergy at Perry's handling of Bromby was well expressed by the Rev. T. M'Kenzie Fraser, who assured the Geelong Ministers' Association that Bromby's theory

> was not a long lived one. Its longevity was curtailed in the same ignominious proportion by a Bishop—his superior in scholarship and science—who in a few gentlemanly and polished sentences of a lecture for which the Christian community is under deep and lasting obligation to him, swept the rash hypothesis out of scientific existence, and courteously consigned it to the limbo of all error.[37]

This procession of learned divines and professors across the stage of the Princess Theatre in the winter of 1869 seems somewhat ludicrous until we realize that these men were not engaged in any academic reconstruction of the English debate, but were doing serious battle against a potent force at work in their own midst, for rationalism had been an active and vocal movement in Victoria for a number of years. By 1869, E. W. Cole, the proprietor of the famous Bourke Street Book Arcade, was sufficiently well known to be described as "daily suffering Persecution for his heretical writings, which the boldest Melbourne papers are afraid to advertise".[38] His *Religions of the World* (1866), *The Real Place in History of Jesus and Paul* (1867), and his *Essay on the Deluge* (1869), all published in Melbourne, are typical rationalist publications, full of the belief in the progress of humanity, insistent upon the necessity to seek and publish the truth wherever it might be found, and scornful of any belief in the supernatural. The Christian belief in the inspired character of the Scriptures was, he declared, but "another similarity in the religions of the world, and another of those expressions of the natural egotism of man by which he invariably places that which belongs to himself on the highest possible level". We can only view these books, he concluded, "one and all, simply as human productions".[39] But Cole's utterances were mild compared to those of his colleague, Henry Keylock Rusden, renegade son of the vicar of East Maitland (see above, Chapter 2), and radical brother of the National Board agent (see above, Chapters 2 and 4). By 1870 Rusden had published five pamphlets dedicated to the proposition that "We are all really atheists now, though only some of us are aware of it",[40] had formed the Liberal Debating Society (later the Eclectic Association of Victoria), had organized its lending library of scientific and rationalist publications and had sponsored a series of Sunday public discussions. In 1871, during a public controversy with Bishop Perry, he made a clear statement of the rationalists' educational argument:

> ... education is most valuable in so far as it is moral. ... Morality is based—not upon religion—but upon men's social nature and necessities. ... That very religious fervour which formerly prompted our ancestors to incremate each other for being conscientious—to subordinate real and natural to imaginary and supernatural duty—is precisely that which now interposes the principal obstacle to the establishment here of an effective (or secular) system of education. ... The suppression of the broad distinction between moral and religious needs and objects is so general, that I grieve to say that I know of no school in Melbourne much superior to the streets for acquiring moral training.[41]

Gregory, who has analysed this rationalist movement in

Defining the Code of Public Education, 1872–1895

some detail, has been careful to warn us that its numbers were always small, but it is hard to escape his conviction that it created an atmosphere of doubt and questioning "which helped to weigh the scales against continuance of the existing alliance between Church and State . . . and to reinforce the political arguments of liberalism against that alliance."[42] It is doubtful if the rationalists were as influential in any other colony as they were in Victoria (though they maintained a weekly journal in New South Wales for nearly two years, and produced some effective pamphlets there),[43] but there seems no doubt that their campaign for secular education must be reckoned as one of the forces which moulded the shape of the new Acts. It is, perhaps, significant that practically every leading newspaper in the colonies eventually endorsed the rationalists' conclusions, even though they deplored their reasoning. Not only the *Age* and *Argus* in Melbourne, but the *Sydney Morning Herald*, the *Queensland Guardian*, the *Brisbane Courier*, the *Register* (South Australia) and the *West Australian* all came, by degrees, to urge a wholly secular solution upon their readers.

The "Common Christianity" Secularists

George Higinbotham (lawyer, editor, Member of Parliament, Minister of the Crown, Royal Commissioner and Chief Justice) forms a link between the first group of secularists, and those who believed that non-sectarian religious instruction should be given in the State schools, for the trend of events carried him from one group into the other. In a short, appreciative study of Higinbotham, Vance Palmer has suggested that his appointment as editor of the *Argus* within two years of his arrival in the colony "brought him into quick touch with the life of his adopted country, acquainted him with its problems, changed him from an immigrant into a citizen. He had to form an opinion on all sorts of questions. . . ."[44] But it could be argued that this experience was too drastic for the young immigrant lawyer of thirty, and forced him to make decisions on matters which he had not thought right through. It is clear, for example, that when Michie's

Education Bill was brought down in 1857 the young editor did not know what stand he was going to take. His early editorials on the Bill (3, 7 October) were cautious and non-committal; ten days later he came out strongly for the Bill, but this decision rested not so much upon his own convictions as upon the advice he had, in the meantime, sought from George William Rusden.[45] Armed with that fanatic's advice, Higinbotham seems to have committed himself to a point of view, the evidence for which was to elude him for the next ten years—a point of view which eventually reduced him to the declaration "I believe I stand alone here".[46] However, by his public pronouncements on the Michie Bill he was committed to the common Christianity group of secularists, and it was in this frame of mind that he entered the Victorian parliament in 1861; one of his first actions was to support Heales' Common Schools Bill (see above, Chapter 4) which appeared, at the time, to be the best compromise measure this group could hope for. In 1866 (by which time he was Attorney-General in the McCulloch Ministry) Higinbotham was appointed chairman of a Royal Commission to inquire into the operation of the Common Schools Act; in this sort of situation he was at his best, and friends and enemies alike paid tribute to his faithful attendance at every session, to his patience with reluctant and tedious witnesses and to the personal responsibility he assumed for the writing of the report.[47]

In January 1867 Higinbotham tabled his report—a sustained and stinging indictment of the Common School system. Substantially less than half the colony's children were enrolled in any type of school, he reported; ". . . the present system of education is inadequate in its scope and extent . . . inefficient in kind . . . enormously and disgracefully expensive".[48] To repair these deficiencies Higinbotham proposed, in a Bill which he introduced in May 1867, to create a Department of Education under a Minister, to make elementary education compulsory, though not free, and to allow the clergy to give "a common system of religious instruction . . . at a certain period of the school day".[49]

Defining the Code of Public Education, 1872-1895

The reasoning which lay behind this solution to the religious difficulty reveals not only the inherent impracticability of the common Christianity solution, but Higinbotham's growing awareness of his own untenable position. Like all the supporters of this solution he had started with the belief that "Religion . . . is an essential part of sound education"[50] and like them he deplored the divisions within the Church which created denominationalism, but by the 1860s he could hardly have escaped the conviction that, even if one restricted oneself to the Christian Church, there was no possibility of devising a non-denominational formula which would satisfy Roman Catholics, and no guarantee that one could devise such a formula for Protestants.[51] But before he would accept the fact that he had committed himself to a hopeless cause, Higinbotham had to go through a distressing process of disillusionment. Closing his eyes to the Catholic refusal to endorse his scheme ("almost all" the clergy supported him, he told the House),[52] and putting the best construction he could upon the Anglican evidence, he went out of his way to placate the clergy. He pointed out that whatever harsh things he might have to say about denominationalism, he did not intend these remarks to apply "directly or indirectly to the clergymen connected with those denominations. I believe that the clergymen of the different sects in this country . . . are foremost in liberality of views in respect of this matter of education".[53] The full weight of his attack on denominationalism was reserved for something he called "the sects themselves", but as plain men might well conclude that he meant the laity, he went on to assure the House that the impediment to his scheme came "not from the laity, but from the sects as corporate bodies".[54] One might imagine that once the clergy and the laity were severed from a denomination one would have little to fear from the dismembered thing that remained, but there was still life in these monsters, he declared.

> Their proceedings are not only injurious to the cause of education, but a disgrace to our social and political system. . . . And the real problem which the State . . . has to address itself

to is—how to get rid of these turbulent intruders upon the peace and welfare of the State household?[55]

This was pitiful reasoning from a man of Higinbotham's stature, and the last three weeks of May 1867 showed him how futile his cause had been, for as soon as he introduced his Bill (7 May) petitions against it flooded in from the Roman Catholic Church and the Church of England. The clergy, to conciliate whom he had gone to ridiculous lengths, had betrayed him, he protested; they had allowed him to gather the impression that he had their support, but now it was apparent,

> and it was never apparent before—that there are at least two large religious bodies which object to any education . . . that is not denominational in its character. I repeat that it is now apparent, for the first time, that the Roman Catholic and Church of England bodies . . . assert a determination to resist any educational scheme that is not denominational.[56]

It seems incredible that this statement could have been made by any well-informed person who had been in the colony since 1854, even when every allowance has been made for the equivocal nature of Bishop Perry's evidence before the Royal Commission. The more one studies the documents connected with the Higinbotham Royal Commission and education Bill, the more one is forced to the conclusion that here was a man who, having espoused a cause rashly and on insufficient evidence, had tried to blind himself to the evidence which had accumulated against his position. Before he withdrew his Bill he made one last attempt to justify this position. It was the clergy after all, he now maintained, who were the opponents of his scheme, while "the lay portion of the community are nearly unanimous" in support. Amid mingled cheers and cries of dissent he declared: "I appeal from the ecclesiastical authorities of those religious bodies to the laymen of this community",[57] but even here he had missed his mark, for he directed his main appeal not to the Anglican laity, who had in educational affairs practically renounced their bishops' authority, but to the Catholic laity who were much less likely to defy episcopal authority.

For the moment Higinbotham was unsure of his direction. The leading Melbourne papers exhorted him to abandon the common Christianity group; the *Age* urged upon him an "absolutely secular" solution and the *Argus*, from whose editorial chair he had once instructed politicians, now told him:

> The phantom of an abstract religion seems to have found no favour with any person but Mr. Higinbotham himself. Nothing, therefore, remains for the state but to refuse to concern itself with religious teaching in any form, and to maintain its schools for secular instruction only.[58]

Higinbotham was slow to take this decisive step, but when in August 1869 T. H. Fellows and Gavan Duffy moved a resolution aimed at reversing the trend towards State control and at allowing a "little free trade in education"[59] Higinbotham finally declared his support of a completely secular system. In a memorable resolution of his own he asked the House to agree:

> That a national system of religious education is at present rendered impracticable by ecclesiastical rivalry and dissensions, and by the unpatriotic policy pursued by the leading Christian sects. That the establishment of a public system of secular instruction, free from the interference of the religious sects, and under the direction of a Minister of the Crown, responsible to Parliament, is urgently demanded by the highest national interests, and calls for the immediate attention of the Legislature.[60]

The secularists had gained another, and a very influential, ally.

However, though Higinbotham and others might defect from the common Christianity group, a very substantial body of citizens remained loyal to its principles, and a man like G. W. Rusden, who first publicly espoused the cause in 1849, could support it unflinchingly for half a century.[61] It could be argued that it was comparatively easy for the

Rusdens of this group to stand their ground for they were never, unlike Higinbotham, called on to translate their principles into legislation, and thereby evaded the practical consequences of their theory, but this argument cannot be applied to Henry Parkes, who must be reckoned in this group. In a parliamentary life which extended over forty years (and included five terms as Premier) there was scarcely a year in which he was not engaged in expounding and defending his educational ideas, but although his political life was full of inconsistencies and although education, like any other issue, was only a pawn in any political game he was playing, he stood unshakeably by the principle which he had embodied in the Public Schools Act of 1866—that secular instruction in government schools should include "general religious teaching as distinct from dogmatical or polemical theology". (See above, Chapter 4.) This was, as Higinbotham discovered, a most unsatisfactory compromise to defend, but whereas the lawyer in Higinbotham had to abandon the compromise when he finally appreciated the weight of evidence against it, the politician in Parkes enabled him to defend it, as an idea, irrespective of the evidence against it. In the Public Schools Act of which he was the author, and in the Council of Education of which he was the first president, Parkes took a fond, paternal interest, blind to their faults, indulgent to their failings and emotional in their defence. Between 1866 and 1880 he made scores of speeches in defence of his brain-children and these speeches reveal that while he was capable of being worn down on this point or that—he could, for example be brought by slow and painful stages to agree that the Council should be replaced by a Department, or that compulsion was necessary—nothing could persuade him to change the "soul of the Bill", as he liked to call it. As the evidence mounted that the Catholic Church (and to a lesser extent the Anglican Church) rejected the Public Schools, he thought it enough to protest his good intentions. "Our system of education . . . had no aggressive spirit", he told an audience at Liverpool in 1871;

Defining the Code of Public Education, 1872–1895

it declared war against no one; it interfered with no one's preconceived opinions, nor did it in any way impair or tamper with any man's faith. . . . It opened the door to every child without distinction as to creed, sect, country, or colour.[62]

As the evidence mounted that the Catholic bishops were prepared to deny the sacraments to Catholic parents who sent their children to the Public Schools, he was content to affirm that "if the parents of the Roman Catholic Church were left free . . . they would as generally avail themselves of the advantages of these schools as any other class in the community".[63] Six times between 1866 and 1880 Parkes defended his Public Schools Act against well-prepared Bills or resolutions; on each occasion he ignored the evidence presented by his opponents and relied on his command of the House, his role of elder statesman, and his eloquence to win the day for him. And even in 1879–80, when it suited his political purposes to discard his cherished Public Schools Act, the religious instruction provisions of it were retained unaltered (see above, p. 176; see below, pp. 218–23).

The "Common Christianity" Denominationalists

The third group whose influence went into the making of the secular Acts were the denominationalists who were prepared to abandon their traditional position in favour of a policy of non-sectarian religious education in the government schools. It has already been argued (see above, Chapter 4) that by the 1860s the overwhelming majority of Presbyterians and Nonconformists were prepared to make this sacrifice for the sake of the voluntary principle; in general their acceptance of this situation was passive, but here or there, individually or in groups, they campaigned actively for non-sectarian education. Thus the Public Schools League of New South Wales (led by a Baptist, the Rev. William Greenwood), the Victorian Education League and the Education League of South Australia rallied a number of Nonconformists and kept up an unrelenting campaign for the preservation of non-sectarian State schools and the abolition of aid to denominational schools.[64] Here

Australian Education, 1788-1900

and there individuals or groups went right over into the ultra-secular camp, as some Presbyterians did in Queensland,[65] but the great majority of non-Anglican Protestants went only as far as the common Christianity compromise—with many misgivings and backward glances.

Essentially this is also the position of the Anglican laity who, by the 1860s, had virtually rejected the legal, social and educational claims of their bishops (see above, Chapter 4). Cable is positive that after 1866 we are only "observing the last scenes of a drama whose plot is already obvious, and the interest centres upon discovering when the curtain will fall, rather than which characters will triumph",[66] but the final scenes of this drama were not without their moments of suspense as the bishops tested the quality of the lay and clerical support they could still command. Some of the Anglican bishops (e.g. Riley in Western Australia and Short in South Australia) were not disposed to challenge lay opinion. Riley, a newcomer to the country, took the advice of his friend Sir Winthrop Hackett, accepted Sir John Forrest's grant of £20,000 as a lump sum compensation for the abolition of aid to his Church and schools, and went off to tell Synod that he was happy about the government's educational plans.[67] Short quietly accepted the laity's attitude, even though some of his clergy rebuked him for his willingness to abandon the denominational principle. As one of them complained,

> if the chief pastor of the Church of England had boldly made common cause with his Roman brother, the result which both really desired would have been wrested from an unwilling Government in the form of grants-in-aid to Anglican, Roman or other distinctive day schools,[68]

but Augustus Short had been in the colony since 1847, and he had long since learnt to appreciate the temper of his flock. Up in Queensland, Bishop Tufnell was less astute and during 1864 and 1865 he joined forces with the Catholic bishop (Dr Quinn) and the two divines set out on a public lecture tour through southern Queensland. Rarely has an

Defining the Code of Public Education, 1872-1895

Anglican bishop in Australia been so reviled by his own followers. As the two bishops moved through Dalby, Toowoomba, Drayton, Ipswich, and so back to Brisbane, and as their meetings became more and more unruly, the newspapers were flooded with protesting letters. The Ipswich *Times* (6 October 1864), after reporting that the bishops' meeting had been marked by "vulgar insults from the front of the audience", the manhandling of interjectors, and the withdrawal of the mayor from the chair, went on to describe Tufnell's position as

> a most pitiable one, for though he unquestionably delivered a very able and telling speech, he was totally unsupported by the members of his own church, who had no other feeling than one of painful humiliation at seeing their head pastor so compromise and degrade himself.

In New South Wales, though Bishop Barker continued to maintain the traditional Anglican position, no amount of exhortation could prevent the steady closing of Anglican schools. When the Council of Education began operations in 1866 there were 161 Anglican schools on its books; by 1878 there were only 71 Anglican schools, and the number of pupils in these schools had fallen by 2,200 despite the over-all increase in population.[69] When Canon Smith of Bathurst was criticized for closing his school, he replied:

> If the people of Sydney had set him an example for the maintenance of Denominational schools he would have tried to follow their example more strenuously; but, as a matter of fact, 100 Denominational schools had been closed before he closed his. What was the use of their fighting in a cause such as this?[70]

In 1879 Bishop Barker was left in no doubt as to the issue when Sir George Dibbs, on behalf of the lay members of Synod, delivered an ultimatum to the clergy. "If the clergy wished for the assistance of the laity", he declared,

> they must face the inevitable doom of the denominational schools . . . separate from their old allies of the Roman Catholic Church in this respect and endeavour to give religious

instruction in harmony with the inevitable course of the law of the land.[71]

The Denominationalists

In ever-hardening opposition to the rise of secularism stood the Roman Catholic Church which, almost alone, made up that group of denominationalists who were prepared to reject the secularists' claims as a matter of principle. During the 1830s, the 1840s, and the 1850s the Catholic hierarchy had approached each new educational issue empirically; Irish, English and Spanish as they were, the bishops had had to adapt their European outlook to the concerns of the impoverished minority group which made up their flock. Distance, moreover, made conference and resolution difficult, but even when they were able to meet (as in the 1862 Provincial Council in Melbourne) their discussion was conducted in terms of the concessions they should be prepared to make in return for State aid. But by 1869, when they next met at a Provincial Council, the bishops spoke with a much more militant voice, for two events had shaped their outlook. In the first place they had had time to judge the effects of the compromise Acts (e.g. the Victorian Common Schools Act of 1862) and they had discovered that the bountiful days of the old Denominational Boards were over. Wherever the new, "general" boards had taken over, they found that regulations had become more specific, government aid less liberal, and freedom of denominational action curtailed. The Catholic impression of this phase in our educational development has been summed up by Fogarty:

> In the third phase, however, most . . . details of management passed into the hands of the central boards; the local authorities retained only a vestige of their original powers. The conditions for qualifying for the government grants were more exacting and where, formerly, aid was given for land, buildings, salaries and books, in the case of the Church schools it was now restricted to salaries and books alone.
> By the sixties and seventies the result of these restrictions was becoming clear; the Catholic schools were gradually being squeezed out of the government system. . . .[72]

Defining the Code of Public Education, 1872–1895

Against this oppression each bishop had fought with whatever weapons he had at hand. In Queensland, Bishop Quinn withdrew his schools from the control of the Board of General Education until certain regulations were relaxed; in Victoria, Bishop Goold refused to recognize the Board of Education after he had quarrelled with its chairman; in South Australia, Bishop Geoghegan (and later Bishop Sheil) tried to make their schools completely independent of State aid. All these were spirited actions, but they did not alter the fact that the acceptance of State aid was becoming a more and more difficult problem to resolve.

While the bishops were adjusting themselves to this oppressive climate, Pope Pius IX published the encyclical *Quanta Cura* with its attached *Syllabus of Errors* (1864), and confronted the Australian hierarchy with a critical situation, for while the Pontiff had written with the European situation uppermost in his mind, every word of his warning applied with a devastating directness to the situation in the Australian colonies. The encyclical itself was an unambiguous condemnation of liberalism in general; the appended "syllabus of the principal errors of our time" categorically condemned eighty manifestations of liberalism, including the belief that education should be "subjected to the civil and political power", and the belief that Catholics could "approve of the system of educating youth unconnected with Catholic faith and the power of the Church".[73]

In the light of this admonition the bishops' task was clear, but the way ahead was full of difficulties. The Catholic Church in Australia had relied for so long on State aid, and had entered into so many compromises with the State, that it was doubtful, by 1869, whether the laity (or the clergy) had any real appreciation of what was meant by Catholic education, any grasp of its essential role in Catholic life, or any will to provide it by sacrifice and effort. So efficiently had the general boards done their work that in name,[74] curriculum, methods of teaching, textbooks and tone, there was little to distinguish one type of school from another, and the ignorant and the simple among the bishops' flocks could well be forgiven for failing to see the difference between the government-assisted Catholic schools and any other government school. Throughout the country Catholic children made up about 18 per cent of the pupils attending non-Catholic schools—a proportion nearly as great as the proportion of Catholics in the population as a whole. More difficult to combat than this indifference born of ignorance, was the indifference born of sophistication, for there were many who, while "calling and deeming themselves Catholics, even sided with infidelity . . . under the seductive banner of 'unbigoted liberalism' ", and preferred "to think with the opponents of their faith, rather than with their pastors and fellow-Catholics".[75] Even the clergy, by and large, were not yet fully seized with the reality of the task before them. To many, the size of the task was unnerving. With the government grant for salaries already amounting to £12,000 a year in New South Wales, with education in Victoria already costing the Church more than £20,000 a year, how could they possibly afford to renounce State aid? ". . . the great majority of the clergy held back", Fogarty wrote. "On the whole they did not seriously entertain any idea of establishing a separate system of their own."[76]

Catholic Reaction to Liberalism

In this challenging situation the bishops decided upon three main lines of action. They must instruct both laity and clergy of the danger in which they stood, and lead them to safer ground; they must, at whatever sacrifice, create schools in which there would be freedom for full denominational action; they must exhort, and warn, and if necessary punish, to establish a sense of Catholic unity on the education issue. These were all necessary lines of action—the *Syllabus of Errors* left no doubt of that—but each was calculated to inspire in the liberal-Protestant mind a political fear of the Catholic Church as an anti-liberal force. This restatement of Catholic ideals, dogma and discipline could not help but collide, head-on, with the whole liberal *ethos* of the late nineteenth century. Worse, this collision of ideologies would

Defining the Code of Public Education, 1872-1895

inevitably expose and inflame the sectarian bitterness and bigotry which has always formed an ugly scar across the Australian mind. It would be difficult to challenge Suttor's conclusion that "The proximate determinant of the Catholics' dissent, and indeed challenge, in this country, was the *Syllabus of Errors* of 1864. . . ."[77] It is often impossible to tell where ideological debate stops and bigotry begins in the educational conflict of the 1870s and 1880s, but it seems clear that it was this sectarian struggle which dominated the final stages of the education debate. It had always been there, as Gregory, Fogarty and Clark agree, but in the closing stages of this struggle between Church and State it assumed a dimension which these three writers have not fully appreciated. It produced the form in which the secular Acts finally passed into law—designed, not to drive religion out of the State schools, but to prevent the Roman Catholic Church from continuing its assault upon the liberal, secular State with the aid of the State's own resources.

There was, of course, nothing peculiarly Australian in this situation. The dilemma of the liberal politician faced with the anti-liberalism of the Catholic Church was a universal situation, and exposed the basic weakness of the liberal creed. In England, for example, while the tenets of his creed drove the liberal to the granting of civic equality in the Catholic Emancipation Act, or the granting of academic equality in the Universities' Tests Act, events such as Newman's conversion, or Manning's conversion, or the re-establishment of the Catholic hierarchy (the "Papal Aggression"), filled him with dread and produced the ambivalent response which Baron von Stockmar had described so clearly to the Prince Consort in 1847:

> The worst point in the attitude of Protestantism towards Romanism is that it cannot venture to be tolerant. Romanism which denounces and excludes every other creed and never surrenders the smallest tittle of its infallibility, forces Protestantism for toleration's sake into acts which are occasionally intolerant in fact. . . .[78]

Caught on the horns of this dilemma a Lord John Russell,

whose liberalism had often brought down upon him the charge of Catholic sympathies, could find himself sponsoring a Bill to prevent Catholic priests from taking territorial titles because he considered "the late aggression of the Pope upon our Protestantism as insolent and insidious".[79] But the English liberal's response to the Papal Aggression of the 1850s was mild compared to his response to the publication of the *Syllabus of Errors* and the declaration of the doctrine of Papal Infallibility (1870). It seemed to Gladstone, Morley records, that the *Syllabus* "challenged modern society in all its foundations, its aims, its principles, in the whole range of its ideas", and the Vatican decisions of 1870 moved him deeply. "For the first time in my life", he told one correspondent,

> I shall be obliged to talk about popery; for it would be a scandal to call the religion they are manufacturing at Rome by the same name as that of Pascal. . . . The truth is that ultramontanism is an anti-social power, and never has it more un-disguisedly assumed that character than in the Syllabus. . . . The proclamation of Infallibility I must own I look upon as the most portentous (taking them singly), of all events in the history of the Christian church.[80]

By 1872 he was declaring that the recent Catholic decrees resembled "the proclamation of a perpetual war against the progress and the movement of the human mind"; by 1874 his pamphlet *The Vatican Decrees in their bearing on Civil Allegiance* commanded a sale of 145,000 copies in twelve months.[81]

To understand the passion which underlay liberal denunciation of the Papacy in the 1860s and 1870s we must pause for a moment and consider the affairs of the Catholic Church in those years. And first we must recognize the tensions which had been created within that Church as it sought to understand and adjust itself to the behaviour of men in one of the most dynamic eras in modern history. At the centre of the Church sat the Roman Pontiff, and central to his thinking was the temporal power of his kingdom. It is hardly to be wondered at that Pius IX, driven from Rome by the Risorgimento in 1848, restored by

Defining the Code of Public Education, 1872–1895

foreign arms in 1850, invaded in 1860 by the Piedmontese revolutionaries and deprived of most of his territories was, by 1864, profoundly distrustful of republican and democratic sentiments. That there was a connexion between these political events and Pius's religious policies in the 1860s and 1870s is hardly to be gainsaid, but as E. E. Y. Hayes has warned we must beware of describing this connexion in too simple terms:

> To pretend that the Pope's attitude towards the irreligious tendencies of his times was not coloured by these happenings on his own doorstep is clearly as absurd as the opposite error, that which pretends that he 'created Catholic dogmas' to spite his enemies![82]

What we also have to take into account, if we are to understand Pius's actions, is the existence, within his Church as well as without, of a powerful intellectual movement which was seeking to reconcile revolutionary lines of scientific and philosophical inquiry with the body of traditional faith, at the very time that he was being confronted with, and despoiled by, armed revolutionary forces. Liberal Catholics, like the Abbé Lamenais, had been silenced by Pius's predecessors when they besought the Church to welcome the intellectual forces of the nineteenth century; the younger generation of liberal Catholics, Montalembert, Döllinger, Acton, found an equally hostile reception from Pius IX. When Montalembert, at a Catholic congress in 1863, spoke against religious intolerance he was condemned by Rome; when Döllinger, a few months later, addressed a congress at Munich and declared that science could not exist in the Church unless it breathed an atmosphere of freedom, he too was rebuked, in the Brief *Tuas libenter*. Acton, sensing that the rebuke to Döllinger also indirectly condemned his journal, the *Home and Foreign Review*, in which he had enthusiastically supported Döllinger, felt obliged to cease publication.[83] In a torture of doubt he wrote in the last issue of the *Review*:

> It would be wrong to abandon principles which have been well considered and are sincerely held, and it would also be

wrong to assail the authority which contradicts them. The principles have not ceased to be true, nor the authority to be legitimate because the two are in contradiction. . . .

Warned, therefore, by the language of the Brief, I will not provoke ecclesiastical authority to a more explicit repudiation of doctrines which are necessary to secure its influence upon the advance of modern science. I will not challenge a conflict which would only deceive the world into a belief that religion cannot be harmonized with all that is right and true in the progress of the present age. But I will sacrifice the existence of the *Review* to the defence of its principles, in order that I may combine the obedience which is due to legitimate ecclesiastical authority, with an equally conscientious maintenance of the rightful and necessary liberty of thought.[84]

That was in April 1864. In December, Pius issued the *Syllabus of Errors* and left the world in no doubt of the Vatican's attitude to liberalism. It can be argued (and was so argued at the time) that the non-Catholic world was not being addressed in the *Syllabus* and therefore had no reason to concern itself with its proscriptions; it can also be argued that the *Syllabus*, being a highly technical theological document, was only capable of being interpreted by the bishops to whom it was addressed. But in fact it was clear to any intelligent reader of the *Syllabus* that Pius IX, with the Italian political situation uppermost in his mind, had condemned the liberal Catholic movement within his own Church; the same intelligent reader could hardly be expected to refrain from asking himself to what extent the proscriptions of the *Syllabus* would determine the behaviour of Catholic subjects within liberal states? Argue it away as Catholic apologists might, Error No. 42, which in effect declared that ecclesiastical law should prevail over civil law where the two were in conflict, meant to a plain man that he was being asked to concede the whole basis of political liberalism.

It was in this atmosphere of apprehension that the liberal world waited upon the outcome of the General Council of the Church which was commanded to assemble in 1869. "The Syllabus", Hayes has written, "was widely regarded

Defining the Code of Public Education, 1872-1895

as a gesture of defiance hurled by an outraged Pope against the nineteenth century. The summoning of the Vatican Council was suspected of being intended to reinforce the Syllabus. ..."[85] The liberal observer was, in fact, hopelessly confused about the purpose of the Council, the Vatican did little to enlighten him and, by default, he took his opinions from the most prolific and lucid polemicists within the Church—the liberal Catholics. The Catholic historian of the Council, Dom Cuthbert Butler, has deplored "the atmosphere of suspicion and hostility" in which the Council sat and the fears stirred up in statesmen's minds "that in some way the acts of the Council were going to issue in a reassertion of the claims to temporal power. . . ."[86] But when we remember that English opinion was informed, almost exclusively, by the reports of two liberal Catholics, Döllinger (in translation) and Acton, we begin to see how this atmosphere of hostility was created. It is probably enough to quote one short passage from Acton's letters to Gladstone to establish this point. In January 1870 he wrote from Rome warning the Prime Minister that papal absolutism had declared war against

> the rights of the Church, of the State, and of the Intellect. . . . We have to meet an organized conspiracy to establish a power which would be the most formidable enemy of liberty as well as of science throughout the world.[87]

True or false, the impression of the Catholic Church which emanated from Rome between 1864 and 1870 was that of an authoritarian and reactionary Church in arms against the liberal, democratic society of the nineteenth century.

This sense of danger recurs amongst the colonial liberals, but here the danger was the more keenly felt because their enemy was so much more numerous. Never less than one-fifth of the population, and by 1870 close to one-third, the Catholics in Australia had always represented to the Protestant mind a very real political danger. Victoria's Registrar-General (a Catholic) was not exaggerating when he told an audience at St. Patrick's College that he had "seen it stated in broad print . . . that Catholics are striving with all their might to obtain more than their due share of influence in the Legislature, and interest in the patronage of the Government".[88] That was in 1856, the first year of responsible government in Victoria. By the time the secular Act came before Parliament in 1872 this Protestant apprehension had hardened into firm belief, and the fact that a Ministry led by the Irish patriot Gavan Duffy had been brought down a few months earlier, when the Premier was charged with an abuse of privilege in favouring Irish Catholics for official appointments, was not lost upon the Protestant electors.

The Hierarchy's Policy after 1869

It is in this setting that we must consider the effect of the bishops' new programme. Back in their own dioceses they set about implementing the decisions they had taken at the 1869 Provincial Council, and in pastorals, sermons, speeches and pamphlets they undertook the detailed instruction of their people.[89] They began by stressing the sacred and inalienable rights of parents and pastors to impart religious instruction to their children, reminding their hearers that they, the bishops, were responsible to God for the souls of the parents and children confided to their care. It was thus impossible, they argued, for any bishop to accept a system of education which did not recognize his guardianship over the education of Catholic children; the function of the State was not to interfere with or control the bishop in the exercise of his guardianship, but to protect, assist and foster him. There were, the bishops warned, three prevailing systems of religious instruction which they could not condone. The first was the system of general, non-dogmatic religious instruction which was unacceptable on three grounds. In the first place, such a system assumed that there was common ground on which Catholics and Protestants might meet, but there was no such common ground in matters of faith. In the second place such a system involved the selection of doctrines—a practice which was presumptuous, impracticable, improper, irreverent and one which Catholics, in Archbishop Polding's words, "dare not allow themselves".

Defining the Code of Public Education, 1872-1895

In the third place, again to use Polding's words, such systems were

> an engine of proselytism of the worst kind—a proselytism not to this or that form of Protestantism, but to the deadliest of all errors, indifferentism—the frightful notion that all religious tenets are mere matters of opinion, that men have neither treasure nor responsibility in the one revealed Divine Truth.[90]

The second system was that of Bible reading, which was not acceptable even if the Douay version were substituted for a Protestant version, for Bible reading, the bishops explained, even under the supervision of a Catholic teacher was neither sufficient nor safe religious instruction. The Church was the divinely inspired custodian of revelation, of which the Bible did not contain the whole; the Bible, of itself, could not be held to speak with authority—that authority belonged to the Church. The third system was that of secular instruction with periods of dogmatic religious instruction provided at certain times of the day. In cases of necessity, the bishops advised, this system could be used by Catholic children as the least harmful of the non-Catholic systems, but inherently the system was erroneous, for it was based upon the delusion that religion could be regarded as an ordinary lesson—like arithmetic or geography a mere subject on the time-table. The truth was that Christian education was a unity in which the secular and the religious could not be separated; every kind of instruction must be interpenetrated by Catholic doctrine, Catholic feeling and Catholic practice. While formal religious instruction was of the highest importance it could not produce its full effect unless it were given in a truly Catholic atmosphere, and unless its doctrines and precepts were woven into the pattern of the whole school day. In short, the bishops explained, they could not approve any type of mixed system. The only type of school acceptable to the Church was one in which there was complete freedom of denominational action—"in which the authority of the Church will be fully recognized, and that method of instruction observed which has for its first object the eternal welfare of souls".[91] These schools, the bishops went on, should be open to government inspection, but "we shall assert our right to our just proportion of the public revenues which are yearly set apart for the education of the people".[92]

This intention to create an independent system of Catholic schools was a direct challenge to the prevailing concept of a national system of schools, but it was likely to be dismissed as an idle threat unless the bishops could translate their words into bricks and mortar. Fortunately for their cause, by the time they met in Melbourne in 1869, the diocese of South Australia had provided them with a pattern of independent schools which they could all follow. In a previous chapter (see above, Chapter 5) we have already noticed Bishop Geoghegan's determination to make himself independent of government assistance, and the nineteen schools he left behind him in South Australia, though make-shift and ill-organized, were the foundations on which his successor, Bishop Sheil, was able to build an imposing structure. In the first five years of his episcopate (1866–71) the new bishop increased the number of his schools to sixty-eight, provided teaching orders in thirty-five of them, and more than doubled their enrolment; the Catholic Press of Australia pointed to the example South Australia had set. Most of the credit for this new system must go to one priest —the gifted, controversial Father Tenison Woods.[93] Called to Adelaide in 1867 to act as Dr Sheil's secretary, he was given charge of educational affairs throughout the diocese, created the office of Director-General (filled by himself), established a Central Council presided over by the bishop, and an effective system of local boards. Thereafter it was he who stimulated the efforts of these boards, examined prospective teachers, inspected the schools, laid down courses of study, methods of teaching and systems of school management, procured (and where necessary wrote) suitable textbooks, and, as editor of a Catholic paper (for there was no limit to his energies), publicized the growing prestige of the South Australian Catholic schools. But his greatest contribution to Catholic education in Australia was undoubtedly his success in staffing the schools with members of a teaching order. For years the bishops had tried to attract overseas teaching orders to their dioceses, but it had proved very difficult to find recruits for such a distant and insignificant part of the Catholic world where the orders were wanted, not to establish fee-paying schools for the well-to-do, but to pioneer remote, bush schools for the poor.[94] Father Woods's solution to this problem was the establishment of an Australian order, the Sisters of Saint Joseph, which he and Mother Mary McKillop founded at Penola in 1867. The success of this innovation was striking. Not only did the presence of the nuns complete the Catholic environment of the schools, but, as they depended entirely on alms, they made it easier for the bishops to risk the loss of government aid. Woods's policy was not accepted by all his colleagues, for some felt that in staffing his schools with nuns he had irrevocably broken with the State and had thereby deprived them of the financial aid they could not afford to renounce, but in general his methods gave a vigorous lead to the other colonies. In Victoria there was too little time for Bishop Goold to organize an effective system of independent schools before the secular decision of 1872 was upon him, but the other bishops, notably Matthew Quinn in Bathurst, James Quinn in Brisbane and Murphy in Hobart, took strength from the South Australian example.

To most Protestants the new Catholic schools were a further proof of the exclusive, divisive character of Catholicism. Here was tangible proof of Catholic hostility to the State, and although there could be no question of forbidding these schools, there was no reason why the State should encourage its own defeat by supporting them. Cut off all aid to Church schools, they reasoned, and the Catholics would soon be brought to their senses; they could not possibly support their schools for long without government aid, and eventually they would have to agree to come into the common schools like anyone else. There were some Protestant thinkers, like the Rev. F. B. Bryce of Orange, who warned that the cutting off of aid would only serve to consolidate Catholic opinion and perpetuate the dual system. Concessions must be made, he urged, in order to keep the Catholic schools within the common system or

> the Roman Catholic children now under the Council of Education in denominational schools, will be handed over to the teaching of the Jesuits. . . . Then there will be no inspection, and nothing to check the full tide of superstition. I, as a Protestant, would much prefer the Roman Catholic children remaining under the Council to letting them go to the Jesuits. The former will make them much better citizens than the latter.[95]

But events had gone too far for compromise by the time Bryce made his protest. The hierarchy had spent a fortune on the creation of these schools (the suffragan bishops of Goulburn, Bathurst and Maitland alone had spent £120,000 in ten years),[96] and it was unthinkable that they should now tamely hand them back to the general boards they had learnt to distrust. They had challenged the State, and there was nothing for it but to go on and win, but to do this they must ensure the full support of the Catholic community. There were still far too many Catholic families unconvinced of their error in allowing their children to attend non-Catholic schools, and unconvinced of their duty to support the new programme. In each diocese therefore the bishops issued the solemn warning that parents who persisted in sending their children to non-Catholic schools had failed to discharge their parental duty, and thereby committed a serious moral offence, were therefore to be regarded as habitually and deliberately living in a state of sin, and as having excluded themselves from the Sacraments.[97] This is a critical point in the struggle, for by this exercise of discipline the bishops confronted the liberal-Protestant mind with an epitome of all that it feared and detested in Roman Catholic thought. To the liberal mind the power to punish men for the exercise of their private judgment in religious matters was tyranny—"this terrible tyranny", as Parkes called it. "As far as I understand the Roman Catholic faith", he declared, "you might as well threaten a person with physical death as threaten him with the withdrawal of the ordinances of his church. You are pushing a man to the brink of a precipice. . . ."[98]

After 1869 it was inevitable that the liberal State and the Roman Catholic Church should abandon their existing educational relationship and establish a new one, but it was by no means inevitable that it should have taken the drastic form which it did. The abolition of State aid to denominational schools was an old issue which had come before the colonial legislatures again and again over the years, but on every occasion liberal opinion had held that no Christian sect should be penalized because its principles and practices differed from those of other sects. It seems clear at this distance that the hierarchy's final bid to secure Catholic unity was so repugnant to the liberal-Protestant mind, and awakened so many fears of Catholic political domination, that only complete rejection of the Catholic case was possible. Academically, the colonial liberals, like their brethren in Europe, had long been aware of the seriousness of the Catholic campaign against liberalism, but suddenly the issue ceased to be academic, became immediate and tangible enough to provoke them to action in defence of their liberalism, and to revive in the minds of thousands who had never considered the matter academically, a latent bigotry.

Abolition of State Aid in Victoria

This moment of crisis, this moment of over-reaching and revulsion, came first in Victoria; once the Catholic Church and the liberal State had joined issue there, the outcome of the conflict could be predicted in the other colonies. In most of them the protagonists were aware that they were repeating, for form's sake, a debate whose outcome could be guessed, and it will be enough if we consider the course of events in only three of the colonies—Victoria, New South Wales and Western Australia.[99] In Victoria the religious difficulty in education was never far from the centre of politics after Higinbotham's abortive Bill of 1867 had stimulated debate, but the education question had become dangerously entangled with sectarianism by the time Charles Gavan Duffy took office as Premier in June 1871. It is hard at this distance to appreciate the violence of the emotions Duffy inspired in Victorian society. An Irish rebel, the close associate of O'Connell, a man who had been arraigned for sedition and treason, he was accepted from the moment of his arrival in Victoria as the political and social leader of the Irish-Catholics. His followers quickly provided him with the necessary property qualification and elected him to the Legislative Assembly in 1856. There his undoubted ability and his experience in the House of Commons soon made him prominent, and within four months he was a member of O'Shanassy's first Ministry. O'Shanassy himself had long been an object of suspicion to the Protestant electors of Victoria, but as Duffy began to eclipse the older man their suspicion and antagonism centred upon the newcomer. By the time he formed his own Ministry in 1871 Duffy was the focal point of sectarian rancour. A year later his Ministry had fallen, but his defeat did nothing to lessen Protestant fears of Catholic political action, for it had been caused by his abuse of patronage in securing appointments for his co-religionists. When Duffy's Ministry fell, the governor refused a dissolution and commissioned J. G. Francis to form a government, but the political practice of the time required his Ministers to present themselves to their constituents for confirmation, and it was in the midst of these elections, and in the shadow of the Duffy scandal, that Bishop Goold issued a Pastoral Admonition on the education issue.

In a statement ordered to be read in all Catholic churches of the diocese on Sunday, 23 June 1872, the bishop told his flock that the Francis Government "boldly and defiantly tell you it is their determination to do away with your schools, and substitute for them Godless schools, to which they will compel you, under penalty (or imprisonment) to send your children". Would Catholics, he asked, tolerate

> a return to that hateful oppression and tyranny which for centuries stamped out Catholic education in the old country?

... be mindful of your conscientious obligations, and refuse your votes to those ... who are in favor of a scheme of Godless compulsory education. He who commits himself by his vote to such a scheme places himself at once in opposition to the Church. . . .[100]

The next morning the Melbourne papers united in denunciation of Goold's tactics. In misrepresenting the compulsory aspect of the Francis Government's education policy the bishop was exploiting the ignorance of many of his followers, they declared; his warning of the consequences of disregarding his advice revealed "the amount of ecclesiastical coercion that will be brought to bear in order to subordinate an Australian policy to the policy of the pontificate." His statement was a "furious anathema", a "wilful calumny" typical of an institution which had "systematically repressed and discouraged the growth of human thought and . . . erect[ed] a huge and hideous fabric of priestcraft over the grave of moral and intellectual freedom". "Beaten in the Legislative Assembly", the *Argus* went on, "Mr. Duffy takes refuge behind the altar".[101]

The election campaign, which had already been marked by sectarian bitterness, now became an open struggle between Catholics and non-Catholics. Edward Cohen told his constituents that his opponent was "the dirty tool of a party who were dissatisfied with everything but the control of State by Church",[102] and both newspapers, on the morning of the election, told their readers that the real issue was simply whether they would or would not submit to "episcopal dictation".[103] The *Argus* brutally affirmed that the Catholics "must be taught that whenever they bring their ecclesiastical organization to bear on political matters, every other party will combine to oppose them, irrespective altogether of the merits of the case".[104] On 26 June 1872 the Francis Ministry was confirmed in office; Bishop Goold's bid "to control the hustings from the altar"[105] had failed, but the full effects of his action had yet to be resolved. How far-reaching and drastic they proved to be is apparent in the behaviour of the Attorney-General-elect, J. W. Stephen.

Australian Education, 1788-1900

The night before Bishop Goold issued his Pastoral Admonition, Stephen had addressed his constituents in the St Kilda Town Hall. He reminded his listeners that he had always opposed any attempt to coerce any sect and that, as a prominent Anglican, he knew that some of his fellow-Anglicans and many Catholics "make it a matter of conscience to have religion taught in their schools. I say let them have it so taught, and compromise with them by giving some aid towards it". But there was a party, he went on, "of whom George Higinbotham is one", which would do all in its power to destroy the denominational schools.

> That I cannot go in for, because I feel that would involve a spirit of persecution, and that is what I and my colleagues, as I understand them, wish if possible to stop short of. But we cannot stand against a torrent. If you run us down in this way, if we are to be persecuted by the leaders of a particular denomination . . . we shall for self-defence have to throw ourselves heartily and entirely with those who are the extreme opponents of that particular denomination and that system of tyranny. . . . I give you fair notice, and I give the world fair notice, and I give the colony fair notice that my future conduct will be entirely guided by the course of events.[106]

The next morning the Pastoral Admonition was read in all Catholic churches, and at St Mary's, St Kilda, Father Corbett chose to embellish his bishop's statement by launching a personal attack on Stephen in which he accused him of venality. Almost immediately Father Corbett discovered that he had been completely misinformed and he wrote at once to Stephen withdrawing the charges ("which I regret to have made"), but the damage had been done.[107] When Stephen went before his constituents again a few nights later, he went with Corbett's letter in his hand. He still affirmed his desire to treat all sects in a spirit of toleration, but he made it clear that the clergy's attempt to misrepresent him and his colleagues would not be tolerated. Amid cheers and interruptions he declared:

> The thin edge of the wedge had already been introduced into the Catholic body and they must allow him to say that the end

of that wedge was a very sharp one. That wedge was education. It had already been introduced, it would be driven home, and it would rend the Catholics asunder.[108]

Three months later it was Stephen who introduced the Education Bill which abolished State aid to the denominational schools.

Abolition of State Aid in New South Wales

The events of 1879-80 in New South Wales are saved from being a stale repetition of the Victorian events by the stature of the antagonists, Sir Henry Parkes and Archbishop Vaughan. They were both formidable men. In 1879, when the conflict reached its most bitter stage, Parkes was sixty-four, but he had lost none of his vigour, and a Ministry he formed eight years later is generally regarded as his most notable. Vaughan was forty-five; he had been five years in the colony and had been Archbishop of Sydney for a little over two years.[109] If, as Fogarty has suggested, Vaughan had been reluctant to force the issue and had been impelled to it by his suffragan bishops, he nevertheless brought to the controversy the strength of his deep scholarship, the compelling force of his character and his remarkable powers of oratory.[110] Both men were outstanding public speakers, and in the closing months of 1879 and the early months of 1880 the people of New South Wales witnessed one of the most passionate and brilliant debates of the late nineteenth century.

It would be ridiculous to suggest that the issue suddenly sprang into life in June 1879, though Parkes often tried to give that impression, for both parties to the conflict had been manœuvring for position for years.[111] The whole development of the hierarchy's programme after 1869 had been a complicated tactical move and, as Professor Martin has demonstrated, Parkes had been engaged in very delicate negotiations with Catholic politicians ever since bankruptcy had forced him to resign his seat in 1870.[112] There can be no doubt that Parkes was virulently anti-Catholic, that he held strong views on the duty of the State to see that all children were educated, and that he had little faith in the

Australian Education, 1788–1900

denominations' capacity or willingness to provide that education. The Churches had suffered a major set-back under the terms of Parkes's Public Schools Act of 1866 (see above, pp. 123–25); the Churches in general, and the Roman Catholic Church in particular, could only have regarded that Act as a first instalment of Parkes's policy. When next he came to power, they must have surmised, there would surely be further limitations placed on their education systems. But the Parkes who returned to power in 1872 was loud in his protestations that there was to be no change in the 1866 Act—and this for the very good reason that the Premier was only in office by virtue of Catholic votes. This strange alliance had been forged in 1870 when Parkes, not yet clear of the bankruptcy court, began to mend his political fences. First, an old but impaired friendship with Charles Gavan Duffy was revived and then, through him, another similar friendship with Edward Butler, the leader of the Catholic party. Butler, promised the post of Attorney-General in the next Parkes Ministry, set to work to organize the Catholic vote and was soon advising Parkes:

> I have begun today to work for you with our people. . . . I have arrangements made . . . that in the northern district I shall communicate with influential persons there and they will get a large amount of the Catholic support throughout the electorates for any person I recommend. . . . Will you say as soon as you can whether you can give me a list of men and as for the western district I want the information for Dr Quinn [Catholic Bishop of Bathurst] before he leaves town.[113]

By the time the election results came in Butler was able to assert: "never has there been a better day's work for the country. . . . Our people stood true to their promises for you. . . ."[114]

For all Butler's enthusiasm he must have been aware how artificial and cynical this alliance was; his own archbishop had long regarded Parkes as the most hateful man he knew,[115] and no Catholic leader could have had any confidence in Parkes's new-found concern for the denominational schools. Nevertheless, for the moment the Catholic schools were safe, and perhaps the exigencies of faction politics would force Parkes into a more binding agreement with the Catholic voters? But all such hopes were illusory. Parkes was constantly assessing the composition of his electoral and parliamentary support and was ever-ready to realign his forces. By 1873 he felt confident enough to break his formal alliance with Butler; by 1876, sensing the growing strength of the secularists, he openly broke with the Catholics on the education question;[116] in June 1879 he stated cryptically that "whenever the Education Question was opened it would not be in favour of Denominational Schools".[117] At this, Fogarty claims, Vaughan and his suffragans realized that unless they moved swiftly the initiative would be lost to them. "They could", he wrote, ". . . put off making a decision—and be caught unprepared as Goold had been in Victoria (by the suddenness of the 1872 Act)—or they could anticipate the seemingly inevitable break and rouse their people before parliament made the next move. The situation was critical. . . ."[118]

Vaughan and his three suffragan bishops met immediately, and the archbishop was at last persuaded that he must act boldly—must "bring things to a crisis", to use his own phrase.[119] Together they composed and signed the provocative Joint Pastoral Letter on Education of June 1879, which Vaughan immediately followed up with five Pastoral Letters of his own; at the same time he delivered a great number of public speeches in and around Sydney, expanding the points he was making in his Pastorals, and answering his critics. The greater part of the Joint Pastoral Letter was taken up with an exposition of the nature of Catholic education, but thereafter the archbishop was mainly concerned to make three points. The most important of these was his condemnation of liberalism, for as he saw so clearly this was the real issue, this was the evil thing to be conquered, this was the "wound in the world's heart . . . the master error of the age . . . the Great Apostasy".[120] The reaction to this attack on liberalism was immediate and violent, for although anyone who could read must have known for years that the Catholic Church condemned liberalism, neither Vaughan (nor Polding before him) had ever gone out of his way to attack it as it manifested itself in Sydney. But now Vaughan had struck not only at liberalism as a system of ideas, but at a tangible manifestation of this creed—the public schools of New South Wales, which their supporters were now appalled to hear described as

> seed plots of future immorality, infidelity, and lawlessness, being calculated to debase the standard of human excellence, and to corrupt the political, social, and individual life of future citizens. . . . I would call these schools "Scavengers' daughters," because they are the most effective instruments invented by man for squeezing very gradually and almost imperceptibly the Catholic faith out of a Catholic people.

It was observable, he went on, that the faith of the children who attended these schools was

> visibly enfeebled, not to allude to their morality: their manners are rough and irreverent: they have little sense of respect and gentleness: they have no attraction for prayer or for the Sacraments; and promise to swell a class which is already far too large in number. Our clergy look on the future of such wild, uncurbed children with grave misgivings. . . . The clergy were continually lamenting the gradual weakening of faith amongst the young, and the "larrikinism" which seemed to be fostered by Public schools.[121]

Nothing could have stung Parkes more than this attack on the schools which he had created, and presided over, with so much pride. With feigned indignation he recalled the many years during which he had protected the Catholic schools from the secularists' attacks, and declared:

> What the secularists had failed to do by their many motions the Archbishop and his associates had contrived to do by one blind move. . . . I felt, in common with tens of thousands that a wanton and libelous attack had been made on our schools. . . . After much consultation it was decided to introduce a Bill to repeal the Act of 1866.[122]

But Parkes was to hear more to disturb and provoke him before the archbishop had finished, for in developing his second main argument Vaughan asserted that since

Catholics could not, under any circumstances, use these "seed plots of future immorality" it followed that they must have separate schools supported from the general revenue to which Catholics had contributed. Anything less than this could only be called tyranny—"a modern monstrosity of cruelty and tyranny": "the tyranny of the majority . . . often more unbearable than that of a single despot".[123] "I will not conceal from you", he told the Irish working men of Balmain,

> that there are signs in the heavens of that which of all things else in a free country is likely to produce such a storm as no bishop or priest would be able to avert. I refer to the spirit of tyranny and persecution that seems as if it was about to be unchained.[124]

And if the Irish were thus aroused, Vaughan asked, who must bear the responsibility? "You all know", he told another audience,

> the world knows, what their faith is to them. It is the light of their eyes and the love of their hearts, entwined, as it is, with an undying patriotism which intensifies and vivifies the very texture of their religion. How can you expect them in this free country tamely to submit to the indignity of being fined or . . . robbed because they educate their young ones according to their conscience? Am I responsible for the deep resentment that springs up spontaneously in the Irish heart when their faith and their civil and religious liberty are trampled on?[125]

To such a question the liberal had to answer "Yes", for in the closing months of 1879 it seemed to him that Vaughan was deliberately exploiting the Irish sense of persecution; by misrepresenting the public schools, and at the same time reiterating the threat of damnation for those who disobeyed the Church's order to vacate them, the archbishop was, as the liberal saw it, exercising an authority over men's minds which was tyrannical. The word "tyranny" occurs in nearly every speech in this debate, and few things reveal so clearly the gulf which separated the liberal and the Catholic mind as the construction each party put upon the word.

In this inflamed state of public opinion Vaughan's third main point, his exhortation to his flock to assert their civic rights, to "organize our strength, and unite as one man",[126] took on a sinister note to the Protestant elector, and although Vaughan continually reminded his flock that they must use only "legitimate pressure" to obtain their just ends, remarks such as "Mark every man who votes on that 26th clause"[127] produced a spasm of political fear.

It would be hard to exaggerate the violence of the controversy provoked by Vaughan's Pastorals and speeches. A study of the Sydney Press between July 1879 and January 1880 reveals a frightening degree of bitterness, and illustrates the extent to which Vaughan's campaign had inflamed and terrified the Protestant majority. By the time the Public Instruction Bill came before the House early in 1880 there was no longer any hope of moderation. In his second reading speech Parkes made no attempt at conciliation. Unabashed, he again reminded his listeners of his record as a champion of the denominational schools, then he went on:

> when the time arrived when not only the secularists opposed religious teaching in the schools but when the denominationalists themselves turned round upon these schools . . . when one audacious prelate at the head of a great denomination denounced our public schools . . . it was when that state of affairs occurred, and connecting that with what was apparent in other English-speaking communities all over the face of the earth that I recognized the necessity for a step. I say that it was when I saw the disposition to establish an ecclesiastical tyranny in the country, dangerous to the liberty of the subject, dangerous to the growth of the free national spirit . . . I thought it best to lend my assistance to the extension . . . of the Act of 1866. . . .[128]

When the time came to vote on the Bill only four, Catholic, members of the New South Wales Parliament opposed it.

Abolition of State Aid in Western Australia

After the Parkes-Vaughan debate there was little left to say; by the time Sir John Forrest reluctantly agreed to abolish State aid to the denominational schools of Western

Defining the Code of Public Education, 1872-1895

Australia (1895) Vaughan was dead, Parkes was dying, and the issue was moribund. Despite their isolation few people in Western Australia could have thought that their education problem was unique or that there would be anything novel about its solution. Weld's dual system of 1871 (see above, Chapter 5) had been an anachronism from the day it was gazetted, and informed opinion had long been convinced that as soon as Western Australia achieved responsible government the secular trend of society would manifest itself in the abolition of State aid.[129] At the end of 1890 the first responsible Ministry took office; almost immediately the secularists began their attack on the existing education system, and the Roman Catholic Church began to rally its forces in its defence.

The arguments of the two parties followed, without variation, the pattern established in the eastern colonies. Liberalism was the great evil of the age, and secular education was "the shibboleth of an irreligious age and the outcome of thoughtless and spurious democracy"; secularism had led to an "alarming" increase of crime in Victoria, New South Wales, Canada and Birmingham, and had increased the incidence of suicide in France; the schools of eastern Australia were "Hot Beds of Immorality" in which children were to be found "doing those acts that make their fathers hang their heads in shame and their mothers' hearts faint with sickening tremours"; from these schools had come "a race of men distinguished only for the lack of every commercial and social virtue".[130] In the face of these evils and the prevailing mood in Western Australia it was imperative that Catholics exercise their political rights against any attempt to "outrage their conscientious convictions". "The time is over", declared the Catholic Press,

> when Catholics will consent to play the part of unresisting victims. . . . As affecting our relations to questions which, like that of education, have a religious as well as a political side, the formation of an association to guide and concentrate the entire political strength of the Catholic body becomes a matter of duty. . . . Its organization must be extended until it

embraces every eligible Catholic within the bounds of Western Australia, and each single member must be educated to an intelligent appreciation of the aims of the Association and an entire willingness to subordinate his own views and predilections to the judgment of the general body. . . . The only unknown element in Western Australian politics is the strength of the Catholic vote. For the future, until the cause of the schools is won . . . it will be given the fullest effect.[131]

The secularists' response to this challenge can be imagined. When Walter James, a member of the Legislative Assembly, discovered that Fr Brereton had been advising his flock on the candidates for whom they should vote, he berated the Catholic Church in words which were almost a paraphrase of the Melbourne *Argus* of 1872. ". . . politics can tolerate no religion", he declared,

> nor tolerate any interference. If we do not teach the lesson now we shall subsequently have to teach it. Whenever a Roman Catholic stands upon independent grounds he can rely upon independent support, but if he comes forward as a religious nominee . . . he should be taught that the State is made for the people and not for any religious body.[132]

"The primary duty of every man", another member told the House, "is to the State as a citizen. Afterwards he can consider the interests of his own Church, but not before".[133]

The Western Australian debate was heated, but it never reached the depths of bitterness found in the eastern colonies —a circumstance which must partly be ascribed to the personal influence of Sir John Forrest and the degree of respect which he and Bishop Gibney felt for each other. When he took office as Western Australia's first Premier, Forrest was already a legend in his own colony, an explorer of international reputation and an administrator of some experience. With his talented younger brother safely installed as Government Whip, and Mayor of Perth, John Forrest settled down to the creation of one of the most personal and paternal governments the country had ever known; when he retired to enter Federal politics he had been Premier of his colony for nearly eleven years—by far the longest uninterrupted term of office enjoyed by any colonial Premier.[134] However, the apparent stability of Forrest's government should not be allowed to obscure the radical changes which occurred in the decade of his premiership. From a tiny settlement of 48,502 in 1890 the colony expanded dramatically to 179,967 by the end of 1900 as the news of the fabulous Golden Mile brought gold-seekers swarming into the colony from the depression-ridden colonies in the east. Overnight Western Australia was confronted with the eastern influences from which it had been so effectively insulated, and as Forrest strove to maintain his supremacy in a colony whose newcomers owed him no allegiance, and at the same time tried to lead his turbulent citizens into Federation, he was faced with a political problem of some complexity.

To a man in Forrest's position the reopening of a question as explosive as the education question was something to be avoided, and as the pressure for educational reform began to mount he told the House that his Ministry had "no intention to disturb the existing Education Act at present. The only direction we would be inclined to go would be to place the department under the control of a Minister".[135] If his critics would withdraw their motions, Forrest went on, he "would consider the matter during the recess, and resolve what is best to be done", but when the House reassembled he protested that he was "not aware of having made any definite promise, and that the Government did not propose to do anything in the matter at present".[136] Late in 1893 Forrest tried to disarm his critics by introducing an Education Bill, but when the opposition saw that the Bill did little more than place public education under a Minister they called the Premier's bluff by inserting a clause refusing State aid to any but existing schools. Forrest immediately used his numbers in the Assembly to reject the new clause, and used the opportunity to read the House a lecture on political tactics. Such a clause as the opposition had proposed would only serve to provoke dissension and uproar, he told the House. "We have to do that which is reasonable, and which is politic, and which is expedient."[137]

In playing this cautious game Forrest was moved by more than considerations of political expediency, for there can be no doubt that he was also influenced by the respect and affection he felt for Bishop Gibney. They were both Western Australians to the core (Gibney had been in the colony for thirty years), and each respected the other's paternal concern for the future of the colony. "There have been pastors more able, more gifted and more cultured" than Gibney, one Catholic historian has written, but there "has never been a better priest, or a greater Australian missionary", and Forrest's letters to Gibney reveal the extent to which he endorsed this judgment.[138] For his part Gibney could tell Forrest, years after he had abolished aid to Catholic schools: "You have been so uniformly kind to me that I could not praise nor thank you too fully",[139] and even at the height of the controversy he could say to a gathering at which Forrest was the guest of honour: "Why, if you did your duty in this colony you would build a temple of fame for the man who is your guest of honour this evening".[140] However, by the beginning of 1894 Forrest must have been wondering how long he could allow his respect for Gibney to affect his political judgment, for it was becoming clearer every day that the Protestant majority in Western Australia was in no mood to continue State aid. All the newspapers of the colony had taken up the cry "Abolish State aid", and at almost every sitting of the House he was confronted by hostile resolutions. The elections of May 1894, which virtually turned upon the education issue, must have shown Forrest the drift of public opinion, and although for a little longer he was able to ignore its pressure it is clear that he was beginning to see the danger in which he stood. In the House the opposition became more truculent; in October, G. T. Simpson moved another resolution forbidding the extension of State aid to new schools. Forrest defeated the resolution by fourteen votes to eleven, but he had to listen to some straight talking in which, amongst other things, the political threat of the Catholic Association was openly discussed. The Vicar-General, one member claimed, was "reported to have said that no further concession is possible. Concessions from whom? It is startling to hear of a religious body talking about making concessions to Parliament and to the Government".[141] One thing, in particular, could hardly have escaped him. Whereas, in earlier years, everyone had quoted English precedents and ignored the experiences of the eastern colonies, now it was the eastern colonies' solution that was being urged, and the English one derided. "Of course I am aware that these denominational schools exist in England", one member protested. "But a different set of things exists there altogether".[142]

Here lay Forrest's political danger. With every increase in eastern migration his policies were becoming less acceptable, and his opposition more formidable. In October he attempted to increase the grant to both government and assisted schools, and found himself out-voted; in the next session a member moved: "That the policy of the Government . . . on the Education question is not satisfactory to this House, nor in accordance with the opinion of the Colony", and Forrest knew that he must give way. He asked the House to give him time to find a solution that would be satisfactory "to all parties concerned, on an equitable and honourable basis", and in August 1895 he proposed:

> That it is expedient that the assisted schools should no longer continue to form part of the public education system of the colony. . . . That a Joint Committee . . . be appointed to consider the terms and conditions on which it will be equitable to amend the law to the above effect.[143]

When the time came to sever the final links between Church and State Forrest demonstrated, at tedious length, the lesson he had learnt from his migrants. "We have been doing a great deal of late years", he explained,

> to bring ourselves practically into line with the other Australian colonies on many of the more important social and political questions of the day. We have now in this colony the same Constitution as the other colonies. . . . In other political questions also, we are rapidly bringing ourselves into line with the more advanced legislation of the sister colonies. This is not

to be wondered at, when we consider that a large number of the people who form the population of this country today are those who have come from other parts of Australia. . . . This bill is one which brings us into line with Australian sentiment and Australian thought on this particular question.[144]

Gibney and his flock accepted Forrest's decision with resignation. Irrespective of the amount of compensation offered, they would prefer to remain within the existing system, the Vicar-General told the Premier, for "we have got on well together".[145] Neither he nor Bishop Gibney had any real hope of reconciliation. Vaughan, who died in 1883, had remained convinced that precipitating the debate on State aid had been a wise tactical move. The violence of his attack must, he realized, produce an equally violent anti-Catholic reaction, but this would be short-lived as men came to see the justice of the Catholic case. "We may, and probably shall, be worse off before we are better off", he reiterated.

> When we have lost everything, then our day will begin. Then we shall make ourselves heard. . . . Our Teaching Orders will hold out an attraction which even non-Catholics will find it hard to resist. . . . Meanwhile the Catholic body will not sleep. . . . Thousands will join them who love order, decency, morality, religion. A reaction will take place in public feeling. And finally, Catholics will get all they ask and all they want. . . .[146]

But Vaughan had misjudged the extent of anti-Catholic feeling in the community. Perhaps he had not been long enough in the country to perceive that his co-religionists were not only politically suspect because they were anti-liberal, but nationally suspect because they were Irish; perhaps his aristocratic, English origins prevented him from feeling the full extent of the anti-Irish prejudice against his flock. Whatever the basis for his judgment, the consequence was that his attack did not so much create a national reaction as provide the occasion for expressing, in legislation, an existing national sentiment. Gibney, who knew his Australia much better than Vaughan did, and who knew the extent

Defining the Code of Public Education, 1872–1895

to which Australian Protestants regarded his Faith as "the tribal religion of the Irish",[147] realized that his Church and the liberal State had broken completely. "At last the doom of the dual system has been positively spoken", he announced. ". . . the struggle . . . has become a hopeless one, doomed to final defeat. . . . Therefore does the Church now freely lay aside her weapons, and ask for 'peace with honour' ".[148]

With Gibney's capitulation the last of the Australian colonies had determined that the State should no longer concern itself to support Church schools, and he and his fellow-bishops could find little reason to face the new century with confidence. Vaughan had predicted that eventually there would be a reaction in their favour, but it was now nearly thirty years since Victoria had cast them off, and there seemed to be no sign in that colony, or in any other, of a spirit of reconciliation. Vaughan might yet prove to be right, but it was hard to forget that J. W. Stephen had introduced the Victorian bill of 1872 with the words: "We wish to create a system of education for the whole country and we do not wish for rival schools."[149]

NOTES

[1] The Acts were: Victoria: The Education Act, 1872; South Australia: The Education Act, 1875; Queensland: The State Education Act, 1875; New South Wales: The Public Instruction Act, 1880; Tasmania: The Education Act, 1885; Western Australia: The Elementary Education Act Amendment Act, 1893 and The Assisted Schools Abolition Act, 1895.
[2] E.g. G. W. Rusden, *History of Australia*, Vol. III, pp. 559, 562.
[3] See Ch. 4, Note 1.
[4] C. M. H. Clark, *Sources of Australian History*, pp. xi, 355, 359.
[5] Four of the five documents he quotes to support this assertion are drawn from *Parl. Deb.* (Vic.)
[6] Western Australia took a separate Act to make this point; see above, Note 1.
[7] *Speeches by Lord Macaulay*, pp. 303–4. For Bacon's and Smith's form of the argument see Francis Bacon, *The Advancement*

of Learning, pp. 12-13; Adam Smith, *An Inquiry into the Nature and Causes of the Wealth of Nations*, p. 353.

[8] *Speeches by Lord Macaulay*, p. 304. For examples of the colonial use of this argument see *Parl. Deb.* (Vic.), Vol. xv, 1557. See also David Blair (Ed.), *Speeches . . . by Henry Parkes*, pp. 218-19; *Parl. Deb.* (W.A.), New Series, vii, 940.

[9] Ibid., 1355.

[10] Smith, loc. cit.

[11] *Parl. Deb.* (Vic.), Vol. xv, 1602; see also 1627, 1630, 1714, 1994. Lowe's actual statement was: "I believe it will be absolutely necessary that you should prevail upon our future masters to learn their letters".

[12] Ibid., 1600-3; see also 1714.

[13] J. J. Bleasdale, *Practical Education*, p. 24.

[14] *Parl. Deb.* (Vic.), Vol. xv, 1627.

[15] T. H. Huxley, *Science and Education*, p. 77.

[16] Ibid.

[17] B. Fitzpatrick, *The British Empire in Australia*, p. 140. Both Grant and Graham Berry claimed that in Victoria the Grant Act alone settled 30,000 farmers between 1865 and 1870, but the true figure was probably nearer 12,000. See Fitzpatrick, op. cit., p. 143, and Clark, op. cit., p. 135.

[18] See Fitzpatrick, op. cit., Ch. 5, and relevant articles in *The Australian Encyclopaedia*.

[19] Fitzpatrick, op. cit., p. 133.

[20] See Fitzpatrick, op. cit.; W. K. Hancock, *Australia*, Ch. 4; F. Alexander, *Moving Frontiers*, Ch. 4; G. V. Portus, 'Americans and Australians', *Australian Quarterly*, June 1942, pp. 30-41. This view is challenged in J. B. Hirst, 'Centralization Reconsidered: The South Australian Education Act of 1875', *Historical Studies*, Vol. 13, No. 49 (Oct. 1967).

[21] For estimates of the work of these boards see Hobart *Mercury*, 1 Jan. 1885; F. A. Milne, 'The Council of Education and its Work', unpublished M.Ed. Thesis, University of Sydney, 1956; P. J. Pledger, 'A critical study of the work of the Board of Education in Victoria, 1862-72', unpublished M.Ed. Thesis, University of Melbourne, 1959.

[22] Report of the Royal Commission on Public Education, 1867, p. v, Tas. H. of A. *Journals*, 1867.

[23] Douglas Pike, 'Education in an Agricultural State', *Melbourne Studies in Education*, *1957-8*, p. 68.

[24] The term Boards of Advice was used in Vic., Tas., S.A.; in N.S.W. similar bodies were called Public School Boards, in Qld. and W.A., District Boards. For an estimate of their effectiveness, see below, Ch. 7.

Defining the Code of Public Education, 1872–1895

[25] Report on the State of Public Education in Victoria, 1877, pp. 38–40, *P. P.* (Vic.), 1877–8.

[26] *Parl. Deb.* (Vic.), Vol. xv, 1343–6.

[27] The Education Act, 1872, sec. 13. Some colonies, e.g. Tas. (1868), W.A. (1871), had introduced the compulsory principle in earlier legislation, but had been unable to enforce it.

[28] *Parl. Deb.* (Vic.), Vol. xv, 1343–6.

[29] *Parl. Deb.* (S.A.), 1875, 383–7. See also Hobart *Mercury*, 27–8 Aug. 1885; Rusden, op. cit., Vol. III, pp. 561–2.

[30] Qld. had adopted the principle of free education in 1869.

[31] *Parl. Deb.* (Vic.), Vol. xv, 1674. Some members of the Jewish community supported the denominational system and were anxious to establish exclusively Jewish schools. Cohen asked them bluntly: "Were we not satisfied with the same amount of liberty as was enjoyed by our fellow citizens; or did we wish to return to our ghettos?" *Australian Israelite*, 7 Mar. 1873.

[32] P. J. Pledger, 'Secularism in Victorian Education, 1855–72', *Journal of Education* (V.I.E.R.), Vol. 3, No. 1, 24–5.

[33] Kenneth C. Cable, 'The Church of England in New South Wales and its Policy towards Education prior to 1880', unpublished M.A. Thesis, University of Sydney, 1952, pp. 131–3.

[34] F. M'Coy, *The Order and Plan of Creation*, pp. 1, 10, 23.

[35] J. E. Bromby, *Pre-Historic Man*, p. 16.

[36] C. Perry, *Science and the Bible*, p. 3.

[37] T.M'Kenzie Fraser, *Lecture on the Theory of Annihilation*, p. 2.

[38] B. S. Nayler, *The Battle of Science*, p. 12.

[39] E. W. Cole, *Jesus and Paul*, op. cit., pp. 51–2.

[40] H. K. Rusden, *The Power of the Pulpit*, pp. 6, 15. See also his *Tough Morsels of Theology; Christ in the Sepulchre; Moral Responsibility; Free Agency; Science and Theology*.

[41] Hokor (H. K. Rusden), *The Bishop of Melbourne's Theory of Education*, pp. 4, 6.

[42] J. S. Gregory, 'Church and State, and Education in Victoria to 1872', *Melbourne Studies in Education, 1958–59*, p. 71.

[43] *The Stockwhip* began publication in Feb. 1875, became *The Satirist* in 1876 and ceased publication in December of that year. See also the anonymous pamphlet *Education Versus Religion*.

[44] Vance Palmer, *National Portraits*, p. 95.

[45] A. G. Austin, *George William Rusden*, p. 122. See also Gwyneth M. Dow, 'Political Factions and Education in Victoria, 1857–8', *Journal of Religious History*, Vol. 6, No. 3 (June 1971).

[46] George Higinbotham, *Public Instruction Speeches*, p. 17.

[47] David Blair, the secretary to the Royal Commission, was astonished to find that the Chairman intended to write the Report himself; ". . . of that Commission", he stated, "Mr Higin-

botham was the originator, as he was subsequently its very life and soul during its existence." See Edward E. Morris, *A Memoir of George Higinbotham*, pp. 150–6.

[48] Higinbotham, op. cit., p. 4.
[49] Ibid., p. 8.
[50] Ibid., p. 18. See also George Higinbotham, *Self Education*, pp. 1–12.
[51] An "agreed syllabus" of religious instruction acceptable to the Protestant denominations in Victoria (and concurred in by the Roman Catholic Church) was not achieved until 1950.
[52] Higinbotham, *Public Instruction Speeches*, p. 6.
[53] Ibid. Either the clergy or Higinbotham had suffered a remarkable change of heart since the day, five years earlier, when he had said that "the greatest enemies to religious education in this country were the Christian clergy of all denominations". *Victorian Hansard*, viii, 1181.
[54] Ibid., pp. 6, 20.
[55] Ibid., p. 7.
[56] Ibid., pp. 17–18.
[57] Ibid., p. 22.
[58] *Age*, 28 May, *Argus*, 6 June 1867.
[59] *Parl. Deb.* (Vic.), Vol. viii, 1832.
[60] Ibid., 1829. For a detailed analysis of Higinbotham's motives at this crisis in his political life see Gwyneth M. Dow, *George Higinbotham: Church and State*.
[61] Rusden, op. cit., Vol. III, pp. 382–4.
[62] Blair, op. cit., p. 317.
[63] Ibid., p. 302.
[64] Greenwood was elected to the N.S.W. Parliament in 1877, and carried the fight into the House.
[65] Report of the Royal Commision on Educational Institutions of the Colony, 1875, Qq. 2174–84; 2210–2311, *P. P.* (Qld.), 1875.
[66] Cable, op. cit., p. 112.
[67] Fred Alexander, *Four Bishops and their See*, pp. 54–62; *Report of the Second Session of the Eighth Synod of the Diocese of Perth*, p. 35.
[68] F. T. Whitington, *Augustus Short: First Bishop of Adelaide*, p. 168.
[69] Figures from Cable, op. cit., p. 114. In Victoria the 214 Anglican schools of 1862 had become 157 by 1871.
[70] Quoted Cable, op. cit., p. 152.
[71] *Freeman's Journal*, 25 June 1879.
[72] Bro. Ronald Fogarty, *Catholic Education in Australia, 1806–1950*, Vol. I, p. 27. Although in the following pages extensive use has been made of Fogarty's material, it must be stressed that the form of the argument is not his.

Defining the Code of Public Education, 1872–1895

[73] Anne Fremantle (Ed.), *The Papal Encyclicals*, pp. 135–52.
[74] In W.A., State-aided Catholic schools were known as "Assisted Schools", in Qld. as "Non-vested Schools", in N.S.W. as "Certified Denominational Schools", in Vic. as "Common Schools", in Tas. as "Public Schools". In most colonies the general board of education insisted on the display and use of these names, and prohibited the display of the name "Catholic School".
[75] *Record* (Bathurst), 1 Feb. 1878; John O'Reilly, *Pastoral Letter on Education*, p. 14.
[76] Fogarty, op. cit., Vol. I, p. 173.
[77] T. L. Suttor, 'The Position of Catholicism in Australia, 1840–1900', A.N.U. Seminar Paper, 11 Aug. 1958, p. 1.
[78] Quoted E. Halévy, *Victorian Years*, p. 369.
[79] Ibid.
[80] John Morley, *The Life of William Ewart Gladstone*, Vol. II, pp. 508, 510–12.
[81] Ibid., pp. 519, 523–4.
[82] E. E. Y. Hayes, *Pio Nono*, p. 241.
[83] Ibid., pp. 266–71.
[84] Quoted Gertrude Himmelfarb, *Lord Acton*, pp. 59–60.
[85] Hayes, op. cit., p. 274.
[86] Dom Cuthbert Butler, *The Vatican Council, 1869–1870*, pp. 11–12.
[87] Quoted Himmelfarb, op. cit., p. 104.
[88] W. H. Archer, *Noctes Catholicae*, p. 2.
[89] The account of Catholic policy which follows is drawn almost exclusively from Fogarty, op. cit.
[90] Archbishop Polding, *Pastoral Letter*, 1859, p. 9.
[91] Decrees on Education adopted by the Archbishop and Bishops assembled in Provincial Council at Melbourne, in April, 1869, A. G. Austin, *Select Documents in Australian Education, 1788–1900*, p. 216.
[92] Ibid.
[93] Woods was a restless man, never at ease in parochial work. In his later years he devoted himself to science, and established a reputation as a geologist, palæontologist and ichthyologist.
[94] Bishop Brady had brought a handful of Sisters of Mercy to Perth in 1846, and some of them later moved to Victoria. Polding brought some Sisters of Charity to Sydney in 1839, and a community of Benedictine nuns in 1849. Quinn brought the Sisters of Mercy to Brisbane in 1861.
[95] F. B. Bryce, Letters in Defence of the Denominational Schools, D. C. Griffiths, *Documents on the Establishment of Education in New South Wales*, p. 158.
[96] Fogarty, op. cit., Vol. I, p. 249.

[97] Ibid., Vol. I, p. 215.
[98] Blair, op. cit., p. 302.
[99] In Tasmania, for example, the editor of the *Mercury*, after reviewing Victoria's education policy, concluded: "As others have done, we shall do sooner or later...." (6 Jan. 1885). As Tasmania did not establish any form of *Hansard*, the debate there must be followed in the Press of 1884–5. For events in Queensland see *Parl. Deb.* (Qld.), xviii, and the Press of 1875. There was practically no debate on the issue in South Australia as the point had been settled in 1851—see above, Ch. 5. The mood of the South Australian Parliament is reflected in Kay's comment: "Mr. Hawker had recently observed that too much was made of the idea of religious strife and discussion here—(Hear, hear)—and that there was very little of it. In that he concurred. The demon had been very successfully buried amongst us, and this was greatly due to the fact that we had no dominant Church, and that religion was unconnected with the State." *Parl. Deb.* (S.A.), 1875, 603.
[100] *Age*, 24 June 1872.
[101] *Argus*, 24 June 1872. See also *Age* of same date.
[102] *Age*, 25 June 1872.
[103] *Argus*, 26 June 1872. See also *Age* of same date.
[104] *Argus*, 28 June 1872.
[105] Ibid., 26 June 1872.
[106] Ibid., 24 June 1872.
[107] Ibid., 24, 26 June 1872.
[108] Ibid., 26 June 1872.
[109] Polding had been made Archbishop of Sydney and Metropolitan of Australia in 1842. Vaughan was appointed his coadjutor in 1873, and succeeded him in 1877.
[110] Fogarty, op. cit., Vol. I, pp. 246–50.
[111] Henry Parkes, *Fifty Years in the Making of Australian History*, p. 308.
[112] A. W. Martin, 'Faction Politics and the Education Question in New South Wales', *Melbourne Studies in Education, 1960–61*, p. 39.
[113] Quoted ibid., p. 42.
[114] Ibid., p. 43.
[115] Ibid., p. 36.
[116] Ibid., p. 46.
[117] Quoted Fogarty, op. cit., Vol. I, p. 159.
[118] Ibid., Vol. I, p. 250.
[119] Ibid., Vol. I, p. 253.
[120] Archbishop Vaughan, *Pastorals and Speeches on Education*,

Defining the Code of Public Education, 1872–1895

First Pastoral, pp. 5–8. Each Pastoral is separately paginated, but the pagination runs consecutively through the Speeches.

[121] Ibid., Joint Pastoral, pp. 11–13, Speeches, pp. 29, 37. Vaughan had already explained that a Scavenger's Daughter was a type of torture press.

[122] Parkes, op. cit., p. 312.
[123] Vaughan, op. cit., Speeches, pp. 18–19, 33.
[124] Ibid., p. 27.
[125] Ibid., p. 52.
[126] Ibid., p. 138.
[127] Ibid., p. 59.
[128] *Parl. Deb.* (N.S.W.), i, 1207.
[129] *Parl. Deb.* (W.A.), 1879, 99–100. See also *Parl. Deb.* (W.A.) New Series, vii, 959.
[130] *Western Australian Record*, 29 Sept., 6 Oct., 22 Dec. 1892, 26 Jan., 13 Apr., 11 May, 6 June, 28 Dec. 1893, 1 Feb., 31 May, 29 Nov. 1894.
[131] Ibid., 25 Jan., 16, 23 Aug. 1894, 14 Feb. 1895.
[132] *West Australian*, 9 Jan. 1892.
[133] *Parl. Deb.* (W.A.), New Series, vii, 945.
[134] See F. K. Crowley, *Sir John Forrest*; F. K. Crowley, *Forrest 1847–1918: Vol. 1, 1847–91, Apprenticeship to Premiership*; G. C. Bolton, *Alexander Forrest: His Life and Times*.
[135] *Parl. Deb.* (W.A.), New Series, ii, 641.
[136] Ibid., 650, iii, 182, 361.
[137] Ibid., v, 879–1107.
[138] P. McCarthy, 'The Foundations of Catholicism in Western Australia', *University Studies in History and Economics* (University of W.A.), Vol. 2, No. 4 (July 1956).
[139] Ibid., p. 61.
[140] *Western Australian Record*, 10 May 1894.
[141] *Parl. Deb.* (W.A.) (New Series), vii, 935–74.
[142] Ibid., 945.
[143] Ibid., viii, 265, 395, 402, 665.
[144] Ibid., 893.
[145] Report of the Joint Select Committee . . . appointed to consider the terms . . . on which it will be equitable to abolish the Assisted School System . . . 1895, p. 17, *V. & P.*, W.A. Parlt., 1895. Fr Bourke had apparently forgotten that the Catholic Church in Western Australia, as in every other colony, had resented the control of the Board of Education and had frequently tried to evade its regulations. See *Parl. Deb.* (W.A.), New Series, vii, 1403, 1468, and G. T. Snooke, 'The Elementary Education Act, 1871–1881', unpublished B.A. Thesis, University of Western Australia, 1951, pp. 31, 54, 59–61.

[146] Vaughan, op. cit., Fourth Pastoral, p. 14. See also First Pastoral, p. 12, Second Pastoral, p. 11, Fifth Pastoral, p. 15.
[147] Suttor, op. cit., p. 5.
[148] *Western Australian Record*, 27 July 1895.
[149] *Parl. Deb.* (Vic.), Vol. xv, 1353.

7

Interpreting the Constitutional Code of Public Education 1872–1900

THE State had triumphed. Now it had to justify its victory, for it had secured the allegiance of some, and the neutrality of others, by promising that, if it triumphed, it would transform the nature of society. Somehow it now had to get the nation's children into the school-room, it had to educate them without direct expense to their parents, and it had to prove that the secular education it intended to give would promote social harmony, raise industrial efficiency, increase political competence and foster national cohesion. The vanquished sought consolation in marking down each unfulfilled promise.

Free and Compulsory Education

The failure of the State to make education free should have surprised none but the most optimistic parent, for even the sponsors of the Education Acts had thought the principle of free education to be a bad one, and after the Acts were passed they lost no opportunity of reminding parents that this sort of charity "would remove the last vestige of pride and independence".[1] The parents, however, with a deplorable

Interpreting the Code of Public Education, 1872–1900

lack of pride, persisted in haggling over the fees and falsely declaring themselves to be paupers until, in despair, Ministers of Public Instruction gave up the attempt to make a profit out of the nation's schools. Again, no one should have been surprised at the failure of the State to make education compulsory. Not only had the Education Acts been intentionally lax on this point (see above, p. 185), but no reliable school census existed and the enforcement of compulsion was, strictly speaking, a responsibility of the weak local boards. In every colony these boards complained of the unpopularity of their duty and the difficulty of finding anyone to perform it. Police Commissioners, without exception, objected that it was not a fitting duty for their officers to perform, and even the promise of an allowance of £6 a year could not entice the police to volunteer, for "the duties of the office being so disagreeable", one constable told the Western Australian authorities, "I am afraid they would clash with Police Duties and bring me into collision with the Settlers."[2] Truancy officers, when they could be found, fought a hopeless battle against the native cunning of the children, the hostility of the parents and the complete inadequacy of their information. "My plan", one truancy officer explained, "was . . . to pick on one of the smaller boys, and threaten pains and penalties, and he would give me the names of the elder boys. . . ."[3] Another admitted:

> I used to commence, say at Swanston Street—I would stand at the corner of the street and count the children that I could see . . . I would then go as fast as I could to another point and do the same thing . . . but repeatedly I counted the same numbers over twice. The children were as active as myself; in fact it would astonish you what a distance those children would travel. I would find them in Spencer Street in the morning, and at the Prahran brick-kilns in the afternoon. . . . One day I found that one school had given a holiday and all my calculations therefore went for nothing. . . .[4]

Factory owners, of course, were reluctant to lose the child labour they had, local boards composed of business men were loath to offend their colleagues by prosecuting, and

Australian Education, 1788-1900

bogus private schools, where a child could mark his attendance each day on the way to work, were not hard to find.[5]

The Education Departments themselves did not make the truancy officers' work any easier by conducting night schools which, although intended to offer education to adolescents or adults, became a refuge for children who were working by day. It was in vain that Departmental officers insisted that attendance at night school did not exempt from attendance at day school; many local boards declared that it did, and refused to prosecute children who could show that they attended at night. That the conduct in these schools was a public scandal hardly worried the members of the local boards for they took good care not to go near them, but the teachers who had to run them came to dread the hours they were forced to spend in the midst of bedlam while their pupils abused and assaulted them, smashed windows and furniture, insulted passers-by and fought blasphemously amongst themselves. The police, though frequently sent for, rarely appeared in enough strength to prevent the neighbourhood being terrorized as the classes swept out at nine o'clock. Here and there an inspector claimed that the night schools in his district were well-conducted, but the overwhelming weight of evidence from teachers and inspectors was that these schools were "an unmitigated evil . . . a disgrace to the colony . . . a great curse . . . a complete failure. . . ."[6]

There is also some evidence to suggest that when the Education Departments realized that compulsion meant the congregation of all classes of children they tried to evade the social consequences of their own regulations by excluding the "gutter children", as they liked to call them, rather than offend the finer feelings of the more respectable parents. In Victoria, for example, a Royal Commissioner declared that "the practice of the department has been to abstain from sweeping these children into our schools, lest they should impair their tone", and he went on to assert that the Department had actually established "ragged schools" for these children in the slums of Melbourne. The ragged school in Little Bourke Street, he reported,

> is in an alley, and the children are frequently taught in the road for want of room inside. Not long ago two Chinese brothels were opened hard by, and the children could watch the customers going in and out during the class work.[7]

Five years later the Secretary of the Education Department denied that his Department had any policy of excluding these children, or that the ragged schools were in any way connected with his Department, but his truancy officers gave evidence that the ragged schools were flourishing, and that the Department was not exerting itself to get these children into the ordinary schools. "The children go inside and out as they like", one officer reported, "and are away selling papers and 'marining', and they give a boy an attendance mark though he has gone out directly after he came into the schools".[8] Victoria's record was bad, but no other colony could afford to criticize it. In Queensland, for example, the compulsory clauses of the 1875 Act were not proclaimed until 1900—the year in which the governor of New South Wales chose the problem of truancy as the theme of his address to the Public School Teachers' Association.[9]

Secular Education

Over the secular provisions of the education Acts a protracted tug-of-war developed. In most colonies the secularists were content to hold the ground they had won, against the efforts of the Bible in Schools League to increase the amount of religious education given in the State schools; in South Australia, for example, the members of the Commission on the Working of the Education Acts (1882) reported that they had distinguished eleven different opinions on religious education, and felt that

> it would be useless for us to enter upon an elaborate investigation of these conflicting opinions with any hope of bringing about unanimity of conviction and practice. . . . After

earnest and mature consideration we recommend that no alteration be made. . . .[10]

In Victoria, however, the tug-of-war was a much more spirited affair. The Education Act of 1872 had contained no reference to religious education, but it had empowered the Boards of Advice "to recommend what use shall be made of school buildings after the children are dismissed from school", and this authority some Boards now used to recommend the holding of classes in religious education. To these recommendations the Minister cautiously agreed, while warning his teachers that they must take no part in these lessons. At the same time the Minister agreed with the secularists (led on this occasion by the Anglo-Israel Association and George Higinbotham) that the Irish National Readers, which were still in use in the schools, were unsuitable because they contained religious material. In 1876 he ordered the replacement of the Irish Readers by the Nelson Readers and instructed his officers to excise from the new books all reference to religious dogma.[11] The English compositors who were set to printing the expurgated Victorian edition of the Nelson Readers must have marvelled at this display of secular righteousness. Where prose or poetry could be conveniently bowdlerized the censors had been satisfied to expunge and substitute ("the Christian mother", for example, had become "the frantic mother"; the "great reformer, John Wycliffe" had become the "celebrated John Wycliffe"), but elsewhere whole poems and articles had been deleted; the "Hymn of the Hebrew Maid" had given way to "The Vision of Belshazzar", "Behold, the Bridegroom Cometh" to "The Turf shall be my fragrant Shrine" and "Paul at Athens" to "Wonders of the Cotton Manufacture". Even then the censors were not satisfied with their handiwork—there remained, they had to admit, a great number of passages "having a religious tendency"; any child set to reading the Sixth Book, for example, would be confronted by such religious expressions as: "In the year 263 before Christ the first Punic war began", and "God helps them that help themselves". There was apparently no end to this solemn farce. Even the intelligent and urbane C. H. Pearson, when ordered by the Legislative Assembly to review the censors' handiwork, could earnestly report that although the passage

> When I think of all that the human hand has wrought, from the day when Eve put forth her erring hand to pluck the fruit of the forbidden tree, to that dark hour when the pierced hands of the Saviour of the world were nailed to the predicted tree of shame, and of all that human hands have done of good and evil since, I lift up my hand and gaze upon it with awe,

had been altered to read

> When I think of all that human hands have done of good and evil, since the day when Eve put forth her erring hand to pluck the fruit of the forbidden tree, I lift up my hand and gaze upon it with wonder and awe,

he felt that the excisions had not gone far enough. The passage, he reported,

> has been altered, so that it no longer gives offence to the religious convictions of Hebrew fellow citizens; but it asserts a theory of the Fall of Man which has never been adopted by the natives of China settled amongst us. It would have been better, I think, to omit the passage altogether.[12]

In the face of this attack the religious instruction party began to rally its forces. The classes which, with the Minister's grudging consent, they were conducting in some schools at the end of the day were not only inadequate, they realized, but positively harmful because of the atmosphere in which they were held. Canon Handfield reported to a Royal Commission in 1883:

> I am teaching now myself at the Central schools after school hours, but I have no very great confidence in what I am doing . . . there is attendance enough, but there is a terrible lack of discipline, and there is a great want of getting a sufficient number of teachers. . . . It is after school, and the entire thing is voluntary, and boy nature is boy nature—wants to get to the playground.[13]

Just how badly Canon Handfield was treated by his pupils it is difficult to tell, for when he was asked "how the boys behaved . . . he merely remarked, with a good-humoured smile, that he did not 'think they were as respectful as formerly'." Handfield's bishop, with less Christian forbearance, declared that at the end of Scripture reading the boys had "shut the books and shied them at his head. . . . No book hit him, but . . . they rained about him on every side. . . ." The headmaster, on the other hand, defended his pupils by pointing out that the books in question were not Bibles ("which would certainly be rather formidable missiles"), but merely copies of Luke's gospel ("weighing less than an ounce each"), and that far from being shied at Canon Handfield's head the books "were merely 'chucked' to the front to the two boys who were appointed to collect them."[14]

However the question of whether the books were "shied" or "chucked" was not the real issue. It is clear from the headmaster's testimony that there were nearly one hundred boys in Canon Handfield's class, and that no teacher was present (or, by regulation, could be present); there can be no doubt that there was a great deal of disorder in this classroom and in every other classroom where religious instruction was given after school hours. In these circumstances the religious instruction party concentrated their campaign upon the demand that the Bible should be restored to the classroom, and the class teacher empowered "to take a course of lessons from the Bible . . . as the basis of moral and historical instruction".[15] Between 1872 and 1900 this simple demand was presented at almost every sitting of Parliament, but neither public meetings, petitions, pledges, deputations, Royal Commission findings nor the eloquence of James Balfour in the Council and Alfred Deakin in the Assembly[16] could move a Parliament which saw how frequently the Bible-in-Schools campaign became entangled with the campaign to restore State aid to Church schools.[17] It was not until 1899 (and then by the narrow margin of thirty-six votes to thirty-four) that the Legislative Assembly agreed to the cautious resolution:

> That, in the opinion of the House, the question of religious instruction in State schools should be referred to a direct vote of

the people. Providing that before the people are asked to vote on the question, the government appoint a commission consisting of the heads of the various denominations registered in Victoria, in order to suggest what religious instruction should be taught in our schools, so that their determination may be placed before the people to accept or reject.[18]

The Commission was duly appointed, and after some months of hard work produced an "agreed syllabus", but as soon as it was apparent that the Roman Catholic Church would not co-operate with the Commission (and presumably intended to use its appointment to reopen the State-aid question) the Parliament took fright and refused to put the Commission's findings before the people. In Victoria, as in every other colony, the religious instruction provisions of the education Acts remained virtually unaltered at the close of the century.

The Failure to Develop Secondary Education

Against this background of religious controversy the new Education Departments went about their task of establishing a national system of education. By the turn of the century they had had (the Western Australian Department excepted) about twenty years in which to show what they could make of the State's triumph, but in every colony their critics insisted that they had failed to justify the trust that had been put in them. Doubtless some of this criticism was ill-informed and some of it was petty, but there can be no doubt that the colonial Education Departments had not only failed to establish an effective system of national education, but that they had tried to escape the consequences of their shortcomings by misrepresentation.

Underlying every weakness in colonial public education was the failure to create a State system of secondary education, for not only had this omission starved the universities of talent, and condemned any effective scheme of technical education to failure, but it had also had a deplorable effect on the State's own primary schools. Without a system of State secondary schools it was impossible to recruit an educated class of teachers for the primary schools, and without an educated class of primary teachers it was impossible to extend or liberalize the primary school curriculum.

The Training of Teachers

The Education Departments had taken over from the Boards of Education a system of teacher training containing three elements—the Model School, the pupil-teacher and the Normal School (or Teachers' College). The Boards, in their turn, had borrowed this system from England where, by Minutes of 25 August and 21 December 1846, the Committee of the Privy Council on Education had tried to devise a means of getting competent teachers into the schools which it had begun to subsidize. As the system operated in England, promising boys and girls of at least thirteen years of age were apprenticed to head-teachers for a period of five years. During those years of indenture the master was rewarded by grants, and the apprentice pursued a course of general and professional studies and submitted to an annual examination. At the end of his five years the apprentice competed by examination for exhibitions which would take him to a Normal School for three years as a Queen's Scholar. It is easy at this distance to deplore the whole principle of the pupil-teacher system, but the English Committee, with no national system of secondary education (and, for that matter, no primary system), was making a distinct advance in establishing even this reprehensible system of teacher-training. There is general agreement amongst educational historians that the Committee's decision marked the beginning of a new era in English education; the new pupil-teachers were "the sinews of English primary education", to use Matthew Arnold's phrase, and any economy should be endured, he pleaded, "rather than that the number of pupil-teachers should be lessened".[19] Inherently faulty as the system was, its worst evils might have been avoided in Australia if it had been carried out as its framers envisaged it, but two colonial modifications combined to distort the original idea: the Australian colonies never established the system as a whole, and the employing authorities became the training authorities.

The effect of these modifications was disastrous. As a child of fourteen the Australian boy (or girl) was engaged by the Education Department at a salary of about £20 a year and apprenticed to one of its headmasters—more often than not the headmaster of the pupil's last school, for appointments were made upon the headmaster's recommendations and the small salary offered made it difficult for a lad to accept a post at any distance from his own home.[20] In this employment he continued for four years, teaching a full day's work in the long school-room under the constant surveillance of the assistant teachers who had classes in the same room, and the occasional supervision of a perambulating headmaster. Before and after school he attended at the headmaster's office and undertook a study of reading, dictation, writing, English grammar and composition, geography, arithmetic and book-keeping. Once a year he sat for his examinations and had his teaching ability assessed by an inspector; if he were successful he received an increment of £10 and his master received a bonus. It was dreary and exhausting work. To stand all day in the long classroom, sandwiched between two other classes, and attempt to keep order in an era of constant and excessive corporal punishment; to be eternally the grist between the lower millstone of insolent pupils little younger than oneself and the upper millstone of the headmaster anxious for his bonus; to face the grind of study at the end of the day under a master scarcely more literate than oneself; to spend the evenings preparing the next day's lessons and cramming for examinations—all this was too much for many of the girls, whose frequent illnesses and absences were annually deplored. With the same frequency the permanent shortage of male pupil-teachers was also reported and deplored, for the colonial lad of spirit was loath to put his neck into this galling yoke.

For most of the young drudges who completed the years of apprenticeship there was no further training, for during most of the late nineteenth century the Normal School which should have been waiting to receive them did not exist;[21] armed with a Licence to Teach they went out to take charge of their own little bush schools, or begin their own tyrant's reign in the long-room. The handful of pupil-teachers who did get into a Teachers' College must have wondered if this rare prize had been worth winning, for they found themselves in the company of another type of student (the matriculated "outsider" who had never been a pupil-teacher) whose accomplishments they could not match. As their lecturers tried to add a little French, Latin, English, science, geometry and history to the students' meagre stock of knowledge it became apparent that even this modest load was too much for most of them to bear for, as the Principal of the Melbourne Teachers' College pointed out, year after year, their education was so defective that even these elementary studies baffled and exhausted them. "Green's *Short History of the English People* is prescribed as the textbook in English history", he reported in 1878.

> The book is a good one, but the subject is the *bête noire* of the trainees, because it bewilders them with its vastness, and dazes them by the strain it puts on the memory. . . . The subject is quite new, scarcely any of them have touched it before. . . . Two books are used in English language and literature —Abbott and Seeley's *Short Lessons for English People* and Craik's *Manual of English Literature and Language*. This last is a voluminous work, and as the subject is as new to the trainees as all the others, and not so generally interesting, it divides the disgust with the history. . . . It is not surprising that the rate of failure has been very high. . . .[22]

Nevertheless, when Frank Tate began to speak out on "the evils of our wretched pupil-teacher system" his views were regarded as little short of heresy.[23] The orthodox view, proclaimed by responsible men in every colony, was strongly in favour of retaining the system; here and there one finds an inspector or headmaster who was prepared to admit that pupil-teachers were perhaps over-worked, but the principle of putting immature, ill-educated, untrained adolescents in charge of children was vehemently supported throughout the nineteenth century.[24] Generally, the defence of the system was based upon the thoroughness of the practical training it gave, but its real attraction to Ministers, inspectors and headmasters lay in its cheapness and its success in producing a docile teaching service. So long as pupil-teachers could be paid a pittance, and given an assistant's work to do, it was no wonder that the system was supported; in New South Wales, for example, pupil-teachers constituted 20 per cent of the teaching service in 1891, and in Victoria 33 per cent as late as 1902. Of course there was always the danger that a clever young upstart like Frank Tate might survive the years of servility with his critical faculties unimpaired, put himself through a university course, excel as a teacher, and then have the impertinence to criticize the system which had nurtured him, but the Frank Tates of the Department were very rare, and officialdom could be confident that each year the Principal of the Teachers' College would be able to report of his graduating students: "The trainees have conducted themselves well. . . . They have been docile, have striven to please."[25]

Payment by Results

If, by any chance, the young teacher still had any spirit left in him after this course of training, the conditions under which he was expected to practise his profession were calculated to grind it out of him, for in most of the Australian colonies in the last quarter of the nineteenth century teachers were engaged under a system of "payment by results" whereby their livelihood was made dependent upon their success in beating the three R's into their unfortunate charges.[26] The discredit for introducing this pernicious system to Australia belongs to Sir James Palmer and his colleagues on the Victorian Board of Education. Called upon by the Common Schools Act of 1862 to distribute a government grant to an ill-organized collection of Board and denominational schools, they found themselves presented with a ready-made solution in the Revised Code which Robert Lowe had just presented to the House of Commons. Lowe and his colleagues in the Palmerston Ministry of 1859-65 were obviously disturbed at the size to which the education grant had grown, and were seeking ways of making a reduced grant serve their purpose when the Report of the Newcastle Commission on "the extension of sound and cheap elementary instruction" suggested to them the possibility of paying the grants to the schools in the form of a capitation grant upon attendance, subject to deductions for faulty teaching. This, Lowe realized, would virtually mean restricting the curriculum to the three R's and the employment of "a lower kind of teacher" (to use his own phrase), but something had to be done to cut the grant, and, as the *Edinburgh Review* reminded him, the education of the poor was undoubtedly "pitched too high". "Hitherto", he told the House,

> we have been living under a system of bounties and protection; now we prefer to have a little free trade. . . . I cannot promise the House that this system will be an economical one, and I cannot promise that it will be an efficient one, but I can promise that it shall be one or the other. If it is not cheap, it shall be efficient; if it is not efficient it shall be cheap.[27]

Ignoring the serious criticisms which the Revised Code had provoked in English educational circles, Palmer quickly imposed the results system upon his Victorian schools and proceeded to find virtues in it which even Lowe had never dreamt of. "It induces regular attendance", Palmer told the Higinbotham Royal Commission,

> it stimulates the teacher, it promotes organization, it ensures uniform progress unto the pupil, and by an equitable distribution of this payment amongst the teachers, and by making this payment dependent on their exertions, it enlists them all heartily in the service.[28]

It was in this form that the Victorian Education Department inherited the system in 1872 and it proceeded to use it, not to apportion payments to aided schools on an equitable basis, but to regiment its own teachers. A portion of

Interpreting the Code of Public Education, 1872-1900

the teacher's salary (at times as little as 50 per cent) was regarded as a fixed amount; the remainder of his salary was calculated upon the attendance and performance of his pupils; the stage was thus set for an elaborate and exhausting contest between teacher and inspector, but to ensure some semblance of fair play the ground rules of the contest were laid out in a detailed series of "standards" by which both contestants knew precisely what a child was supposed to have learnt by a certain age. Within this framework of rules teacher and inspector were free to exercise their ingenuity and guile. Attendance rolls could be falsified, children's ages misreported, talented pupils with infectious diseases kept at school, backward children discouraged from attending and copies of an inspector's questions passed quickly ahead of him from school to school. The teacher was fighting for his livelihood, and could only hate the man who had the power, on a brief annual visit, to take part of it from him. "I had . . . an examination this day week", John Rae told a Royal Commission in Victoria,

> and I was held responsible for a family of five who had left the district. They are counted total failures . . . and I had no more power to bring them than I had to bring the man in the moon. . . . Children from country districts sometimes came in from seven, eight and nine years old, not acquainted with the alphabet, and they raise the average age of others so much that teachers have to lose. . . . An examination was conducted in my school when the thermometer was at 106, and a child fell down in a fainting fit, but she was counted against me. The inspector would take neither her copybook nor sewing. . . . Even when the child is ill in bed, not able to raise its head from the pillow, it is counted a total failure against us.[29]

For his part the inspector generally retaliated by protesting his liberality. "Here is a case at Bordertown", Mr L. W. Stanton pointed out to a Royal Commission in South Australia,

> where there is a mark, "needlework excused for deformity." . . . Here is another at Glenburnie, in 1880, where three children were examined, and in consequence of their doing so

badly I asked the teacher for an explanation, and he said they had been irregular in their attendance. I said—"But why did you not point this out before I began?" He replied, "I thought they might do well, and that I would risk it." I exempted those children afterwards, and thus allowed the teacher to take the risk, as he put it, but not to take the penalty. . . . Here is another at Compton Downs, in 1881, where I excused the drill of the whole school in consequence of the teacher having been ill for a month, and having handed in a medical certificate. . . .

But if the inspector was pushed far enough his real attitude to the contest became clearer. When the Chairman asked Stanton why he had failed some pupils in writing he asserted that

> while we have Darnell [a series of copybooks] in the schools Darnell must be followed where he gives instructions that in the m's and n's the second stroke has to come from the bottom of the previous one, and not from the top. . . . I am constantly pointing out some of these minute things to the teachers. . . . I say the down strokes must be complete. . . . I am not advocating Darnell's system. . . . All I say is that even a bad system is better than none at all. . . . When the children afterwards write quickly their individuality comes out, but it should be suppressed beforehand, not only in the way of moral training, but in order to improve the writing itself. . . . I think all the inspectors are agreed that there should not be latitude in this respect, as it will be productive of evil.[30]

In some astonishment one of the Commissioners asked: "If I thoroughly understand you, you stated that it was quite possible for a child to be failed in writing, even though he writes better comparatively than another child who is not failed in the same class?" "Yes", the inspector replied, "because we take the copybook as our standard in judging what is better and what is inferior. . . . I think in their training there ought to be a certain amount of suppression and repression. . . ."[31] When, as a refinement of the whole evil system, it was determined that the headmaster's salary should depend in part upon his assistants' results a reign of terror in the colonial classroom was assured.

Interpreting the Code of Public Education, 1872–1900

The Status of the Teacher

A tyrant to the pupils the teacher might be, but to his superiors in the new Education Departments he was a servant who had to be taught his place. It was a fairly easy lesson to teach. Defectively educated, trained in the pupil-teacher tradition, forced to conform by the payment-by-results system, the departmental teacher had little power to resist his masters; he had neither the protection of an effective professional organization nor the disciplined, critical intelligence that might have come from a university education. On the one side lay the threat of exploitation, on the other the danger of conformity.

How narrow the path was between these dangers became apparent during the sittings of the Victorian Royal Commission of 1882–84. In an interim report the Commissioners declared that political patronage had reached serious proportions in the Department—that both appointments and promotions had been influenced by Members of Parliament, and that it was

> of the highest importance . . . that a system of appointment and promotion of departmental officers and teachers should be as early as possible established by law. . . . Any regular system of appointments and promotions must be based upon a classification of officers. . . . All subsequent promotions should be regulated in reference to the classification laid down in the general system.[32]

The Minister immediately obliged with a Public Service Act which gave teachers the status of public servants and, early in 1885, published the first classified roll of teachers and schools. In the meantime, however, he had disclosed the price teachers were to pay for this security. Late in 1882 the headmaster of State School No. 1278, La Trobe Street, Melbourne (Mr E. Parnell) had, in giving evidence before the Royal Commission, revealed the fact that he had thought a departmental directive on discipline to be foolish, and had ignored it. In October he received a letter from the Secretary of the Department ordering him to explain his conduct, and in reply to his explanation, a second letter which told him that "The Minister of Public Instruction . . . considers that your conduct is deserving of the severest censure. . . . A persistence in conduct so openly subversive of all discipline will be incompatible with your retention in the service." Parnell had the good sense to lay both these letters before the Commission (which was still sitting) and the Commissioners, disturbed at this attempt to intimidate a witness, appealed to the governor "to take such steps . . . as shall secure the recognition and observance of the privileges of witnesses already examined and hereafter to be examined by us. . . ." The Minister, when appraised of the position, protested that his action had been "taken with a view solely to the maintenance of proper discipline in the Department . . . and without any desire or intention of invading the privileges of the Commission, or the rights of any of the witnesses." The Minister added that he had since informed all officers "that they may give their evidence frankly, fully and truthfully without fear of departmental censure or injury to their position". To this the Commissioners objected that the Minister's instruction to his officers could only lead to the impression "that the examination by the Commission of the officers of the Department is conducted by virtue of a concession of the Department, rather than in the exercise of the authority entrusted to the Commission by the Crown to enquire into the administration of the Department." Under pressure, the Minister finally agreed to withdraw his letter to Parnell, and concur in an Order-in-Council for the protection of witnesses.[33]

It was not only in Victoria that Royal Commissioners had to contend with authoritarian Ministers; both in South Australia (1882-3) and Queensland (1888) they had to report difficulty in getting Departmental teachers to testify, "they . . . being evidently influenced by the fear of ultimate unpleasant results to themselves".[34] What the Royal Commissioners of the 1880s had encountered was not so much Ministerial tyranny, but the arrogance of ambitious senior officers who, taking advantage of weak Ministerial leadership, had begun to build their own little empires within the

Interpreting the Code of Public Education, 1872–1900

Education Departments. The Ministers of Public Instruction were rarely the villains their senior officers made them out to be. Admittedly it was possible for the Inspector-General in Western Australia to be severely reprimanded by his Minister (E. H. Wittenoom), who declared that he was, "to say the least of it, surprised to find that you had been criticizing the Department",[35] but the situation in Western Australia was an unusual one, for the Inspector-General had only been in the colony for a few weeks and the Minister was a member of a Ministry which had been in office for more than six years. In the other colonies, where a Ministry was lucky to survive for more than eighteen months, and where an Inspector-General was likely to have had twenty or thirty years' experience, stretching back into the Board of Education days, Ministers were rarely able to dominate their departments. As the Queensland Royal Commissioners pointed out:

> Although the administration of the Department is vested in the Minister for Public Instruction, it seems practically to be in the hands of the Under Secretary and the General Inspector. . . . There is abundant evidence that the administration is conducted in an arbitrary, capricious and often unfeeling manner, and all in the name of "The Minister," who seems to be a convenient medium for the exercise of the most autocratic management. . . . The Inspector-General has exercised his powers in the name of "the Minister" in such a manner as to bring the staff into a frame of mind very short of rebellion.[36]

The Local Boards

The first stage in this aggrandizement, as Pearson pointed out in 1877, was the centralization of power which should have been shared with other agencies. The Victorian Education Department had only been in existence for five years, he reported, but already "the leading principle . . . has been to substitute supervision from Melbourne for local co-operation. . . . The department has been over-trustful in itself. . . ."[37] As Pearson went on to point out, the only real safeguard against an autocratic Minister or an ambitious Inspector-General was the authority vested in the local

Boards of Advice, but they, by their very nature, were practically doomed from their inception. Australia had never had a strong tradition of local government, and the framers of the education Acts had been reluctant to give the local boards any real power; nevertheless, they might have succeeded if anyone in authority had wanted them to succeed, but all the evidence points to an intention to ignore them. They might have succeeded, Pearson believed,

> if the department had gradually divested itself of its own authority where the school boards were prepared to take up the work. But the department has been . . . unduly doubtful of the zeal and intelligence that were prepared to second it throughout the country. The result has been that many boards have been discouraged, and many competent members have withdrawn from seats on them. . . .[38]

In Western Australia, where local boards had been established under the Elementary Education Act of 1871, the "empire-builders" had been even more ruthless. Within a year the Central Board was asserting that

> we cannot shut our eyes to the fact that unless members of the District Boards, as a rule take more direct and personal interest in carrying out the principles of the Act . . . the success of the Elementary Education Act will not be so decided as at first we had reason to believe it would be.[39]

But the Central Board's own Minutes tell another story. In June 1873 the Swan District Board was informed that "The Central Board declines to enter into the Question whether the Elementary Education Act is interpreted correctly or otherwise by them"; in October 1873 the Fremantle District Board was informed that "The Central Board declines to recognize any right on the part of a District Board to criticize their conduct". By the end of 1874 the Rev. J. Withers, a member of the Bunbury District Board, was convinced that the District Boards were a dead letter. "The action of the Central Board", he wrote,

> has all along been *high-handed* and unyielding. The advice and suggestions, not only of this Board, but of every Board with whose proceedings I have become acquainted, have been set

Interpreting the Code of Public Education, 1872-1900

aside, snuffed out, and in many cases treated with covert contempt, and seldom if ever met by argument.[40]

In Queensland, the District Boards were never allowed to function at all; although provided for in the State Education Act of 1875 they were not established in the regulations promulgated under the Act. Throughout the 1880s Royal Commissions continued to deplore the decline of the local boards and to suggest ways by which they could be revitalized, but they were fighting in a lost cause. The passing of the local boards might well be dated 29 August 1881, the day on which the correspondent of the Cranbourne Board of Advice wrote to the Secretary of the Victorian Education Department:

> Sir,
> I am directed by the above Board to report to your Department that the bar of one of the locks on door of State School No. 2068 is broken, and that the Board wish to be informed what is best to be done with a view to having it repaired.[41]

When a government department had reduced the hardheaded dairy-farmers of Cranbourne to this degree of impotence there was obviously nothing left to fight for.

The Role of the Inspector-General

With Ministers in and out of office so frequently, and with the local boards moribund, the Inspectors-General had a dangerous accumulation of power in their hands. The more sycophantic of their subordinates were quick to see which way the wind was blowing, and began to trim. No report, it seemed, could be considered complete without a peroration in praise of "the system". In 1877 the district inspector at Warrnambool (Thomas Brodribb) provided his colleagues with a model of the panegyric they should write. "Victoria", he declared in concluding his annual report,

> may now rejoice in the fact that schools are brought within reach of almost every little cluster of families, these schools being well furnished, liberally provided with educational requisites, carefully organized, and conducted under a rigid system of inspection and control . . . and if our system, with

all its advantages, does not become the parent of excellence, we may feel sure that the fault will then lie with the teachers and their inspectors and not with the Legislature that devised so liberal a provision.[42]

The fact that Brodribb quickly outstripped his colleagues and became Secretary of the Victorian Education Department was probably not lost upon his subordinates, but if any were slow to learn the need for conformity "the system" had ways of silencing them. Conferences of inspectors, at which their views might be aired, could be abandoned, adverse reports from them could be rejected or expurgated and in the last resort they could be dismissed; even the great Brodribb was eventually tumbled from office when, forgetting the way in which he had climbed, he spoke back too sharply to his superiors.[43] By 1900 the annual reports issued by the Departments of Education were so edited and expurgated that neither the Ministers, whose reports they were supposed to be, nor anyone else had much chance of discovering the truth about the condition of public education.[44] Summing up the findings of his Royal Commission, Theodore Fink told the Victorian Parliament that despite the gross inefficiency he had discovered in the Education Department its annual reports "had year by year, with parrot-like identity of expression, referred to the efficiency of the system being maintained". The sentence, he concluded, "must have been kept in type. . . ."[45] But those who had only the annual reports to guide them remained happy in their ignorance, and vied with one another in praising the condition of public education. ". . . we might well be proud of our Education Department", one member of the New South Wales Parliament declared; ". . . it was the best system of public instruction in the Southern Hemisphere"; another announced that it was as good as that "in any part of the world", and a third thought it "was perhaps . . . the finest in the Universe". Members of the Victorian Parliament were no doubt delighted to hear that their education system "was far and away superior to that of . . . New South Wales. . . ."[46]

Interpreting the Code of Public Education, 1872–1900

It seemed as though nothing could stop this adulatory nonsense. For over twenty years Royal Commissions had been telling the people of Australia that their Departments of Education were being mismanaged, but it was as though their reports had never been written. In Queensland, for example, though the Royal Commission of 1888 declared that the Inspector-General and Under-Secretary were "unsuccessful administrators of this important department"[47] the Inspector-General (D. I. Ewart) was rewarded with the office of Director of Education when that position was created in 1905, and continued to mismanage his department, insult his teachers and retard educational progress until his retirement in 1909. In South Australia, where no one doubted the harsh efficiency of the Inspector-General (J. A. Hartley), there were many who found his arbitrary conduct intolerable and feared that he was grinding the life out of the schools, but though the Premier might complain of Hartley's "red tape, love of power, uniformity, doctrinairism and non-allowance for human weakness in teachers and scholars",[48] and though the Parliament might resolve to inquire into his régime nothing was ever done to stop his abuse of power. It was only after his death in 1896 that the full extent of the damage he had done forced itself upon the South Australian conscience.

Turn-of-the-century Criticism

It was, in fact, not until the end of the century that any colony awoke to the fraud which the educationists had been practising upon the Australian public. The 1870s and 1880s had been, by and large, years of prosperity and careless optimism, though towards the end of the 1880s some independent souls had begun to question the direction society was taking; with the 1890s came depression, a crippling drought and the most bitter and protracted strikes the country had ever known. While the depression called into question the country's industrial and commercial efficiency, the strikes raised fundamental questions about the structure of Australian society; the militant republicanism displayed by the strikers at Barcaldine, the resort to arms by both strikers and government, and the punitive use of the courts were events which shocked, and made critical, a people who had thought they were building a new and just society. Probably never before or since have the Australian people questioned themselves so closely; rarely have they read and argued so earnestly. Henry George's *Progress and Poverty*, Edward Bellamy's *Looking Backward*, Gronlund's *Co-operative Commonwealth*, Dawson's *German Socialism*, Ruskin, Carlyle, Disraeli, Dickens and the Fabians all contributed to the colonists' soul-searching; William Lane's Utopian attempt to found a New Australia in Paraguay, the creation of the Australian Labour Party, the challenge of the *Bulletin*, and the Federation issue all demanded that men should examine the society in which they lived, and declare their vision of its future.[49] "The impulse towards Utopianism was at once a sign of faith in the future and uncertainty about the present", Vance Palmer has written,

> for towards the end of the eighties many people were beginning to wonder where the political policies of the different colonies were leading. Was the dream being fulfilled—the dream of a self-contained country, secure from the outer world, developing its own resources, and gradually building up a society that would be a pattern for free men everywhere? Or had they come to an impasse?[50]

By the late 1890s this question had still not been resolved, but with returning prosperity it was at least possible to think of reconstruction.

It is difficult to determine, with any exactness, the steps by which a vague and generalized public discontent becomes a desire or demand for reform. It is equally difficult to determine how this desire or demand becomes structured in such a way that it succeeds in its object; that is, why, short of violence or the threat of violence, should a government concede that its policies have possibly been wrong and should be changed or, at least, appraised by an independent authority with a view to change?

These are deep questions and are more the business of the

Interpreting the Code of Public Education, 1872-1900

political scientist than the educational historian, but the sequence of events in Victoria (to take an example) which turned a generalized public discontent about its system of education into specific demands for reform, thence into political threat and finally into the condemnatory findings of a protracted Royal Commission might prove instructive to both types of scholars.

Even a cursory glance at this sequence of events suggests the direction in which some of the answers might lie. The Pearson Royal Commission of 1877 (see above, p. 255) was probably not intended seriously by the Premier (Graham Berry) who authorized it; certainly Pearson was a very distinguished scholar and educationist, but he was also a politician and the appointment smacked of jobbery.[51] Nevertheless Pearson produced an excellent and critical report—about which nothing was done—and a quarter of a century was to elapse before the Fink Royal Commission reports of 1899-1901 brought action from the government. As a generalization, then, we could say that political action is not taken at the first indication of criticism. In fact the Victorian evidence suggests that a long period of time is needed to allow a sustained campaign of criticism to develop: a campaign which emanates from a number of responsible sections of the community, and which enlists the support of the Press (preferably as a matter of conviction rather than expediency) and, finally, opposition politicians of integrity. The Victorian evidence also suggests that if the campaign is to succeed there must eventually be a political situation in which the government finds it politically dangerous to resist inquiry, and there must be a financial situation in which some reforms at least can be paid for without arousing an outcry from sections of the community not concerned with the specific reform issue.

The Fink Commission in Victoria

The evidence for these tentative generalizations will appear if we start, not at the beginning, but towards the end of the process as it manifested itself in Victoria.

Late on the night of 6 December 1898, while the Legislative Assembly was stolidly debating the Estimates, Alfred Deakin rose to speak on the sum proposed for the Education Department. Of the State Schools, he admitted, he had had no direct experience, but he had had the opportunity of speaking to a number of visiting experts who had told him:

> Victoria was in its education system in the lowest rank, that it was little better than the worst, and that it was far behind the mother country. They stated that the bookishness, the mere memory training, and ordinary teaching of our schools were such as were practised in the mother country ten or fifteen years ago. . . . Without actual experience, one was not competent to pass judgement, but he must say he was staggered, and painfully staggered, to find that every expert whom he had had an opportunity of meeting or communicating with had expressed an unfavourable opinion.[52]

Emboldened by Deakin's example, other members continued the attack. R. T. Vale declared that the Victorian Education Department was "the largest sweating concern in the colony", J. N. Cook told the Minister for Public Instruction that if he would "pass by the head officers in the department for the nonce, and ask for confidential reports from the inspectors . . . and the head teachers . . . the honourable gentlemen would have an eye-opener", and M. K. McKenzie called for a Royal Commission. "They must", he declared, "have reliable information . . . which went to the very root of our national progress in the future."[53]

The significance of this criticism, as I have suggested, did not lie in its novelty. In 1892 the *Australasian Schoolmaster* had carried reports of Frank Tate's criticisms of teacher-training in Victoria, and in 1898 attentive readers of the Melbourne *Herald* would have noticed several articles on the need for educational reform, but Tate, after all, was only an obscure lecturer at the Melbourne Teachers' College, and the *Herald* articles had been too mild and infrequent to stir public opinion. The significance of Deakin's attack lay in the reputation of the man who now challenged the government to refute his charges—and the weight of the support he could command. Deakin had not held office in a Victorian Ministry since 1890, for after the fall of the Gillies-Deakin Ministry he had resolved to

> remain in politics, but only as an independent member, having determined not to take office or accept party leadership, so as to enjoy the privilege of speaking my mind without the restraint which these imply. I especially desire to devote what energies I have to the Federal cause. . . .[54]

But his years as a private member had increased rather than diminished his influence. Ever since the Imperial Conference of 1887, where he had rallied the colonial delegates in opposition to Lord Salisbury's policy of ceding the New Hebrides to the French, Deakin had been building a reputation as the recognized leader of the Federal movement; by June 1898 when the people of Victoria voted (100,520 to 22,099) to accept the Commonwealth Bill he held an unrivalled position in public life, and could have boasted that he had been invited to join every Ministry formed in Victoria since 1890. Power, moreover, had not corrupted him; in twenty years of political life he had, no doubt, made many enemies, but none of them ever doubted his integrity. To the Victorian Parliament of 1898 Deakin's charges must have constituted a *prima facie* case against the administration of public education.

However, even Deakin's influence might not have been enough to force the issue; the House was within a few days of prorogation and the Turner Ministry might reasonably have hoped that the charges would be forgotten in the long Christmas recess. The next morning's edition of the *Age* destroyed these hopes. Mr Deakin's remarks, wrote the editor, "created a very perceptible sensation in the House, it being recognized that they meant thorough enquiry, and if necessary drastic action in the near future". The extent to which David Syme, through the *Age*, could manipulate Victorian politics has never been accurately measured, and the popular belief that he could make and unmake governments probably needs to be accepted with reservations, but his influence on his 100,000 readers cannot be doubted, and in an age of lax party discipline and frequent coalitions there were few Premiers who were prepared to defy him on an important issue.[55] That Syme regarded educational reform as an important issue soon became apparent. He had, before Deakin's speech of 6 December, published a few articles and editorials on technical education, but now he took the matter up in earnest. There was more than coincidence to Syme's and Deakin's simultaneous attacks. Deakin had been a protégé and friend of Syme's since he began writing editorials and articles for the *Age* in 1878, and although Syme had fought against Deakin's Federal plans until mid-1898, the two men were again closely associated in the latter part of the year. By August, Deakin was again writing editorials for the *Age*, and dining with Syme; by December, when Syme was under attack in the House, it was Deakin (and the Premier) whom he summoned to confer with him.[56]

Deakin's interest in public education had never been a dominant one. A cultivated man, who had been educated at Melbourne Grammar School and had taught for a short time at All Saints' Grammar School, he had had no actual experience of the State schools and had never concerned himself deeply with their problems. When he was Chief Secretary in the Gillies-Deakin Ministry (1886-90) he had had the good sense to offer C. H. Pearson the Education portfolio, and he had consistently opposed the secular character of the public schools, but there his interest appears to have ended. On the other hand, his philosophical nature forced upon him a general interest in the function and the process of education, and almost by accident other interests also led him to a study of educational thought. Ruskin, for example, he first met in the role of art critic (*Modern Painters*), but under the spell of the art critic's prose style he went on to read everything that Ruskin wrote, and found himself carried away by the social critic in *Unto This Last* and the educational critic in *Sesame and Lilies*. Again, it was as literary figures that he first encountered Matthew Arnold and George Meredith when he visited England in 1887, but in both of them he also found serious educational thinkers;

years later, in summing up the Meredith he had known well for over twenty years, Deakin recalled him as a "full-blooded nature despising prudery and asceticism, his chief antipathies were the restraints imposed upon youth and capacity, the narrowness and pedantry of education. . . ."[57]

In Melbourne, in the closing months of 1898, the same fortuitous meetings with educationists went on. Eleven years before, Deakin had been the guest of Sir George Trevelyan (the nephew and biographer of Macaulay); now he found himself host to Trevelyan's son, Charles, and his travelling companions, the famous socialists, Sidney and Beatrice Webb. Young Trevelyan had just completed a term on the London School Board and Sidney Webb, who had been a major witness before the Bryce Commission on secondary education, and the founder (with Beatrice) of the London School of Economics, was properly regarded as the main driving force behind the Fabian campaign for educational reform in England.[58]

His chairmanship of the Technical Education Board of the London County Council (1893–1898) had provided him with unrivalled experience as an educational administrator. The Webbs and Trevelyan were, therefore, formidable critics—and they found a great deal to criticize. "We have also looked carefully into the working of the State education, both here and in N.S.W. and Queensland", Beatrice wrote to her sister. "The Education here is in a deplorable state . . . and the State education remains where it was 20 years ago."[59] It was our impression, she recorded in her diary,

> that the Victorian system of education had fallen behind, that the fees charged for all subjects other than the three R's has resulted in these subjects not being taught at all, that the free grant of scholarships to secondary schools and university, which the State had initiated in the good times had been dropped, that there was no attempt to provide "Higher Grade Schools" and that lastly the University itself had not gained a firm grip on the life of the community. . . .
> The most discouraging failure of Victoria is the state of its Civil Service. . . . The pernicious rule that seniority is to govern promotion . . . is ruining the Victorian civil service.

Australian Education, 1788-1900

... The staff of the State schools seems to be selected on the same principle. Beginning by pupil teaching, without normal training, the individual rises into one class after another—the only difference being that the number of marks he gains from the inspectors of his work governs his progression on the ladder of the graded hierarchy. But once he has gained his footing in a class by a due number of marks, his selection for a particular vacancy is entirely dependent on seniority, no attention being paid to the character of the school or special circumstances he is required to deal with. University men or women who choose to devote themselves to elementary teaching have to climb up in precisely the same way as if they began as pupil teachers. Altogether education is in a bad way.[60]

That much of this criticism was conveyed to Deakin is clear from his Estimates speech; it is significant that on at least one occasion when Deakin conferred with Sidney Webb and Trevelyan he was accompanied by David Syme.[61]

Whether Deakin and Syme agreed to launch a campaign for educational reform can only be a matter of conjecture. If they did, Syme quickly narrowed the scope of Deakin's criticism, for while Deakin had deplored the spirit of the whole system, Syme concentrated his campaign upon the deficiencies of technical education. In doing this Syme was not only being consistent with his life-long interest in Victoria's industrial prosperity, but he was putting himself at the head of a movement which had already made its influence felt in the colony, for there was, as the headmaster of Wesley College put it, "a public craze about the matter".[62] The Chamber of Manufactures, the Chamber of Mines, the Trades Hall Council, the Royal Agricultural Society, the Working Men's College, the University of Melbourne and the Protectionist Association had all been represented at meetings, or on deputations, which had urged greater government interest in technical education, before December 1898.[63] Syme, as Professor La Nauze has suggested, "did not always create waves, but sometimes rode on their crests";[64] using Deakin's speech to give him impetus Syme now scrambled on to the powerful breaker of technical education. On 9, 10 December he published two long articles designed to show the progress made in South Australian technical education; on 25 January he set out the steps Victoria must take to match the progress being made in New South Wales and South Australia, and warned the Turner Ministry that "a liberal provision in these directions will be amongst the most profitable expenditures of the State"; on 14 February he switched his attack to agricultural education, but three days later swung back to his main target by advising the Victorian Association for the Promotion of Technical Education that he declined the position of Vice-President because he could best serve their cause by remaining outside their Association. In March, when the Melbourne University took up the issue and suggested a new degree course in Mining Engineering, he supported the suggestion enthusiastically.[65]

Under this attack Turner's Minister for Public Instruction, Alexander Peacock, sought first one way of escape and then another. Anxious to avoid any general inquiry into a department which he had administered for five years, and concerned to protect the Inspector-General, whose pupil he had been, Peacock had immediately countered Deakin's charges by declaring that the only weakness in the system was the condition of technical education; this, he asserted, he had already taken in hand by appointing a sub-committee of Cabinet to study it, and by planning to send one of his officers to report on conditions outside Victoria.[66] Syme waited until the beginning of March to see what would come of Peacock's promises, and then he hit hard. The need for improved technical education, he declared, was

> the ABC of the workman's primer. Knowledge wins; education takes the palm. There is not a member of the Turner Cabinet who will not yield the readiest assent to it. But intellectual assent is a meaningless mockery if it be not followed by its equivalent in action. They know perfectly well what they ought to do; they form the most commendable resolutions that they will do it; and then sit down apparently satisfied with the exceeding virtue of their resolves.[67]

The idea of a Cabinet sub-committee on technical education

Interpreting the Code of Public Education, 1872–1900

"looked feasible enough", Syme went on, "but nothing has come of it".[68] The Minister had certainly sent one of his officers to New South Wales, "but no living soul outside the department can find that anything has come of the report furnished". The Minister, it was said, was contemplating a plan whereby elementary technical education would begin in suitable primary schools. "Not a single syllable has since been heard of the scheme", Syme commented. ". . . Why is the Government of Victoria lagging?" he asked. "Has it reached to that stage described as 'Rest and be thankful'? If so, it is a dangerous place to drift to." These were ominous words from the *Age*, but still Peacock tried to avoid an inquiry. At the laying of a foundation stone for a new wing at the Ballarat School of Mines he announced a plan for introducing kindergarten and "hand and eye" work under overseas specialists, and went on to express his confidence in the School of Mines and the progress being made in technical education.[69] These were bad tactics. The Education Department had never exercised effective control over the Schools of Mines, many of which had fallen into decay, and the Department's administration could only be seen in the worst possible light if the Schools of Mines were examined closely. Syme ignored Peacock's new promises, dispatched a reporter to the country and early in May published three scathing articles on Victoria's Schools of Mines. Each School was examined in turn, its deficiencies brutally exposed, its staff, equipment and curriculum ridiculed. If this, Syme declared, was what the Turner Ministry meant by technical education, it was a national scandal and a flagrant waste of public money.[70] Two days later Turner announced that a Royal Commission, under the chairmanship of Theodore Fink, a private member, would be appointed "to investigate the important question of laying down a practical scheme of technical education". The *Age* had no hesitation in claiming that it had precipitated the Commission.

Syme had got what he wanted. Peacock had escaped a general inquiry. The system, it seemed, could not be questioned. Then, dramatically, the situation changed. Seizing upon that part of his commission which instructed him "generally to recommend what means should be adopted for the better provision of a systematic and graduated course of technical instruction", Fink proceeded to inquire into the general administration of public education, and his first two Progress Reports (issued 10 July and 29 November 1899) were damning indictments of the whole system. It was in vain that the one Departmental officer on the Commission (C. R. Long) protested at this extension of the inquiry and refused to sign the reports; Fink and the rest of the Commissioners were not to be deterred. Early in 1900, before the Commission had even begun its work on technical education, Peacock (now out of office) was forced to sit in the House and hear Fink declare that the Education Department

> had been quite stationary—not only dead to reform, but for the past ten years . . . it had actually gone back. There could be no doubt that as far as public education was concerned this colony had been living in a fool's paradise. . . . From the Inspector-General downwards almost every branch of the system needed a thorough overhaul.

The Inspector-General himself, Fink conceded, was diligent, but he was

> utterly wanting in all the qualifications for that position. He had no grasp, no capacity, no determination, no coherence of expression at all . . . [and was] utterly unqualified to do anything to prevent the department drifting from one reactionary position to another.[71]

Why Fink should have decided to use his commission in this way is not clear. The simplest explanation would be that as a close friend of Deakin he was convinced that the original charges made in December 1898 should be investigated. Fink was a minor political figure, but he was a man of considerable standing in both legal and commercial circles in Victoria, and would have had no hesitation in pursuing this unpopular line of action even to the detriment of his own political advancement. We know that Fink could, on occasions, act altruistically, as he did in 1899 when, after a period of sixteen days as a member of the McLean Ministry, he resigned from the Cabinet because he felt that the Treasurer had been needlessly vindictive towards the defeated Ministry.[72] We also know that he could, on occasions, act in the most self-interested way, as he did by using his legal acumen to extricate himself from the consequences of bankruptcy during the financial crash of the 1890s.[73]

In one sense, of course, Fink's motives are not of paramount importance. He was only one, albeit the chairman, of seven royal commissioners and he could neither have exploited their commission to the limit nor limited the scope of that commission without their consent. Once he opened his inquiry he was confronted with a mass of evidence from all the parties who had initiated and sustained the campaign for an inquiry, and this was so overwhelmingly critical of the existing system that no amount of skilful report writing could have obscured its significance.

The Reform Movement in the other States

Whatever his motives, then, Fink produced a report so condemnatory of public education in Victoria that no government could ignore it. Moreover it constituted a challenge to every other State in Australia. The irresponsible politician of New South Wales, or Tasmania or Queensland, could pretend for a little longer that the Victorian disclosures only proved how backward that State was compared to his own, but responsible opinion in these States was beginning to accept the possibility that the conditions Fink had uncovered probably existed in every other Education Department.

In June 1901, the Attorney-General of New South Wales (B. R. Wise) found the courage to question the belief that his government was administering the best system of public education in the world, and declared that he was prepared to "lay rude hands upon the ark of the covenant".[74] The next day, one of the most respected figures in the University

Interpreting the Code of Public Education, 1872–1900

of Sydney, Professor Francis Anderson, admitted that he, too, was "unable to join . . . the conspiracy of adulation . . . or the conspiracy of silence. . . ." which surrounded the system of public education. "The parrot cry of the most perfect system is echoed and re-echoed", he declared, but in fact "a radical alteration" in the New South Wales system was needed. The teachers of New South Wales, he went on, were "in the grip of the system, and at the mercy of the machine"; they constituted "a 'close' body. No outsider is admitted to the ranks. . . ." They were afraid to speak out, he realized, but in their hearts they knew that the manual training given in their schools was "a sham and a delusion", and the pupil-teacher system "a shame and a disgrace . . ."[75] It took six months to convince the Premier that public opinion was behind this attack. As late as December he was protesting that he "had been under the impression that the State system of education was an admirable one. . . . It had turned out thousands of bright boys and girls every week",[76] but his Minister of Public Instruction, knowing that the campaign had been taken up by the Leader of the Opposition (J. H. Carruthers), who had been Parkes's Minister of Public Instruction and was an authority on technical education, realized that reform could not be postponed much longer. Like Peacock in Victoria, however, he tried to avoid a general inquiry; in March 1902 he appointed G. H. Knibbs (Lecturer in Surveying at the University of Sydney) and J. W. Turner (Principal of the Fort Street Training College) as Commissioners to inquire into the development of education abroad and to make recommendations for the reorganization of the New South Wales system. Their Report rivalled Fink's in its unpalatable disclosures.[77]

In 1904 the Tasmanian Government commissioned W. L. Neale (a South Australian inspector) to investigate its system of primary education; in 1905 the Premier of South Australia, while paying due homage to Hartley's memory, admitted that education in his State was "lagging behind". "I conceive it to be my duty to see to this, and remedy it", he went on.

Australian Education, 1788-1900

We have reached that stage in our national life where the old must give place to the new. . . . All the facts show that the time has come for a change. . . . I see . . . that the great battle of the future between the nations will be for the supremacy of trade, and if the people of Great Britain and Australia are not equipped with the best technical and other education, they must inevitably go down in the struggle.[78]

In Queensland D. I. Ewart protected his empire to the last, but even before his retirement (1909) the Minister had made it clear that with the appointment of his successor the whole system of public education would have to be overhauled.[79]

All these developments, of course, lie outside the chronological limits of this study, but they are relevant to any discussion of the state of public education in Australia at the turn of the century. They make it clear that, at the moment when the Australian colonies were accepting the responsibilities of federation and nationhood, they had clearly failed to educate their citizens for the national status they were assuming. The colonial statesmen could hardly plead that they had not been warned of the shabby civilization they were developing; a long line of visitors and migrants (men like Sir Charles Dilke, Anthony Trollope, J. A. Froude, Marcus Clarke) had tried to awaken the Australian to his danger. The most perceptive of them, Francis Adams, had, in imitation of his idol, Matthew Arnold, tried to make us see the colonial type of Barbarian and Philistine we were producing. "Everywhere", he lamented,

> are the thumb marks and the great toe marks of the six-fingered, six-toed giant, Mr. Arnold's life-long foe, the British Philistine. . . . The Australian public cares little that, in the State schools which it has founded . . . dead dry intellectual knowledge is rampant—that "asinine feast of sow-thistles and brambles," as Milton disgustedly puts it, "which is commonly set before our youth as all the food and entertainment of their tenderest and most docile age"—"inanimate gerund-grinding" as Carlyle equally disgustedly called it—gerund-grinding and spiritual cockatoo screeching. . . .

But Adams, though he was to despair of life itself and die by his own hand, believed that the Australians might find their own salvation. "Perhaps one of these mornings", he wrote,

Interpreting the Code of Public Education, 1872–1900

the . . . public will wake up, tired of listening to the chatter of the religious and secular dogmatists gathered together like eagles over the carcase of "Religion without Superstition" and there may arise a curiosity and a care for Higher Education. . . . And, perhaps, some day poor little Culture, putting off the cumbrous armour with which the gerund and the cockatoo want to load him, taking his sling in his hand and a few smooth stones from the brook, may smite great Goliath in the forehead, and cut off his head, and there be a signal rout of all the Philistines, even unto Gath and Gaza and the utmost borders of the land.[80]

NOTES

[1] *Parl. Deb.* (S.A.), 1890, 1659.
[2] Western Australian Education Department Files, 89/88. (J.S.B.).
[3] Report of the Royal Commission . . . upon the existing General Condition of Education, 1882–4; Minutes of Evidence, Q. 3433, *P. P.* (Vic.), 1884.
[4] Ibid. Qq. 3688–90.
[5] Ibid. Qq. 3777–94, 3852, 4013–20. See also Douglas Pike, 'Education in an Agricultural State', *Melbourne Studies in Education, 1957–8*, p. 79.
[6] Report of the Royal Commission . . . 1882–4, op. cit.; see 'Night Schools' in index. See also remarks on Night Schools in Annual Reports of Minister of Public Instruction.
[7] Report on the State of Public Education in Victoria, 1877, p. 10, *P. P.* (Vic.), 1877–8.
[8] Report of the Royal Commission . . . 1882–4, op. cit.; Minutes of Evidence, Qq. 200–6, 3746–55, 4198–205.
[9] E. R. Wyeth, *Education in Queensland*, p. 158; *Sydney Morning Herald*, 26 June 1901.
[10] Final Report of the Commission on the working of the Education Acts, 1882, p. vii, *Proc. Parlt.*, (S.A.), 1883–4. See also Pike, op. cit., pp. 63–6; Wyeth, op. cit. Ch. 6.
[11] Report of the Royal Commission . . . 1882–4, op. cit., Qq. 592–3 and Appendix D.
[12] *V. & P.*, Vic. Leg. Assembly, 1877–8, Paper C17. It should be added that Pearson was unhappy about his task. He protested: "The propriety of mutilating the works of a standard author is always doubtful. . . . Altogether these passages do not seem so important as to constitute any real objection to the use of the series." For Pearson's own views on the place of religious instruction see the *Victorian Review*, Vol. 3, No. 14, Dec. 1880. See also John Tregenza, *Professor of Democracy: The Life of Charles Henry Pearson.*

[13] Report of the Royal Commission . . . 1882-4, op. cit., Qq. 337-9.
[14] Ibid., Appendix P.
[15] *Argus*, 8 Oct. 1878.
[16] Andrew Harper, *The Hon. James Balfour*, pp. 183-208; Walter Murdoch, *Alfred Deakin*, p. 178.
[17] Report of the Royal Commission . . . 1882-4, op. cit.; Report of the Chairman, pp. 7-12.
[18] *Parl. Deb.* (Vic.), Vol. xci, 249. For the secularists' response to this campaign see *Argus*, 8 Oct. 1878; Marcus Clarke, *Civilization Without Delusion*.
[19] Quoted W. F. Connell, *The Educational Thought and Influence of Matthew Arnold*, p. 237.
[20] This picture of the colonial pupil-teacher is a composite one drawn from the Ministers' Reports in the various colonies.
[21] A Teachers' College was not opened until 1876 in S.A., 1902 in W.A., 1906 in Tas., 1914 in Qld. In N.S.W. short, improvised courses were conducted in borrowed rooms from 1867 on, but it was 1906 before the Blackfriars School was converted into a Teachers' College. Victoria opened a Normal School in 1855, closed it in 1859, re-opened it as the Central Training Institute in 1870, moved it to a new site as the Melbourne Teachers' College in 1889, closed it in 1893 and re-opened it in 1900.
[22] Report of the Minister of Public Instruction, 1877-8, p. 211, *P. P.* (Vic.), 1878.
[23] *Australasian Schoolmaster*, Nov. 1892, June 1895. Frank Tate had been appointed to the staff of the Melbourne Teachers' College in 1889. He became a district inspector in 1895.
[24] See the evidence given before any colonial Royal Commission or Select Committee on Education in this period.
[25] Report of the Minister of Public Instruction, 1877-8, op. cit., p. 213.
[26] Vic. paid its teachers under this system from 1863 to 1905; Tas., S.A. and W.A. all experimented with it in the last quarter of the century. Qld. and N.S.W. who prided themselves on having avoided its evils nevertheless employed a similar system which might be called "promotion by results".
[27] Quoted J. W. Adamson, *English Education, 1789-1902*, pp. 226, 230.
[28] Report of the Royal Commission . . . upon the operation of the system of Public Education, 1867, p. 37, *P.P.* (Vic.), 1867.
[29] Report of the Royal Commission . . . 1882-4, op. cit.; Minutes of Evidence, Qq. 11458-69.
[30] Final Report of the Commission on the working of the Education Acts, 1882, op. cit., Qq. 7207, 7261-73, 7372.

Interpreting the Code of Public Education, 1872–1900

[31] Ibid., Qq. 7363–7.
[32] Report of the Royal Commission . . . 1882–4, op. cit.; Second Report, p. vi.
[33] Ibid., Appendix I.
[34] Report of the Commission on Education, 1888, para. 25, *V. & P.*, Qld. Leg. Assembly, 1889. See also Final Report of the Commission on the working of the Education Acts, 1882, op. cit., p. iv.
[35] Western Australian Education Department Files, 843/97. (J.S.B.)
[36] Report of the Commission on Education, 1888, op. cit., paras. 28, 32, 55.
[37] Report on the State of Public Education in Victoria, 1877, op. cit., p. 4.
[38] Ibid.
[39] Report of the Central Board of Education, 1872, p. 3, *V. & P.*, W.A. Leg. Council, 1873.
[40] Quoted G. T. Snooke, 'The Elementary Education Act, 1871–1881', unpublished B.A. Thesis, University of Western Australia, 1951, pp. 21, 25.
[41] Letter Book of the Cranbourne Board of Advice. (In the possession of Mr M. James, Toorak Teachers' College, Melbourne.)
[42] Report of the Minister of Public Instruction, 1876–7, p. 41, *P. P.* (Vic.), 1877–8.
[43] Report of the Commission on Education, 1888, op. cit., paras. 29, 31. Royal Commission on Technical Education, 1899–1901; Second Progress Report, p. 43, *P. P.* (Vic.), 1899–1900. See also R. J. W. Selleck, 'The Strange Case of Inspector Robertson', *Melbourne Studies in Education, 1964*.
[44] Ibid., pp. 52–5.
[45] *Parl. Deb.* (Vic.), Vol. xciii, 3578–9.
[46] *Parl. Deb.* (N.S.W.), First Series, cix, 4163; Second Series, vii, 2902, iii, 2913. *Parl. Deb.* (Vic.), Vol. xc, 3400.
[47] Report of the Commission on Education, 1888, op. cit., para. 30.
[48] Quoted C. E. Saunders, 'John Anderson Hartley and Education in South Australia', unpublished B.A. Thesis, University of Adelaide, 1958, p. 38.
[49] See C. M. H. Clark, *Select Documents in Australian History, 1851–1900*, p. 563; C. M. H. Clark, *Sources of Australian History*, Ch. 5; Vance Palmer, *The Legend of the Nineties*, passim.
[50] Palmer, op. cit., p. 70.
[51] See John Tregenza, op. cit., Ch. 8.
[52] *Parl. Deb.* (Vic.), Vol. xc, 3397–400.

[53] Ibid., 3401–7.
[54] Deakin to Royce, 5 June 1892, quoted Murdoch, op. cit., p. 129. The definitive biography of Deakin is J. A. La Nauze, *Alfred Deakin, a Biography*.
[55] See J. A. La Nauze, *Political Economy in Australia*, pp. 99–100.
[56] On 15 Dec. 1898 Frank Madden, M.L.A. had charged Syme with improper practices under the Land Act of 1865. Alfred Deakin, Diary, 20 Dec. 1898. (In the possession of Professor J. A. La Nauze, A.N.U.).
[57] Quoted Murdoch, op. cit., p. 196. For an example of Meredith's interest in education see his novel *Lord Ormont and his Aminta* (1894).
[58] See A. G. Austin (Ed.), *The Webbs' Australian Diary, 1898*.
[59] Beatrice Webb to Kate, Lady Courtney, 15 Nov. 1898. (B.L.E.P.S.)
[60] Austin, op. cit., pp. 74 and 87.
[61] Deakin, Diary, op. cit., 19 Oct. 1898. Another of Deakin's informants may have been Frank Tate who was an old friend and who visited Deakin's home on 4 Nov. 1898.
[62] *Age*, 15 Dec. 1898. There are a few *Age* articles on the need for general educational reform (e.g. in the issues of 22 Feb., 4 Mar. 1899), but the overwhelming weight of the *Age* attack is on technical education.
[63] Ibid. 18, 20 Oct., 16 Nov. 1898. There had been a Technological Commission in Victoria from 1869 to 1890; Pearson issued a Report on Technical Education in 1888 and presided over a Commission on Technical Education in 1889. A Departmental committee also reported on technical education in 1891.
[64] La Nauze, *Political Economy*, op. cit., p. 99.
[65] *Age*, 20, 25 Mar., 4, 5 Apr. 1899.
[66] *Parl. Deb.* (Vic.), Vol. xc, 3410–11.
[67] *Age*, 2 Mar. 1899.
[68] Ibid. In fact Peacock had appointed a board to advise the Cabinet sub-committee, but all its members were officers of the Departments of Education or Agriculture. One of them (H.W. Potts) and the Secretary (W. J. Skewes) survived as members of the Fink Commission. *Age*, 31 Jan. 1899.
[69] Ibid., 15 Apr. 1899. For the history of these institutions see Royal Commission on Technical Education, 1899–1901, op. cit.; Final Report, pp. 148 et seq. See also Stephen Murray-Smith, 'A History of Technical Education in Australia', unpublished Ph.D. Thesis, University of Melbourne, 1966.
[70] *Age*, 5, 8, 10 May 1899.
[71] *Parl. Deb.* (Vic.), Vol. xciii, 3569–70.
[72] *Argus*, 21, 25 Dec. 1899.

[73] Michael Cannon, *The Land Boomers*, Chs. 16, 17.
[74] *Sydney Morning Herald* (Evening Edition), 26 June 1901.
[75] Ibid., 27 June 1901. Anderson's speech was badly reported in the Press; for the complete text of his speech see Francis Anderson, *The Public School System of New South Wales*.
[76] *Sydney Morning Herald* (Evening Edition), 11 Dec. 1901.
[77] There were, in fact, a series of reports tabled during 1903, 1904 and 1905—see Bibliography. In general Turner, as befitted a senior officer of the Education Department, was cautious and placatory, but Knibbs felt no need for restraint. "It is the inferiority of our whole educational system", he wrote, "which has made the task of the Commissioners a difficult one". Commission on Primary, Secondary, Technical and other Branches of Education, 1903-5; Report Mainly on Secondary Education, 1904, p. 11, *P. P.* (N.S.W.), 1904.
[78] Quoted T. H. Smeaton, *Education in South Australia from 1836 to 1927*, pp. 99-102.
[79] Wyeth, op. cit., pp. 156-7. In Western Australia the Education Department was only established in 1893, and was saved from the fate of its eastern counterparts by the importation of (Sir) Cyril Jackson as Inspector-General in 1896. Jackson, who had had extensive experience in England, found a great deal to criticize in the Western Australian system, but because his department had not had time to settle into bad habits, and because the colony, thanks to its gold-fields, was prosperous, he had comparatively little difficulty in making it the superior of any other Education Department in Australia before he left the country in 1903.
[80] Francis W. L. Adams, *Australian Essays*, pp. 55, 62-3.

Select Bibliography

This bibliography has been arranged according to the following classification:

A. Manuscript Material.
B. Printed Material.
   1. Official and Semi-official Documents.
   2. Books and Pamphlets.
   3. Articles.
   4. Newspapers.
C. Unpublished Theses.

A. Manuscript Material

Angas Papers. (S.A.A.)
Appendix on Eccelesiastical Establishments, Schools and Charitable Societies (Bigge Report). C.O. 201/127. (P.R.O.)
Bishop Broughton Papers (microfilm copy). (M.L.)
Bonwick Transcripts, Box 27; Biography, Vol. 1; Missionary, Vol. 5, Box 53. (M.L.)
Bourke Papers, Uncat. MSS, Set 403. (M.L.)
Correspondence of Thomas Hobbes Scott. Vol. 1. (M.L.); and C.O. 201/147. (P.R.O.)
Deakin, Alfred, Diary for 1898. (In the possession of Professor J. A. La Nauze, Ernest Scott Professor of History, University of Melbourne.)
First Report of the General Committee of Education, 1848. (J.S.B.)
Hassall Correspondence. Vol. 2 (M.L.)
Inward Correspondence of the Denominational Schools Board, Port Phillip District, 1848–51. (S.L.V.)

Select Bibliography

Letter Book of the Cranbourne Board of Advice. (In the possession of Mr M. James, Toorak Teachers' College, Melbourne.)
Marsden Papers. Vol. 1. (M.L.)
Minutes and Correspondence of the Education Committee, Western Australia, 1847–9. (J.S.B.)
Minutes of the First Conference of the Australian Wesleyan Methodist Church, 1855. (Methodist Conference Office, 288 Little Collins Street, Melbourne.)
Miscellaneous Letters Received by the Board of National Education, New South Wales, 1848–51. (M.L.)
New South Wales: Governors' Despatches. Vol. 5, 1823–4. (M.L.)
Nicholson Correspondence. (In the possession of Mr P. J. Williams, Eaglemont, Victoria.)
Papers of Sir George Arthur. Vols. 12, 13. (M.L.)
Passfield Papers, Letters, 1892–99. (B.L.E.P.S.)
Reddall Papers. (M.L.)
Report of the Commissioners for investigating the manner in which the system of Public Education in Van Diemen's Land is carried out, 1845. (T.S.A.)
Rusden, G. W., Diary. (S.L.V.)
Webb, Beatrice, Diary for 1898. (B.L.E.P.S.)
Western Australian Education Department Files. 89/88, 843/97. (J.S.B.)

B. Printed Matter

1. *Official and Semi-official Documents*

Aid From Public Funds to Roman Catholic Schools in Western Australia, *V. & P.*, W.A. Leg. Council, 1870–1.
Annual Reports of the Board of Education, 1840–8, *V. & P. & P.*, V.D.L. Leg. Council, 1840–9.
Annual Reports of the Commissioners of National Education in New South Wales, 1849–53, *V. & P.*, N.S.W. Leg. Council, 1849–53.
Annual Reports of the Commissioners of National Education in Victoria, 1852–62, *V. & P.*, Vic. Leg. Council to 1856, thereafter *P.P.* (Vic.).
Annual Reports of the Inspector of Schools, 1850–3, *V. & P. & P.*, V.D.L. Leg. Council, 1850–3.
Annual Reports of the Minister of Public Instruction, Victoria

Australian Education, 1788–1900

1872–1900, Queensland 1875–1900, South Australia 1875–1900, New South Wales 1880–1900, Tasmania 1885–1900, Western Australia 1893–1900 in relevant Parliamentary Papers.

Coghlan, T. A., *General Report on the Eleventh Census of New South Wales* (Sydney, 1891).

Commission on Primary, Secondary, Technical and other Branches of Education: Interim Report on Certain Parts of Primary Education, 1903; Report Mainly on Secondary Education, 1904; Preliminary Report on Technical Education Generally, 1904; Report on Agricultural, Commercial, Industrial and other Forms of Technical Education, 1905, *P.P.* (N.S.W.), 1903–5. (The Knibbs-Turner Report.)

Copies or Extracts of Correspondence respecting the Clergy Reserves in Canada: 1819–40, Part 1, *Great Britain and Ireland: Parliamentary Documents*, Vol. 26, 1813–40.

Debates (S.A. Leg. Council), 1851.

Documents and Correspondence Relating to the Establishment and Dissolution of the Corporation of Clergy and School Lands in the Colony of New South Wales. *Great Britain and Ireland: Parliamentary Documents*, Vol. 19, 1838–9.

Final Report of the Commission on the Working of the Education Acts, 1882, *Proc. Parlt.* (S.A.), 1883–4.

First Report of the Commission appointed to enquire into the State of Education; Final Report from the School Commissioners, *V. & P.*, N.S.W. Leg. Council, 1855–7. (Wilkins, Turton, Levinge Report.)

Fraser, Malcolm A. C., *Seventh Census of Western Australia* (Perth, 1901).

Hansard (Vic.), iii, xi.

Historical Records of Australia, Series I. Vols. i–xxvi; Series III. Vol. v.

Historical Records of New South Wales, Vol. I, pt. 2.

Hobart Town Gazette, 1838–54.

Papers Relative to Public Education in Western Australia, 1870, *V. & P.*, W.A. Leg. Council, 1870–1.

Parl. Deb. (N.S.W.), First Series, cix; Second Series, i, iii, vii.

Parl. Deb. (Qld.), xviii.

Parl. Deb. (S.A.), 1875, 1890.

Parl. Deb. (Vic.), Vols. viii, xv, xc, xci, xciii.

Parl. Deb. (W.A.), 1879; New Series, ii, vii, viii.

Select Bibliography

Proceedings of the Education Conference, 1904, *P.P.* (Qld.), 1904.

Report from the Select Committee appointed to take into consideration the Question of Public Education, 1853, *V. & P. & P.*, V.D.L. Leg. Council, 1853.

Report from the Select Committee on Education, 1852, *V. & P.*, Vic. Leg. Council, 1852.

Report of Commissioners appointed by His Excellency the Governor to enquire into the state of Superior and General Education in Tasmania, 1860, Tas. H. of A. *Journals*, 1860.

Report of the Board of Inspection of the Public Schools of the Island, 1853, *V. & P. & P.*, V.D.L. Leg. Council, 1853.

Report of the Central Board of Education, 1872, *V. & P.*, W.A. Leg. Council, 1873.

Report of the Central Board of Education, 1889, *M. & V. & P.*, W.A. Parlt., 1890–1.

Report of the Commissioner of Inquiry into the state of the Colony of New South Wales, 1822; Report of the Commissioner of Inquiry on the Judicial Establishments of New South Wales and Van Diemen's Land, 1823; Report of the Commissioner of Inquiry on the State of Agriculture and Trade in the Colony of New South Wales, 1823, *House of Commons Papers*, 1822, Vol. 20, 1823, Vol. 10. (Bigge Report.)

Report of the Commission on Education, 1888 *V. & P.*, Qld. Leg. Ass., 1889.

Report of the Joint Select Committee . . . appointed to consider the terms . . . on which it will be equitable to abolish the Assisted School System . . . 1895, *M. & V. & P.*, W.A. Parlt., 1895.

Report of the Royal Commission on Public Education, 1867, Tas. H. of A. *Journals*, 1867.

Report of the Royal Commission on the Educational Institutions of the Colony, 1875, *P.P.* (Qld.), 1875.

Report of the Royal Commission . . . upon the Administration, Organization and General Condition of Education, 1882–4, *P.P.* (Vic.) 1882–4. (The Rogers–Templeton Report.)

Report of the Royal Commission . . . upon the operation of the system of Public Education, 1867, *P.P.* (Vic.), 1867. (The Higinbotham Report.)

Report of the Second Session of the Eighth Synod of the Diocese of Perth (Perth, 1893).

Australian Education, 1788–1900

Report of the Select Committee of the House of Assembly appointed to report upon a system of Education, 1861, *Proc. Parlt.* (S.A.), 1861.

Report of the Select Committee on Education, 1844, *V. & P.*, N.S.W. Leg. Council, 1844.

Report on the State of Public Education in Victoria, 1877, *P.P.* (Vic.), 1877–8. (The Pearson Report.)

Royal Commission on Education: First, Second, Third, Fourth, Fifth and Final Reports, 1899–1901, *P.P.* (Vic.), 1899–1901. (The Fink Report.)

South Australian Government Gazette, 1851.

Third Report of the Commissioners of Colonial Inquiry into the Receipt and Expenditure of Colonial Revenue, 1830, *Great Britain and Ireland: Parliamentary Documents*, Vol. 5. 1826–38.

Western Australian Government Gazette, 1848, 1855.

2. Books and Pamphlets

A'Beckett, T. T., *A Defence of State Aid to Religion* (Melbourne, 1856).

A Brief History of Education in Western Australia, 1829–1937. Typescript prepared by the Education Department of W.A., 1937.

A Charge Delivered to the Clergy of the Diocese of Tasmania at the Primary Visitation by Francis-Russell Nixon, Lord Bishop of Tasmania (London, 1848).

A Colonist, *A Plea for Common Schools* (Sydney, 1857).

Adams, Francis W. L., *Australian Essays* (Melbourne, 1886).

Adamson, J. W., *English Education, 1789–1902* (C.U.P., 1930).

Akenson, Donald H., *The Irish Education Experiment* (London, 1970).

Alexander, Fred (Ed.), *Four Bishops and Their See* (Univ. of W.A. Press, 1957).

Alexander, Fred, *Moving Frontiers* (M.U.P., 1947).

An Account of the Proceedings of the Laity and Clergy of the Church of England in South Australia, occasioned by the publication of certain Minutes of a Meeting held at Sydney by the Australasian Bishops in October, 1850 (Adelaide, 1851).

Anderson, Francis, *The Public School System of New South Wales* (Sydney, 1901).

Archer, W. H., *Noctes Catholicae* (Melbourne, 1856).

Arnold, Thomas, *Passages in a Wandering Life* (London, 1900).

Select Bibliography

A Speech Delivered at the General Committee of Protestants on Wednesday, August 3rd, 1836, by the Bishop of Australia (Sydney, 1836).

Auchmuty, J. J., *Irish Education; A Historical Survey* (Dublin, 1937).

Austin, A. G., *George William Rusden and National Education in Australia* (M.U.P., 1958).

Austin, A. G., *Select Documents in Australian Education, 1788–1900* (Melbourne, 1963).

Austin, A. G. (Ed.), *The Webbs' Australian Diary, 1898* (Melbourne, 1965).

Barrett, John, *That Better Country: The Religious Aspect of Life in Eastern Australia, 1833–1850* (M.U.P., 1966).

Battye, J. S., *Western Australia: A History from its Discovery to the Inauguration of the Commonwealth* (O.U.P., 1924).

Bickford, James, *An Autobiography of Christian Labour, 1838–88* (London, 1890).

Blair, David (Ed.), *Speeches on Various Occasions . . . by Henry Parkes* (Melbourne, 1876).

Bleasdale, J. J., *Practical Education* (Melbourne, 1870).

Bolton, G. C., *Alexander Forrest: His Life and Times* (M.U.P., 1958).

Border, Ross, *Church and State in Australia, 1788–1872: A Constitutional Study of the Church of England in Australia* (London, 1962).

Bromby, J. E., *Pre-Historic Man* (Melbourne, 1869).

Brose, Olive J., *Church and Parliament: The Reshaping of the Church of England, 1828–1860* (London, 1959).

Burke, Edmund, *Works*, 8 vols. (London, 1861).

Burton, A. (Ed.), Wollaston Journals, Vol. I. Typescript. (M.L.)

Burton, A. and Henn, U. (Eds.), *Wollaston's Albany Journal* (Perth, 1955).

Burton, A. and Henn, U. (Eds.), *Wollaston's Picton Journal* (Perth, 1948).

Burton, W. W., *The State of Religion and Education in New South Wales* (London, 1840).

Butler, Dom Cuthbert, *The Vatican Council, 1869–70* (London, 1962).

Cairns, A., *A Lecture on the Mutual Relations and Duties of Church and State* (Melbourne, 1856).

Cannon, Michael, *The Land Boomers* (M.U.P., 1966).

Clark, C. M. H., *Select Documents in Australian History, 1788–1850* (Sydney, 1950).

Clark, C. M. H., *Select Documents in Australian History, 1851–1900* (Sydney, 1955).
Clark, C. M. H., *Sources of Australian History* (London, 1957).
Clarke, Marcus, *Civilization Without Delusion* (Melbourne, 1880).
Cleverley, John F., *The First Generation: School and Society in Early Australia* (S.U.P., 1971).
Cole, E. W., *Essay on the Deluge* (Melbourne, 1869).
Cole, E. W., *Religions of the World* (Melbourne, 1866).
Cole, E. W., *The Real Place in History of Jesus and Paul* (Melbourne, 1867).
Connell, W. F., *The Educational Thought and Influence of Matthew Arnold* (London, 1950).
Crowley, F. K., *Australia's Western Third* (London, 1960).
Crowley, F. K., *Forrest, 1847–1918: Vol. 1, 1847–91. Apprenticeship to Premiership* (U. of Q. Press, 1971).
Crowley, F. K., *Sir John Forrest* (U. of Q. Press, 1968).
Denison, Sir William, *Varieties of Vice-Regal Life* (London, 1870).
Dow, Gwyneth M., *George Higinbotham: Church and State* (Melbourne, 1964).
Duncan, W. A., *Lecture on National Education* (Brisbane, 1850).
Ferguson, W. T. and Immelman, R. F. M., *Sir John Herschel and Education at the Cape, 1834–1840* (Cape Town, 1961).
Fitzpatrick, Brian, *The British Empire in Australia* (M.U.P., 1949).
Fitzpatrick, Kathleen, *Sir John Franklin in Tasmania* (M.U.P., 1949).
Fogarty, Bro. R., *Catholic Education in Australia, 1806–1950*, 2 vols. (M.U.P., 1959).
Frankel, Charles, *The Case for Modern Man* (New York, 1956).
Fraser, T. M'Kenzie, *Lecture on the Theory of Annihilation* (Melbourne, 1870).
Fremantle, Anne (Ed.), *The Papal Encyclicals in their Historical Context* (New York, 1956).
Geoghegan, P. B., *Pastoral Letter to the Clergy and Laity of the Diocese on the Education of Catholic Children* (Adelaide, 1860).
Goodman, G., *The Church in Victoria during the Episcopate of the Rt. Rev. C. Perry* (London, 1892).
Greenwood, Gordon (Ed.), *Australia: A Social and Political History* (Sydney, 1955)
Griffiths, D. C., *Documents on the Establishment of Education in New South Wales, 1789–1880* (A.C.E.R., 1957).

Select Bibliography

Hale, Mathew, *A Letter . . . on the Education Question* (Perth, 1871).
Halévy, E., *The Liberal Awakening* (London, 1949).
Halévy, E., *The Triumph of Reform* (London, 1950).
Halévy, E., *Victorian Years* (London, 1951).
Hammond, J. L. and Hammond, Barbara, *The Bleak Age* (London, 1947).
Hancock, W. K., *Australia* (London, 1945).
Harper, Andrew, *The Hon. James Balfour* (Melbourne, 1918).
Hartwell, R. M., *The Economic Development of Van Diemen's Land, 1820-50* (M.U.P., 1954).
Hasluck, Alexandra, *Portrait With Background: A Life of Georgiana Molloy* (O.U.P., 1955).
Hawtrey, C. L. M., *The Availing Struggle: A Record of the Planting and Development of the Church of England in Western Australia, 1829-1947* (Perth, 1950).
Hayes, E. E. Y., *Pio Nono: A study in European politics and religion in the nineteenth century* (London, 1954).
Higinbotham, George, *Public Instruction Speeches* (Melbourne, n.d.).
Higinbotham, George, *Self Education* (Melbourne, 1862).
Himmelfarb, Gertrude, *Lord Acton: A Study in Conscience and Politics* (London, 1952).
Howell, P. A., *Thomas Arnold the Younger in Van Diemen's Land* (Tasmanian Historical Research Association, 1964).
Hutchins, William, *A Letter on the School Question* (Hobart Town, 1839).
Huxley, T. H., *Science and Education* (London, 1899).
James, G. F. (Ed.), *A Homestead History* (M.U.P., 1949).
King, Hazel, *Richard Bourke* (O.U.P., 1971).
Knight, Ruth, *Illiberal Liberal: Robert Lowe in New South Wales, 1842-1850* (M.U.P., 1966).
Knaplund, Paul, *James Stephen and the British Colonial System* (Madison, 1953).
La Nauze, J. A., *Alfred Deakin, a Biography* (M.U.P., 1965).
La Nauze, J. A., *Political Economy in Australia: Historical Studies* (M.U.P., 1949).
Landor, E. W., *The Bushman; or Life in a New Country* (London, 1847).
Lang, John Dunmore, *Account of the Steps taken in England with a*

view to the Establishment of an Academical Institution or College in New South Wales (Sydney, 1831).
Lang, John Dunmore, *An Historical and Statistical Account of New South Wales*, 2 vols. (London, 1840 and 1852).
Lang, John Dunmore, *Phillipsland: Its Present Condition and Prospects* (London, 1847).
Leslie, Shane (Ed.), *From Cabin-Boy to Archbishop: The Autobiography of Archbishop Ullathorne* (London, 1941).
Loch, John, *An Account of the Introduction and Effects of the System of General Religious Education Established in Van Diemen's Land in 1839* (Hobart Town, 1843).
Lovat, Lady Alice, *The Life of Sir Frederick Weld* (London, 1914).
Macartney, H. B., *State Aid to Religion and Education* (Melbourne, 1856).
M'Coy, F., *The Order and Plan of Creation* (Melbourne, 1869).
McMahon, John T., *One Hundred Years* (Perth, 1946).
Madden, Thomas More (Ed.), *The Memoirs of Richard Robert Madden* (London, 1891).
Mill, John Stuart, *On Liberty* (London, 1945).
Morris, Edward E., *A Memoir of George Higinbotham* (London, 1895).
Murdoch, Walter, *Alfred Deakin* (London, 1923).
Murphy, James, *The Religious Problem in English Education: The Crucial Experiment* (Liverpool University Press, 1959).
Nayler, B. S., *The Battle of Science* (Melbourne, 1869).
Nixon, Francis Russell, *A Charge Delivered to the Clergy of Tasmania . . . on Thursday, 22nd May, 1851* (Hobart Town, 1851).
Nixon, Francis Russell, *A Charge Delivered to the Clergy of the Diocese of Tasmania . . . on Tuesday, 22nd May, 1855* (Hobart Town, 1855).
O'Brien, Eris, *Life and Letters of Archpriest John Joseph Therry*, 2 vols. (Sydney, 1922).
O'Brien, Eris, *The Foundation of Australia* (Sydney, 1950).
O'Reilly, John, *Pastoral Letter on Education* (Port Augusta, 1889).
Palmer, Vance, *National Portraits* (M.U.P., 1948).
Palmer, Vance, *The Legend of the Nineties* (M.U.P., 1954).
Parkes, Henry, *Fifty Years in the Making of Australian History*, 2 vols. (London, 1892).
Perry, C., *Science and the Bible* (Melbourne, 1869).
Pike, Douglas, *Paradise of Dissent* (Melbourne, 1957).
Polding, John Bede, *Pastoral Letter* (Sydney, 1859).

Select Bibliography

Proceedings at a Meeting of the Members and Friends of the Protestant Association . . . June 19, 1839 (London, 1839).
Ramsay, A. M., *How the Money Goes* (Melbourne, 1856).
Rankin, Donald H., *The History of the Development of Education in Western Australia* (Perth, 1926).
Reilly, J. T., *Reminiscences of Fifty Years' Residence in Western Australia* (Perth, 1903).
Roberts, William, *Memoirs of the Life and Correspondence of Mrs. Hannah More*, 4 vols. (London, 1835).
Robson, L. L., *The Convict Settlers of Australia* (M.U.P., 1965).
Roe, Michael, *Quest for Authority in Eastern Australia, 1835–1851* (M.U.P., 1965).
Ross, James Clark, *A Voyage of Discovery and Research, 1839–43* (London, 1847).
Rusden, G. W., *History of Australia*, 3 vols. (Melbourne, 1897).
Rusden, G. W., *National Education* (Melbourne, 1853).
Rusden, H. K., *Christ in the Sepulchre* (Melbourne, 1867).
Rusden, H. K., *Free Agency* (Melbourne, 1868).
Rusden, H. K., *Moral Responsibility* (Melbourne, 1868).
Rusden, H. K., *Science and Theology* (Melbourne, 1870).
Rusden, H. K., *The Bishop of Melbourne's Theory of Education* (Melbourne, 1871).
Rusden, H. K., *The Power of the Pulpit* (Melbourne, 1877).
Rusden, H. K., *Tough Morsels of Theology* (Melbourne, 1866).
Shaw, A. G. L., *Heroes and Villains in History: Governors Darling and Bourke in N.S.W.* (S.U.P., 1966).
Smeaton, T. H., *Education in South Australia from 1836 to 1927* (Adelaide, 1927).
Smith, Adam, *An Inquiry into the Nature and Causes of the Wealth of Nations* (Edinburgh, 1859).
Smith, S. H. and Spaull, G. T., *History of Education in New South Wales* (Sydney, 1925).
Speech of Thomas George Gregson Esq. in the Legislative Council on the state of Public Education in Van Diemen's Land (Hobart Town, 1850).
Speeches by Lord Macaulay (O.U.P., 1952).
Suttor, T. L., *Hierarchy and Democracy in Australia, 1788–1870* (M.U.P., 1965).
Sweetman, Edward, *The Educational Activities in Victoria of the Rt. Hon. H. C. E. Childers* (M.U.P., 1940).

The Autobiography of Archbishop Ullathorne (London, 1891).
The Speech of the Lord Bishop of Australia in the Legislative Council upon a System of General Education, on Tuesday, 27 August, 1839 (Sydney, 1839).
Tregenza, John, *Professor of Democracy: The Life of Charles Henry Pearson* (M.U.P., 1968).
Vaughan, Roger William Bede, *Pastorals and Speeches on Education* (Sydney, 1880).
Whitington, F. T., *Augustus Short: First Bishop of Adelaide* (Adelaide, 1887).
Wilkins, William, *National Education: An Exposition of the National System of New South Wales* (Sydney, 1865).
Withers, W. B., *The History of Ballarat* (Ballarat, 1870).
Wyeth, E. R., *Education in Queensland* (A.C.E.R., n.d.).

3. *Articles*

Allott, Kenneth, 'Thomas Arnold the Younger, New Zealand, and the "Old Democratic Fervour" ', *Landfall*, Vol. 15, No. 3 (Sept., 1961).
Arnold, W. T., 'Thomas Arnold the Younger', *The Century Magazine*, Vol. LXVI, No. 1 (May, 1903).
Austin, A. G., 'The Bush Boarding School in the Port Phillip District', *Journal of Education* (V.I.E.R.), Vol. 3, No. 3.
Barrett, John, 'The Gipps-Broughton Alliance, 1844. A Denial Based on the Letters of Broughton to Edward Coleridge', *Historical Studies: Australia and New Zealand*, Vol. 11, No. 41 (Nov. 1963).
Barron, T. and Cable, K. J., 'The Diary of James Stephen, 1846', *Historical Studies*, Vol. 13, No. 52 (April 1969). (Formerly *Historical Studies: Australia and New Zealand*.)
Burns, R. J., 'Archdeacon Scott and the Church and School Corporation', Turney, C. (Ed.), *Pioneers of Australian Education* (S.U.P., 1969).
Burroughs, Peter, 'Wakefield and the Ripon Land Regulations of 1831', *Historical Studies: Australia and New Zealand*, Vol. 11, No. 44 (April 1965).
Cavanagh, F. A., 'State Intervention in English Education', *History*, Vol. 25, No. 98 (Sept. 1940).
Charlesworth, M. J., 'The Liberal State and the Control of Education', *Melbourne Studies in Education, 1967* (M.U.P., 1968).
Cleverley, J. F., 'Governor Bourke and the Introduction of the

Select Bibliography

Irish National System', Turney, C. (Ed.), *Pioneers of Australian Education* (S.U.P., 1969).

Davey, Lois, Macpherson, Margaret, Clements, F. W., 'The Hungry Years: 1788–92', *Historical Studies: Australia and New Zealand*, Vol. 3, No. 11 (Nov. 1947).

Dow, Gwyneth M., 'Political Factions and Education in Victoria, 1857–8', *Journal of Religious History*, Vol. 6, No. 3 (June 1971).

Ewers, J. K., 'Governor Kennedy and the Board of Education', *Journal of the Western Australian Historical Society* (1947).

Fitzpatrick, Kathleen, 'Mr. Gladstone and the Governor: The recall of Sir John Eardley-Wilmot from Van Diemen's Land, 1846', *Historical Studies: Australia and New Zealand*, Vol. 1, No. 1 (Apr. 1940).

Goodin, V. W. E., 'Public Education in New South Wales before 1848', *Journal and Proceedings*, R.A.H.S., Vol. 36, Parts 1–4 (1950).

Gregory, J. S., 'Church and State, and Education in Victoria to 1872', *Melbourne Studies in Education, 1958–59* (M.U.P., 1960).

Grose, Kelvin, '1847: The Educational Compromise of the Lord Bishop of Australia', *Journal of Religious History*, Vol. 1, No. 4 (Dec. 1961).

Grose, Kelvin, 'William Grant Broughton and National Education in New South Wales, 1829–1836', *Melbourne Studies in Education, 1965* (M.U.P., 1966).

Hirst, J. B., 'Centralization Reconsidered: The South Australian Education Act of 1875', *Historical Studies*, Vol. 13, No. 49 (Oct. 1967). (Formerly *Historical Studies: Australia and New Zealand*.)

Hooper, F. C., 'The Point Puer Experiment', *Journal of Education* (V.I.E.R.), Vol. 3, No. 1.

Howell, P. A., 'Bishop Nixon and Public Education in Tasmania', *Melbourne Studies in Education, 1967* (M.U.P., 1968).

King, Hazel, 'The Humanitarian Leanings of Governor Bourke', *Historical Studies: Australia and New Zealand*, Vol. 10, No. 37 (Nov. 1961).

King, Hazel, 'Villains All', *Journal of the Royal Australian Historical Society*, Vol. 53, Part 1 (March 1967).

Lawry, J. R., 'Bishop Tufnell and Queensland Education', *Melbourne Studies in Education, 1966* (M.U.P., 1967).

McCarthy, P., 'The Foundations of Catholicism in Western

Australia', *University Studies in History and Economics* (Univ. of W.A.), Vol. 2, No. 4 (July 1956).

McLachlan, N. D., 'Bathurst at the Colonial Office, 1812-27: A Reconnaissance', *Historical Studies*, Vol. 13, No. 52 (April 1969). (Formerly *Historical Studies: Australia and New Zealand*.)

Martin, A. W., 'Henry Parkes: Man and Politician'; 'Faction Politics and the Education Question in New South Wales', *Melbourne Studies in Education, 1960-61* (M.U.P., 1962).

Morrison, Allan A., 'Charles Lilley', *Journal and Proceedings*, R.A.H.S., Vol. 45, Part 1 (1959).

Philipp, June, 'Wakefieldian Influence and New South Wales, 1830-1832', *Historical Studies: Australia and New Zealand*, Vol. 9, No. 34 (May 1960).

Pike, Douglas, 'Education in an Agricultural State', *Melbourne Studies in Education, 1957-8* (M.U.P., 1958).

Pike, Douglas, 'Wilmot Horton and the National Colonization Society', *Historical Studies: Australia and New Zealand*, Vol. 7, No. 26 (May 1956).

Pledger, P. J., 'Secularism in Victorian Education, 1855-72', *Journal of Education* (V.I.E.R.), Vol. 3, No. 1.

Portus, G. V., 'Americans and Australians', *Australian Quarterly*, June 1942.

Saunders, G. E., 'The State and Education in South Australia, 1836-1875', *Melbourne Studies in Education, 1966* (M.U.P., 1967).

Selleck, R. J. W., 'The Strange Case of Inspector Robertson', *Melbourne Studies in Education, 1964* (M.U.P., 1965).

Stannus, M. H., 'Education and the Liberal Ideal', *Melbourne Studies in Education, 1971* (M.U.P., 1971).

Turney, C., 'The Rise and Decline of an Australian Inspectorate', *Melbourne Studies in Education, 1970* (M.U.P., 1970).

Turney, C., 'William Wilkins—Australia's Kay-Shuttleworth', Turney, C. (Ed.), *Pioneers of Australian Education* (S.U.P., 1969).

Wyatt, Ransome T., 'A Wine Merchant in Gaiters', *Journal and Proceedings*, R.A.H.S., Vol. 35, Parts 3-5 (1949).

4. *Newspapers (Years Used)*

Adelaide Observer, 1867.
Age (Melbourne), 1867, 1872, 1898, 1899.
Argus (Melbourne), 1851-7, 1867, 1872, 1878, 1899.
Atlas (Sydney), 1844-8.
Australasian Chronicle, 1840.

Select Bibliography

Australasian Schoolmaster and Literary Review, 1892–5.
Australian (Sydney), 1826–8.
Australian Israelite, 1873.
Colonial Times (Hobart), 1856.
Empire (Sydney), 1850.
Freeman's Journal (Sydney), 1874, 1879.
Fremantle Herald, 1867–71.
Gazette (Perth), 1840, 1847.
Geelong Advertiser, 1849.
Hobart Town Daily Courier, 1856.
Inquirer (Perth), 1841, 1843, 1846–7, 1856.
Launceston Examiner, 1843–5.
Liverpool Courier, 1836.
Mercury (Hobart), 1885.
Monitor (Sydney), 1829.
Moreton Bay Courier, 1846, 1850.
Mount Alexander Mail, 1856.
Port Phillip Christian Herald, 1846.
Record (Bathurst), 1878.
South Australian, 1846.
South Australian Register, 1852.
Southern Australian, 1844.
Stockwhip (later *Satirist*) (Sydney), 1875–6.
Swan River News, 1847.
Sydney Gazette, 1807.
Sydney Morning Herald, 1839, 1842, 1851, 1901.
Tasmanian Church Chronicle, 1852–3, 1856.
Times (Ipswich), 1864.
True Colonist (Hobart), 1839.
Weekly Register (Sydney), 1848.
West Australian, 1892.
Western Australian Record, 1892–5.

C. Unpublished Theses

Cable, Kenneth C., 'The Church of England in New South Wales and its Policy toward Education prior to 1880', unpublished M.A. Thesis, University of Sydney, 1952.

Milne, F. A., 'The Council of Education and its Work', unpublished M.Ed. Thesis, University of Sydney, 1956.

Murray-Smith, Stephen, 'A History of Technical Education in

Australia', unpublished Ph.D. Thesis, University of Melbourne, 1966.

Phillips, W. A. P., 'A Précis of Uncompleted Research on the Social History of Western Australia, 1829-70', unpublished Statement, University of Western Australia, 1951.

Phillips, W. A. P., 'Education and Society in Western Australia, 1829-56', unpublished B.A. Thesis, University of Western Australia, 1951.

Pledger, P. J., 'A Critical Study of the Work of the Board of Education in Victoria, 1862-72', unpublished M.Ed. Thesis, University of Melbourne, 1958.

Saunders, C. E., 'John Anderson Hartley and Education in South Australia', unpublished B.A. Thesis, University of Adelaide, 1958.

Snooke, G. T., 'The Elementary Education Act, 1871-81', unpublished B.A. Thesis, University of Western Australia, 1951.

Suttor, T. L., 'The Position of Catholicism in Australia, 1840-1900', A.N.U. Seminar Paper, 11 Aug. 1958.

Index

Act to Promote the Building of Churches and Chapels (W.A.), 89, 92
Acton, Lord, 206, 208
Adams, Francis, 272
Adelaide, 57, 91, 98, 102, 150, 166,
Age, 192, 196, 262–9
Agnosticism, 113, 149, 157, 174, 177, 190–2
  See also Secularism, Rationalism
Airds, 9
Albany, 169 (n. 29)
Albert, Prince Consort, 204
Albury, 54
All Saints' Grammar School, 263
An Account of the Introduction and Effects of the System of General Religious Education Established in Van Diemen's Land in 1893, 79
Anderson, Sir Francis, 271
Angas, G. F., 99, 101
Anglo-Israel Association, 242
Antigua, 158
A Plea for Common Schools, 117
The Argus, 128, 192, 196, 216
Armidale, 55, 57
Arnold, Matthew, 177, 246, 263, 272
Arnold, Thomas, 70 (n. 60), 88, 139–42, 147, 167 (n. 1), 170 (n. 60)
Arthur, Colonel George, 21–2, 72–5, 80
Assisted Schools Abolition Act (W.A.) 173, 183
Association . . . for Maintaining in V.D.L. the Principles of the Protestant Reformation, 144
Atlas, 46, 50
Australasian Schoolmaster, 261
Australian, 17, 22, 29 (n. 46)
Australian Agricultural Company, 15
Australian Labour Party, 260

Bacchus, Marsh, 57
Bacon, Francis, 178

Balfour, James, 244
Ballarat School of Mines, 268
Balmain, 222
Baptismal Regeneration, 121
Baptist Church, 102, 120, 147, 198
Barcaldine, 260
Barker, Bishop Frederick, 122, 200
Barlee, F. P., 159–62
Bathurst, 11, 52–4, 200, 213
Bathurst, Earl, 8–13, 18–22
Battersea, 58
Bell, Dr. Andrew, 8–9
Bellamy, Edward, 260
Benson, Rev. William, 102
Bentham, Jeremy, 99
Bernard, W. D., 108 (n. 37)
Bible in Schools League, 241
Bigge, J. T., 9–13, 16, 17, 21
Bligh, Captain William, 4, 5
Board of Education:
  South Australia, 105, 165
  Tasmania, 78, 82, 83, 87
  Victoria, 184, 249
  Western Australia, 156
Board of Inspection (Tas.), 141–5
Bonwick, James, 78
Bordertown, 251
Botany Bay, see Sydney
Bourke, Sir Richard, 26, 33–43, 45, 48, 49, 51, 54, 57, 62, 72–4, 122
Bowen, Sir George, 134–5
Bradbury, Thomas, 87
Bradley, James, 9
Brady, Bishop John, 93, 96, 97, 153–4
Brandy Creek, 183
Bereton, Rev. H., 225
Brisbane, 59, 117
Brisbane Courier, 192
Brisbane, Sir Thomas, 12, 13, 14, 33, 41–9, 61, 74, 77, 78, 87, 143, 165
British and Foreign School Society, 8,
Brodie brothers, 57
Brodribb, Thomas, 257–8

Bromby, Rev. J. E., 190
Brookfield, 56
Broughton, Bishop W. G., 31 (n. 66), 36–8, 39, 40, 42, 43, 46, 47, 49–50, 68 (n. 27), 74, 75, 79, 121, 123
Brown, John, 99
Bryce Commission, 265
Bryce, Rev. F. B., 212
Bulletin, 260
Bunbury District Board, 256
Buninyong, 65
Burke, Edmund, 3, 37
Bush Boarding Schools, 63–7
Bussell family, 90
Butler, Dom Cuthbert, 208
Butler, Edward, 219–20
Butters, Rev. M. L., 164

CABLE, K. C., 120–1, 121–2, 189, 199
Calcutta, diocese of, 91
Camden, 64
Canada, 12, 26
Canning, George, 23–4
Carlyle, Thomas, 260
Carruthers, J. H., 271
Cartwright, Rev. Robert, 9
Castlemaine, 132
Catholic Emancipation Act, 23, 25, 204
Central Board of Education:
  South Australia, 106–7
  Tasmania, 145–8
Chamber of Manufactures, 266
Chamber of Mines, 266
Chaplains, 6, 9, 79, 91, 102,
Childers, H. C. E., 62, 127
Christian Brothers, 61
Church and School Corporation, 12–26, 33, 72
Church of England:
  and denominational education, 60–2, 161–2, 164–5, 216–17
  and liberalism, 43–4, 74, 147–8
  and National Society, 8–9
  and systems of general education, 36–8, 43, 45–7, 55, 65, 78–9, 82–3, 87, 94, 98, 107, 120–3, 126, 128–9, 134, 140–5, 155–6, 161–2, 164–5, 193–9
  status of, 6, 7, 17, 18, 19, 22–3, 26, 33–4, 72–3, 76, 87–9, 91, 93, 102, 121–3, 144–5
  See also Church and School Corporation, Evangelicalism, Oxford Movement
Clark, C. M. H., 174–7, 182, 204
Clarke, Andrew, 92–3

Clarke, Marcus, 272
Clergy Reserves, 12
Cobb and Co., 183
Cohen, Edward, 180, 187–8, 189, 216
Cole, E. W., 190–1
Collisson, Rev. M., 102
Colonial Office, 1, 7, 9, 10, 12, 13, 22, 23, 25, 31 (n. 78), 39, 49, 75, 80–1, 84, 85, 95–100, 105, 112, 122, 139, 149, 153, 155, 158–9
Colonial Schools, 92–4
Commissions on Education:
  Queensland (1888), 254–5, 259
  South Australia (1882), 240–2, 251–2, 253
  Tasmania (1860), 148, (1867), 148, 185
  Victoria (1867), 193–6, 250; (1877), 185; (1882–4), 243–4, 251, 253–4; (1899–1901), 258, 260–69
Committee of the Privy Council, 246
Common Christianity, 116, 132–3, 135, 156, 166, 167, 187–200
Common Schools Act (Vic.), 119, 133, 193, 201, 249
Compton Downs, 252
Compulsory Education, 185–6, 239–40
Conference of Australasian Bishops (1850), 121, 144, 165
Cook, J. N., 261
Coolgardie, 183, 226
Co-operative Commonwealth, 260
Corbett, Rev. J. F., 217
Council of Education (N.S.W.), 123, 185, 197–8, 200, 213
Courtney, W., 108 (n. 37)
Cranbourne Board of Advice, 257

DALBY, 200
Dalley brothers, 183
Daly, Sir Dominick, 158
Darling, Sir Ralph, 14–18, 24–6
Darnell's copybooks, 252
Darwin, Charles, 189–90
Davies, Archdeacon R. R., 83, 141, 145
Deakin, Alfred, 244, 260–9
Denison, Sir William, 81, 85, 87, 88, 139–45
Denominational Schools Board:
  New South Wales, 51, 60, 65, 66
  Victoria, 61, 65, 66, 123–4, 126, 129–30
Department of Education:
  Victoria, 193, 240–51, 250–61, 252–4, 257–61, 268–9
  Western Australia, 276 (n. 76)

Index

Dibbs, Sir George, 200
Dickens, Charles, 260
Dilke, Sir Charles, 272
Disraeli, Benjamin, 260
Docker, Joseph, 57
Döllinger, J. J. I. von, 206, 208
Drayton, 200
Duffy, Sir Charles Gavan, 196, 209, 215–6, 219
Duncan, W. A., 50, 61, 117
Dunne, Very Rev. W. J., 148

EARDLEY-WILMOT, Sir John, 83–5, 105
Edinburgh Review, 250
Education Act:
  South Australia, 173, 182
  Tasmania, 173, 182
  Victoria, 149, 173, 182, 220
Education Committee (W.A.), 94, 95, 96, 98, 151, 152, 155
Education League of S.A., 198
Eedle, David, 157
Elementary Education Act (Forster's) 162, 176
Elementary Education Act (W.A.), 149–50, 162–3, 256
Elementary Education Act Amendment Act (W.A.), 173, 183
Empire, 117, 124
Essay on the Deluge, 191
Eureka, 132
Evangelicalism, 75, 121–2
Ewart, D. I., 259, 272
Exeter Hall, 100

FABIANS, 260, 265
Fawkner, J. P., 126
Federation, 173, 225, 226, 260, 262
Fellenberg, P. E. von, 101, 110 (n. 95)
Fellows, T. H., 179, 196
Ferguson, Sir James, 161
Field, Barron, 13
Fink, Theodore, 258, 261–70
FitzGerald, Captain Charles, 95–8, 151–3, 157
Fitzpatrick, Brian, 183
Fitzpatrick, Kathleen, 85
FitzRoy, Sir Charles, 49–51, 122
Fogarty, Bro. Ronald, 135 (n. 1), 143–4, 174–7, 201, 203, 218, 220, 223 (n. 72)
Forbes, Rev. James, 65
Forrest, Alexander, 225
Forrest, Sir John, 199, 224, 225–9
Francis, J. G., 215–16

Franklin, Sir John, 75–80, 85, 104
Fraser, Rev. T. McK., 190
Free education, 186–7, 238–9
Fremantle, 89, 169 (n. 29)
Froude, J. A., 272

GAWLER, Lieut.-Colonel George, 103
Geelong, 55, 57, 190
Geoghegan, Bishop P. B., 119, 129, 143, 166, 167, 202, 211
George, Henry, 260
German Socialism, 260
Gibney, Bishop Matthew, 159–60, 225–30
Giddy, Davies, 2
Giles, William, 102–3
Gilles, Osmond, 99
Gipps, Sir George, 39, 41–9, 57
Gladstone, W. E., 82–5, 105, 205, 208
Gleaner, 29 (n. 46)
Glenburnie, 251
Glenelg, Lord, 39
Gobarralong, 60
Goderich, Lord, 19, 23–6
Gold discoveries:
  Victoria, 127
  Western Australia, 183, 226
Goold, Bishop J. A., 202, 212, 215–17, 220
Gorham judgment, 121
Gouger, Robert, 102
Goulburn, 213
Gould, John, 75
Great Disruption, 120
Greenwood, Rev. William, 198, 233 (n. 64)
Gregory, J. S., 112–14, 128, 174–7, 191–2, 204
Gregson, T. G., 82, 86
Grey, Earl, 24
Grey, Sir George, 102–3, 105
Griffiths, C. J., 57
Griver, Bishop Martin, 170 (n. 63)
Grose, Kelvin, 49
Grote, George, 98

HACKETT, Sir Winthrop, 199
Haines, W. C., 129–33
Hale, Bishop Mathew, 156–7, 161–3
Hall, Very Rev. W., 141–2, 145
Hamersley family, 90
Hampton, Dr. J. S., 158–9
Hancock, Sir Keith, 184
Handfield, Rev. H. P., 243–4
Hanson, Richard, 99
Harrington Street Public School, 146
Hartley, J. A., 259, 271

295

Hartwell, R. M., 16
Hastie, Rev. Thomas, 65
Hawdon, Joseph, 57
Hayes, E. E. Y., 206, 207
Heales, Richard, 133, 193
Heidelberg, 57
Herald, 261
Herschel, Sir John, 78, 107
Higinbotham, George, 133, 150, 192–8, 214, 217, 242, 250,
Hobart, 78, 140, 142, 146
Holland, 86
Home and Foreign Review, 206
Howard, Rev. C. B., 102
Hunter, Captain John, 5
Hunter Valley, 54, 55, 62
Hutchins, Archdeacon William, 75–8
Hutt, John, 89, 92
Huxley, T. H., 177, 180, 181, 189, 190

INDEPENDENT Church, 72, 76, 102, 119, 120, 147, 198–9
Inquirer, 94, 95
Inspection of schools, 59–60, 131–2, 240, 250–2
  See also Inspectors-General
Inspectors-General, 255, 257–9, 267, 269
Ipswich, 200
Irish National System, 34–8, 40, 45–7, 52, 53, 57, 61, 96–7, 105, 115, 116–17, 146, 155, 166, 187
  See also National Schools Board
Irish Readers, 242
Irwin, Lieut-Colonel F. C., 92–4

JACKSON, Sir Cyril, 276 (n. 76)
James, Walter, 225
Joint Pastoral Letter, 220
Jugiong, 60

KALGOORLIE, 183, 226
Kay, Dr. James, 58, 177
Kennedy, Captain Arthur, 156–9
Kimberley, 183
Kinchela, John, 52–4
King, Captain P. G., 4, 5
King's School, Canterbury, 47
King's School, Parramatta, 33, 37
Kingston, George, 99
Knaplund, Paul, 22–3
Knibbs, G. H., 271

LABILLIÈRE, C. E. de, 57
La Chalotais, Louis-René de, 1–2
Lamenais, Abbé, 206

La Nauze, J. A., 266–7
Lancaster, Joseph, 8, 42
Land Acts, 181–2
Lane, William, 260
Lang, Rev. J. D., 18, 19, 38, 50–1, 120
La Trobe, C. J., 85, 126, 130
La Trobe Street School, 253
Laud, Archbishop, 122
Launceston, 142, 146
Launceston Examiner, 83
Learmonth brothers, 65–6
Learmonth, Dr. J., 55
Lefroy family, 90
Levinge, Thomas, 115
Liberal Debating Society, 191
Liberalism, 33, 34, 42, 43–4, 74, 99, 112–14, 118, 119, 149, 157, 174, 176, 187, 202, 203–9, 213–14, 220–21, 224
Lilley, Charles, 134
Lillie, Rev. Dr., 141
Liverpool, Lord, 23–5
Local Boards of Advice, 185, 242, 255–7
Loch, John, 79, 80, 82–4
Lochee, Francis, 94
London Missionary Society, 5
London School of Economics, 265
London University, 77
Long, C. R., 269
Looking Backward, 260
Lovett, William, 100
Lowe, Robert, 46–7, 50, 179, 250
Lyell, Sir Charles, 189

MACARTHUR, William, 64–5
Macartney, Rev. H. B., 57
Macaulay, Lord, 124, 177, 178
M'Coy, Frederick, 189–90
McCulloch, Sir James, 193
Mackenzie, D., 57
McKenzie, M. K., 261
McKillop, Mother Mary, 212
Macquarie, Colonel Lachlan, 5–10
McQueen, Thomas, 5
Madden, R. R., 96
Maitland, 36, 213
Manning, Cardinal H. E., 204
Manual of English Literature and Language, 248
Margaret Street Public School, 146
Marsden, Rev. Samuel, 6, 7, 9
Martin, A. W., 117, 218
Martin, James, 123
Melbourne, 54, 64, 117, 189–92, 201, 239–41, 253, 260–69
Melbourne Grammar School, 264

Index

Meredith, George, 264
Methodist Church, 2, 7, 60, 62, 73, 76, 119–20, 147, 164, 198
Meyers, John, 108 (n. 37)
Michie, Archibald, 128, 132, 133, 192
Mill, John Stuart, 3, 177
Mining, 182–3, 226
Ministers of Education, 253–5, 257–8
Mitchell, Sir Thomas, 15
Model School, 51, 57, 58, 62, 114, 246
Modern Painters, 263
Molesworth, Sir William, 99
Molloy, Georgiana, 89, 90, 156
Monitor, 29 (n. 46)
Monsell, W., 154
Montalembert, Comte de, 206
Moonta, 182
Moore, Samuel, 90
More, Hannah, 2
Moreton Bay Courier, 59, 133
Moreton Bay District, see Queensland
Morphett, John, 104
Mount Bischoff, 182
Mount Cameron, 183
Mount Lyell, 183
Murphy, Bishop Daniel, 212
Murphy, Sir Francis, 57, 125
Murray, Sir George, 24

Nash, R. W., 94, 96
National Education, 131, 136 (n. 6)
National Schools Board:
New South Wales, 49–62, 64–6, 114–15, 117, 125–6, 134
Queensland, 135
Victoria, 61, 65–6, 125–6, 130–2
see also Irish National System
National Society for the Education of the Poor, 8
Naylor, Rev. F. B., 74
Neale, W. L., 271
Nelson, 140
Nelson Readers, 242–3
Newcastle, 11
Newcastle Commission, 250
New England District, 54–5
New Hebrides, 262
Newman, Cardinal J. H., 204
New Norcia, 93
New South Wales, 1–27, 33–67, 72, 74, 83, 85, 88, 105, 112–25, 143, 175, 182, 187, 189, 192, 197–8, 200–1, 203, 213–14, 218–23, 241, 249, 258–9, 265, 266, 270–1
New Zealand, 88, 104, 139–40, 158
Nicholson, Sir Charles, 51, 57, 133–5

Night Schools, 240
Nixon, Bishop F. R., 79, 80, 82, 144–7, 165
Non-vested schools, 115, 133, 135
Normal schools, 39, 140, 246, 248
See also Teachers' Colleges

O'Connell, Daniel, 215
Oldham, William, 102
Orphan School, 86
O'Shanassy, Sir John, 126, 129–33, 167, 215
Oxford Movement, 121, 165
Oxley, John, 14–15

Palmer, Sir James, 249–50
Palmer, Vance, 192–260
Palmerston, Lord, 250
Papal Aggression, 204
Papal Infallibility, 204–5
Paraguay, 260
Parkes, Sir Henry, 16, 114, 117–19, 122–5, 197, 213–14, 218–20, 221, 223–4, 270
Parnell, E., 253–4
Parramatta, 9, 33, 36
Pastoral Admonition, 214–16
Patriotic Four, 106
Patriotic Six, 82
Payment by results, 249–53
Peacock, Sir Alexander, 267–9
Pearson, Charles H., 185, 243, 255–6, 261, 264, 273 (n. 12)
Peel, Sir Robert, 23
Peel, Thomas, 88
Penola, 212
Perry, Bishop Charles, 128, 190, 191, 195
Perth, 150, 154, 225
Perth Girls' School, 151
Peters, D., 57
Phillip, Captain Arthur, 1, 4–5, 88
Pilbara, 183
Pine, Sir Benjamin, 158
Pius IX, 119, 202, 205–7
Pledger, P. J., 188
Plunkett, J. H., 51, 58
Polding, Archbishop J. B., 44, 46, 209–10, 221
"Police" view of education, 178–9
Port Chalmers, 139
Port Jackson, see Sydney
Portland, 54, 55
Port Philip Christian Herald, 65
Port Philip District, see Victoria
Pownall, Rev. G. P., 152
Prahran, 239

297

Australian Education, 1788–1900

Presbyterian Church, 12, 18, 19, 37, 42, 60, 63, 65, 73, 75, 119, 120, 141, 147, 198–9
Priestley, Joseph, 3
Primary Education Act (Qld.), 133–5
Progress and Poverty, 260
Proposed Plan for General Education (Vic.), 126
Provincial Council (1862), 118, 201; (1869), 148, 201, 209, 211
Public Instruction Act (N.S.W.), 173, 176, 182, 223
Public School Teachers' Association, 241
Public Schools Act:
  New South Wales, 122, 176, 197–8, 219
  Tasmania, 148
Public Schools League of N.S.W., 198
Public Service Act (Vic.), 253
Pupil-teacher system, 246–7, 253, 265–6, 270

Quanta Cura, 202
Queensland, 48, 54, 112, 133–5, 175, 182, 199–200, 202, 212, 235 (n. 99), 241, 254–9, 268, 271
Queensland Guardian, 192
Queen's Scholars, 246
Queenstown, 146
Quinn, Bishop James, 143, 199, 202, 212
Quinn, Bishop Matthew, 212, 219

Rae, John, 251
Ragged Schools, 240–1
Raikes, Robert, 2
Railways, 183–4
Rationalism, 190–2
  See also Agnosticism, Secularism
Reddall, Rev. Thomas, 8–9, 19, 28 (n. 19)
Register, 192
Religions of the World, 191
Revised Code, 249–50
Rice, Spring, 39
Richmond, 142
Riley, Bishop C. O. L., 199
Riley, J., 57
Roach, Patrick, 57
Roadnight, W., 57
Robe, Major F. H., 70 (n. 60), 103–6
Roman Catholic Church:
  and denominational education, 62, 93, 94, 118–19, 129, 201–30
  and liberalism, 201–30
  and Protestant attitude towards, 36, 38, 79, 93, 113, 201–30

Roman Catholic Church (*contd.*)—
  and systems of general education, 18, 42–6, 55, 60, 65, 76, 87, 93–8, 107, 118–19, 121, 125, 129, 140–4, 146, 147, 153–67, 194–8, 201–30
  See also Church and School Corporation
Royal Agricultural Society, 266
Royal Commissions on Education, see Commissions on Education
Rusden, Rev. G. K., 36, 54
Rusden, G. W., 51–65, 117, 130–2, 193
Rusden, H. K., 191
Ruskin, John, 260, 263
Russell, Lord John, 23, 204
Ryan, Very Rev. M., 166–7

St Kilda, 217
St Mary's Church, 217
Salisbury, Lord, 262
Schiller, J. C. F. von, 180
Scott, D., 59–60
Scott, Archdeacon T. H., 10–22, 26, 88–9
Scripture Extracts, 35, 60, 155
Sectarianism, 65, 113, 149, 157–8, 173, 174, 177, 204–5, 215
Secularism, 113, 114, 124, 127, 132–3, 148, 173, 174, 189–96, 221, 224–5, 241–5
  See also Agnosticism, Rationalism
Select Committees on Education:
  New South Wales (1844), 45–6, 50, 64, 120; (1854), 115
  South Australia (1851), 106; (1861) 163–4
  Tasmania (1853), 141, 115–16
  Victoria (1852), 129, 131, 166
Separation:
  Queensland, 112, 134
  Victoria, 112, 125–6
Serra, Bishop, J. M. B., 153–5
Sesame and Lilies, 264
Sheil, Bishop L. B., 202, 211
Shepperdson, J. B., 102
Short, Bishop Augustus, 91, 98, 107, 156, 164–5, 199
Short History of the English People, 248
Short Lessons for English People, 248
Simpson, G. T., 227
Sisters of Mercy, 93, 154
Sisters of Saint Joseph, 212
Smith, Adam, 178, 179
Smith, Rev. L. A., 200

Index

Society for the Preservation of Religious Freedom, 103
Society for the Promotion of Christian Knowledge, 61
Society for the Propagation of the Gospel, 5, 6, 49, 90
Sorell, 76
South Australia, 70 (n. 60), 98–107, 119, 175, 182, 185, 198, 199, 202, 211–13, 235, 241, 251, 254, 259, 266, 271
South Australian Register, 104
South Australian School Society, 101–2
Southern Australian, 103
Southern Cross, 183
Spencer, Herbert, 189
Squatters, 40, 46–7, 48–9, 56–7, 64–6
Stanhope, 56
Stanley, Lord, 35, 40, 52, 82, 83, 105
Stanton, L. W., 251–2
State Education Act (Qld.), 173, 182, 257
State secondary education, 245–6
Stephen, James, 22–4
Stephen, J. W., 186, 216–17, 230
Stephens, Edward, 103
Stirling, Sir James, 92
Stockmar, Baron von, 206
Stow, T. Q., 102
Strzelecki, Count de, 75
Swan District Board, 256
Sydney, 1, 3, 5, 8, 19, 36, 54, 62, 64, 88, 91, 134, 200, 221–3, 270–1
Sydney Cove, see Sydney
Sydney Diocesan Church Society, 122
Sydney Morning Herald, 192
Syllabus of Errors, 119, 202, 203–5, 207, 208
Syme, David, 263–4

TABLE of Minimum Attainments, 115
Tasmania, 1, 24, 70 (n. 60), 72–88, 104, 105, 106, 139–48, 167 (n. 1), 175, 182, 185, 212, 234 (n. 99), 270, 271
Tasmanian Church Chronicle, 145, 147
Tasmanian Society of Natural History, 75
Tate, Frank, 248, 249, 261
Teachers' Colleges, 246, 248, 249, 261
See also Normal Schools
Technical education, 245, 264–9
Telegraph, 183–4
The Faith and Duty of a Christian, 78
Therry, Rev. J. J., 18

The Real Place in History of Jesus and Paul, 191
The Vatican Decrees in their bearing on Civil Allegiance, 205
Thomas's Plains, 183
Tingcombe, Rev. H., 55
Toowoomba, 200
Trades Hall Council, 266
Training of teachers, 246–9
See also Normal Schools, Teachers' Colleges
Transportation, 81, 149
Trevelyan, Sir Charles, 265
Trevelyan, Sir George, 265, 266
Trollope, Anthony, 272
Truancy, 239–41
True Colonist, 86–7
Tuas libenter, 206
Tufnell, Bishop E. W., 135, 199–200
Turner, J. W., 271
Turner, Sir George, 262, 267–8
Turton, Samuel, 115

ULLATHORNE, Very Rev. W. B., 68 (n. 22)
Universities, 58, 59, 245, 253
Universities Tests Act, 204
University of Melbourne, 265, 266–7
University of Sydney, 134, 270–1
Unto This Last, 264

VALE, R. T., 261
Van Diemen's Land, see Tasmania
Vasse, The, 156
Vaughan, Archbishop R. W. B., 218–24, 229–30
Victoria, 40–1, 48, 55, 58, 61, 62, 85, 112, 115, 125–33, 149, 174, 175, 182, 186–7, 189–96, 198, 202, 203, 212, 214–18, 239–41, 242–5, 249, 250–1, 253–4, 255, 258, 260–9
Victorian Association for the Promotion of Technical Education, 267
Victorian Education League, 199
Voluntaryism, 100–6, 119–20, 122, 149, 156, 174, 177

WAGGA, 56, 67
Wakefield, E. G., 25, 99
Wallaroo, 182
Wangaratta, 57
Wannon, The, 57
Warrnambool, 257
Webb, Beatrice, 265
Webb, Sidney, 265, 266
Webster, Corporal William, 5

299

Weekly Register, 50
Weld, Sir Frederick, 158–63, 167, 224
Wellington, Duke of, 23–5
Wesley College, 266
West Australian, 192
Westbury, 142
Western Australia, 88–98, 175, 182–3, 199, 223–30, 239, 255, 256, 276 (n. 79)
Wilkins, William, 57–63, 66–7, 114–17, 118
Wilks, John, 100
Willson, Bishop R. W., 79, 142–5, 147, 148
Wilson, Rev. N., 55
Wimmera River, 55

Wise, B. R., 270
Withers, Rev. J., 256–7
Wittenoom, E. H., 255
Wittenoom, Rev. J. B., 94
Wollaston, Rev. J. R., 89, 91
Wollongong, 39
Woods, Rev. Tenison, 211–12
Working Men's College, 266
Wyatt, William, 106

YARRALUMLA, 61
Yass, 52
Yilgarn, 183
Young, Sir Henry, 106
Yuroke, 57

ZEAL, William, 180

DANFORTH LIBRARY / NEW ENGLAND COLLEGE

00039312

LA 2101 .A8 1976

Austin, Albert G

Australian education, 1788-1900

NOV 2 0 RET'D

WITHDRAWN
FROM
NEC LIBRARY

DEMCO

THE AUSTRALIAN COLONIES
in the second half of the nineteenth century

See also back end papers

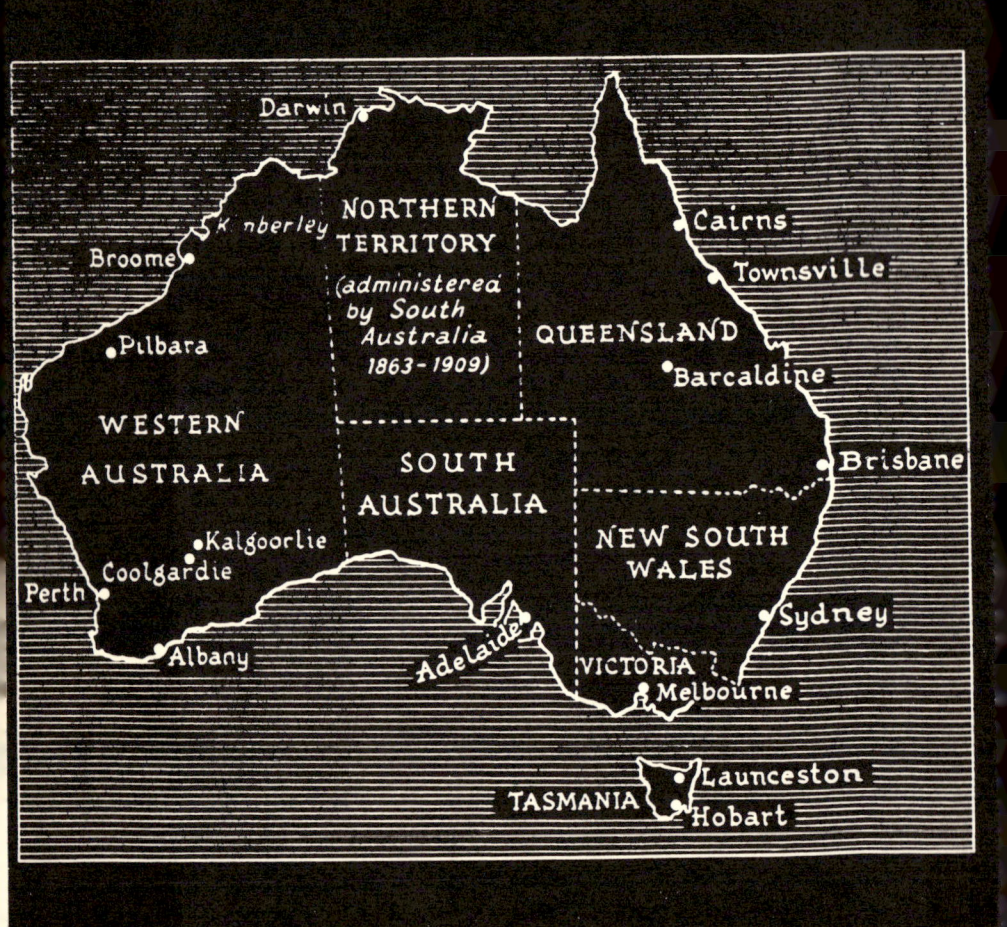

- Darwin
- Kimberley
- Broome
- Pilbara

NORTHERN TERRITORY
(administered by South Australia 1863-1909)

- Cairns
- Townsville

QUEENSLAND
- Barcaldine
- Brisbane

WESTERN AUSTRALIA
- Kalgoorlie
- Coolgardie
- Perth
- Albany

SOUTH AUSTRALIA
- Adelaide

NEW SOUTH WALES
- Sydney

VICTORIA
- Melbourne

TASMANIA
- Launceston
- Hobart

0 50 100 150

Approximate scale of miles for the enlarged sections